Shalom,
JAPAN

Shalom, JAPAN

A Sabra's Five Years
in the Land of the Rising Sun

Shifra Horn

Translated from Hebrew by Ora Cummings

KENSINGTON BOOKS

KENSINGTON BOOKS are published by

Kensington Publishing Corp.
850 Third Avenue
New York, NY 10022

Library of Congress Card Catalog Number: 96-077145
ISBN 1-57566-111-X

First Printing: November, 1996
10 9 8 7 6 5 4 3 2 1

Printed in the United States of America

Shalom, JAPAN

Welcome to Japan

I boarded the crowded tourist section of the airliner taking me to Japan, my knees knocking with preflight nerves. I moved down the cabin's narrow aisle, and glanced covertly at the dozens of faces on either side. All of the passengers were Japanese.

They sat tidily and compactly in their cramped seats, safety belts already fastened. Most of the men wore three-piece suits, with impeccably knotted ties. The women, whom I studied closely, were dressed in elegant outfits, each with a pair of high-heeled shoes set neatly by her feet. All had shining, perfectly groomed black hair.

This crowd of people seemed to be waiting, with silent patience, for the conductor of a philharmonic orchestra to raise his baton and begin a concert. I tiptoed to my seat.

The flight would take twenty hours. I had almost resigned myself to my fear of going up in the air in a hermetically sealed metal tube. Then my overactive imagination reminded me of every plane that ever skidded off a runway, or landed in the middle of a road, or sucked in a bird and crashed into a mountain.

The sight of the Japanese man and woman in seats 24-A and B brought home the fact that I had to spend the last day of my life squeezed uncomfortably beside them in seat C. I shoved my things untidily into the carry-on compartment, jarring the origami-like folds with which the other passengers had stowed away their clothes.

I settled into my seat and swallowed sleeping pills, my shaking body firmly fastened by the safety belt, which would magically guard me against any danger. I planned to curl up in one of those thin woolen blankets and cushion the impact of the inevitable crash.

I was ready to strike up a conversation with my neighbors, and pump them for information on Japan, the best nightspots, interesting tourist and recreation sites to visit, and so forth. The couple beside me might even become my first Japanese friends.

But they were already asleep. I looked around at the other passengers, also drowsing in the plane's excruciatingly uncomfortable seats. They looked as if they were happily stretched out on their futons at home.

Even the difficult and noisy takeoff, which caused the plane to tremble like a sinking ship and made me dig my nails into my palms until they bled, did not wake them up.

They remained in blissful coma for hours. Nothing disturbed their preternatural calm: not the captain's booming voice, speaking in English with a thick Swedish accent, nor the flight attendant's high-pitched Japanese.

The clanking food carts finally did the trick. Japanese biological clocks seemed to reset naturally for the random hours at which the crew served meals, ignoring day and night, breakfast and dinner times.

Their eerie silence was interrupted by enthusiastic slurps of noodle soup. Cups were filled with green tea and passed out. The cabin resounded with loud, hissing sips.

A Japanese who drinks tea or eats noodles quietly simply isn't enjoying them, I was to learn.

As soon as the trays were cleared, my fellow passengers fell asleep once more. I was left awake to monitor the plane, listen to the ominous racket of the engines, and search red-eyed for signs of fire on the wing.

The deep silence was broken only by the voice of the captain explaining our flight route, or announcing the in-flight movie, which was watched by an audience of one. Me.

I had given up prowling the aisle in search of another insomniac, and contemplated the couple next to me. Despite all the trays of food they had consumed, despite the gallons of tea they had poured into themselves, they lay motionless, eyes shut. They were a miracle of physiology. Not once during the endless flight did I have to stand up to let them go to the toilet.

They never exchanged a word in their brief periods of wakefulness, nor did they speak with any of their countrymen. They certainly never spoke to me, the stranger who strangely could not fall asleep, in spite of all the sleeping pills floating about in the wine inside my stomach.

During the stopover at Anchorage, Alaska, my Japanese traveling companions all jumped to their feet as one army and dashed out of the plane to the lavatories or the duty-free shops. With empty bladders, and transparent bags full of whiskey, cigarettes, cosmetics, and smoked salmon, they returned to the plane and arranged their new purchases, in perfect order, in the luggage racks above their heads. Then, in perfect order, they fell asleep again.

About five minutes before the official announcement that our plane was about to land at Narita Airport, all the sleeping beauties opened their eyes and, as if under joint orders, put on their shoes and stretched their limbs in a way that did not disturb their neighbors, and carefully folded the soft airline blankets. All this was done calmly and quietly, with no fuss and with no unnecessary words.

I first heard the voice of my fellow passenger on this long and sleepy journey when our plane's wheels touched down on the runway. Red-faced and earnest, he turned to me and uttered the first and last sentence I heard from him in the twenty hours of the flight: "Welcome to Japan."

We were now permitted to unfasten our seat belts and make our way to the exits. Only then did the passengers move into the aisles. The plane was vacated, calmly, quietly, in single file. Relaxed, fresh, and well rested, their clothes clean and unrumpled as if they had just left home, the passengers walked slowly down the plane's exit chute.

Bleary-eyed and puffy from lack of sleep, with stiff limbs and swollen ankles, I moved along the walkway, scanning Narita's dozens of exits and giant passenger halls and the thousands of Japanese people scurrying back and forth between them.

In the enormous passport control hall, I watched the queue of Japanese, standing one behind the other, straight-backed, each clutching a red-bound passport with the emblem of the rising sun engraved on it, under a sign which declared that this counter would check "Japanese Only." A sign over a nearby counter explained that it would accept "Aliens." A scraggly, weary, and shapeless line of creatures zigzagged its way to the aliens' counter. I pulled my luggage behind me and dragged my feet toward my fellow outsiders.

After carefully scrutinizing and comparing my haggard, exhausted face with the fresh and healthy one smiling out from my picture, a somber official stamped my passport and returned it to me. I made my way to Customs and then out to the exit hall. I walked faster now, looking for my Tokyo driver. Suddenly I felt a heavy, white-gloved hand grasping my shoulder. Alarmed, I turned to face a uniformed Japanese official, who indicated that I should accompany him. I was propelled to the passport control desk. My legs weak with fear. My passport was taken back and turned over and over in the white-gloved hands of officialdom, which took it to a back room for further examination. I was quick to grab the passport as soon as they gave it back, before anyone changed his mind, and dragged myself and my luggage away to the exit hall. Once again, I was followed by that same official, and the same white-gloved hand was placed on my shoulder, and once more I was called back to the passport control desk. With tears of frustration and desperation and more than a little suspicion, I placed my irreproachable passport, back on the desk. After a few minutes I noticed that the clerk was not even bothering to look at it, and I picked up my scattered belongings and stole away quietly toward the exit. With one foot already in the exit hall, I was asked by the guard to wait in a side room. Another uniformed official came in and, in stuttering English, asked me to accompany him. Helpless, I dragged my suitcase after him, imagining Japanese-style torture chambers and prison cells crawling with rats and cockroaches, where I would be forced to spend the rest of my innocent life. With shaking knees, paralyzed with fear, I was led into the same exit hall which I had left a few minutes before. The uniform, stoically silent throughout our walk, stopped suddenly and, with a Prussian click of his heels, saluted, held out his hand, and gestured expansively that I was free to go. I couldn't resist asking the reason for the delays and the three baffling times I had been obliged to return to the passport control desk.

"*Sumimasen passporto.* Your passport, please." he demanded firmly.

I regretted my impulsiveness and chronic curiosity and pulled my passport from its warm hiding place on my stomach, placing it on the outstretched white glove. The glove's finger moved over the foreign letters inscribed on the passport's blue cover, with the gold menorah on front and stopped at the word "Diplomat." That same finger pointed triumphantly at the exit desk, to which I had been led that last time. The desk carried the sign "For holders of diplomatic passports only."

Suddenly I understood. I was traveling on a diplomatic passport, which meant that I was only allowed to leave the terminal through the exit designated for holders of such passports. I had made the fateful mistake of having my passport stamped at a desk meant for ordinary aliens, and that was why I had to retrace my steps and leave by the exit officially designated for people like me.

Once sure that I fully understood the matter, the uniform turned to me and, with a sharp, ceremonial click of his heels, said, "Welcome to Japan," and ushered me out.

How to Survive in a Strange World

Organizing the Garbage

*T*he car pulled up to a redbrick building with the rather pretentious name of "Royal Yoyogi's Garden House." My husband, who had arrived in Tokyo two months previously, opened the door to our apartment and ordered me to remove my shoes. "Don't forget you're in Tokyo," he said dryly, before giving me a chance to recover from the two-hour ride from the airport. "From now on you're going to behave like a Japanese lady."

The Embassy's driver, Gimunshi helped carry in all my bags and baggage. He didn't even wait to be thanked before leaving with my husband, who was in a hurry to get back to work. I was absolutely exhausted.

Wearily I surveyed my new domain, which my husband had rented in my absence. A huge, empty living room bore witness to the very important role I would be required to play: diplomatic hostess. A quick glance confirmed that more than seventy people could be convivially crowded into this room. Encouraged by this thought, I examined the rest of the apartment. Besides two futons, which did wonders to raise my spirits after the long sleepless hours, the apartment was quite bare.

I made my way to the futons, happy that I had somewhere to collapse at last. As I was peeling off my clothes, a sharp ring reverberated through the empty rooms.

I felt my way to the door, confused by the dozens of cupboard doors lining the walls of the dark, narrow corridor, and cursed whoever had so rudely disturbed my plans.

"This can't wait," said the sour-faced, toothless concierge in English. He introduced himself as Kato and positioned himself in my doorway. "You must come with me at once."

I followed him with bleary eyes. Sleep was all I wanted after my long flight, but I was unable to get this across to him in the meager Japanese I had mastered before leaving Israel.

Kato shuffled ahead of me quickly, not even turning his head back to see if I was following him.

When we reached the building's underground parking lot, he stopped and, with great ceremony, opened a green metal door. He led me into the Royal Yoyogi's vast garbage room, which was easily as big as our own living room. I stared at him in apprehension. Kato smiled.

I followed him, doing my best to make some sense of his explanations. Like a proud chef, Kato lifted up the lids, one after another, of the brightly polished garbage cans. Each move he made was accompanied by lengthy explanations in Japanese sprinkled with a few words of English. He must have noticed my quizzical expression, because he demanded relentlessly that I stick my head into the cans. I did as he said, passing from can to can.

"*Vakarimas ka.* Do you understand?" he asked impatiently.

"*Vakarimas.* Understand," I lied.

Shamed and confused, I returned to the apartment, trying to forget the incomprehensible guided tour of the garbage in seventeen hours of good healthy sleep. The following day, I phoned the secretary of the Israeli Embassy in Tokyo.

"What's with the garbage?" I asked. He answered with a burst of laughter.

"You're going to have to learn how to throw away your garbage," he explained, still laughing.

"What do you mean, 'learn'?"

"Go down and spend a few minutes in your garbage room and make sure you look into all the cans." I could hear giggling in the background.

I went down to the garbage room, and looked all around, hoping there was no one there to catch me. One by one, I examined the cans and lifted up their lids. Not a single cat jumped out at me, nor was I overcome by the usual stinking fumes.

The first one I opened was filled with empty food cans, aluminum foil, bottle tops, and various metal kitchen utensils.

The second can was filled with all sorts of plastic objects. Its immediate neighbor contained glass and the little can next to it was filled with used batteries. Only the two cans at the side contained the familiar household garbage, oozing the stinking, fermenting juices of organic matter.

On the walls were shelves full of books, magazines, and newspapers, which gave a rather intellectual and studious air to the room. The book-lined walls reminded me of an elementary school library. The books were arranged side by side, and the magazines held together with white ribbons in thick, tidy parcels. A seemingly brand-new stereo system and two modern Sony television sets at the entrance completed the scene. Did the Japanese make a habit of reading, or listening to classical music, or watching TV while throwing away their garbage?

And on the matter of newspapers, books, and magazines, my son, then aged nine, was in for a real surprise. It took a few months of living in Japan for me to understand his unusual and enthusiastic willingness to take down the garbage, even when the cans in the apartment were almost empty. Only after I noticed that the mattress on his bed was raised by several inches of graphically illustrated pornographic magazines did I discover the secret of his sudden desire to help with household chores. Delighted at the treasure trove of erotic, informative literature he had found, my son turned the huge garbage room into his own private library. Thus the plastic garbage cans in my kitchen were forever empty and his informal sexual education became ever richer, in descriptions of every imaginable pose, deviation, and sin devised by mankind.

It took me a while to understand what the almost-new TVs and stereo systems were doing in the garbage room. The Japanese don't usually repair broken electrical equipment. Nor do they sell their old appliances when a new model comes on the market. So, for example, in the same year that compact discs came into fashion, the Japanese threw out all their old stereo systems and quickly acquired the new equipment.

Anyone touring the streets of Japan cannot be blamed for thinking that the country is one giant junkyard for electrical equipment. Everywhere you look you see TV sets: on the sidewalks, on the street, in public parks, and beside bus stops. Every time we went for a walk around the block, we counted at least ten abandoned color TV sets. Most of these sets were in working order, and the others had only minimal damage, such as a missing switch or a broken antenna. There they sit, almost brand-new, for anyone to pick them up and take them home. If the TV is still serviceable, its Japanese owner takes the trouble to wind up its cord and tie it with a white ribbon. If the TV is beyond repair, the electrical cord is cut, so that no one makes the mistake of carrying home a useless set. The constant innovations in the Japanese electronics industry create a situation where the garbage rooms are full of modern, serviceable electrical equipment, including large fax machines (which have been replaced by the smaller, more sophisticated models), VCRs, computers, satellite dishes, small cookers, washing machines, microwave ovens, food processors, and small refrigerators, most of them clean and in good working order.

All these appliances looked as if their owners had taken the trouble of cleaning them before throwing them away, except one: the domestic toaster. These were sooty, and greasy. Toasters only cost about $20. After a few months, the Japanese prefer to throw it out, rather than clean it, and simply buy another one instead.

And I haven't even mentioned the decorated Japanese plates, thrown out because one piece in the set was broken, glass ornaments, pictures for which there was no longer any room, carpets, furniture, and bed linen—a lot of that—futons, blankets, and pillows. When the Japanese move house, they prefer to throw out their old sheets and blankets and buy new ones instead.

Those who come to live in Japan don't have to buy a thing. A three-day turn around the neighborhood and you'll find everything you need to furnish all the rooms in your house, including furniture, bedding, electrical appliances, and even houseplants in fancy pottery containers. If a plant has so much as one drooping leaf, or a wilted flower, it will be sent to the garbage room and a new one will take its place.

Delighted by the garbage room in our apartment building, and full of good intentions to make my own modest contribution to world ecology, I went straight out and bought five trash cans in varying sizes and colors, which filled the small kitchen in our apartment.

It wasn't easy to get used to this new concept, and I made a few mistakes here and there. The little plastic spool which had once held the camera film found its way into the organic waste, and once a broken jam jar was trashed with the metals. Accidents of this sort were accompanied by deep shame on my part and dozens of apologies—*"Gomenasai"*—to Kato, who always snooped and searched in my plastic bags of trash. He would grunt to himself in displeasure, pull out the offending objects, and wave them in front of my blushing face.

Actually, I was sympathetic to Kato's disapproval. From time to time, the Japanese press published statistics proving that this recycling did indeed constitute a significant savings to the nation's economy. This attitude to ecology and recycling is so well developed in Japan, that if a neighbor were to catch you throwing away unseparated trash, you would be likely to find yourself facing a neighborhood tribunal. Many of Tokyo's older areas have a neighborhood watch committee. Once a week, dressed in protective rubber boots and gloves, the ladies of the region rummage in and separate the neighborhood garbage, each to its own category. By afternoon, large piles of neatly folded and tied paper (almost like origami), piles of glass and piles of metals, accumulate on the sidewalk. Recycling vans circle the neighborhood to pick them up and to give the ladies gifts of toilet paper, fragrant soaps, and paper napkins—incentives for their work.

Houses in Japan are usually small and crowded and all sorts of things accumulate: objects received as gifts, spur-of-the-moment purchases, or things found in the garbage and hauled home. These things, which take up a great deal of space, can sometimes constitute a real threat to household serenity. The Japanese found a solution for this, too. Instead of simply throwing this stuff away, it is sold in flea markets all over the country, where entire Japanese families—children, old people, and even dogs—flock to the giant recycling festivals. The aim of these flea markets, if you are not a merchant, is to rid yourself, as ecologically and efficiently as possible, of your own personal trash, to enjoy the festive atmosphere and company, and to make a few pennies' profit. In these markets, ten dollars can buy you the latest ski equipment. Fifty dollars gets you a computer; new toys cost pennies, and you can buy designer clothes for the price of a bowl of soup.

The Japanese have solved the problem of domestic garbage, but there remains one particular ecological issue for which no solution has been found. The Japanese are decimating the tropical rain forests of South America to produce disposable chopsticks, which they use for traditional and hygienic reasons. The average Japanese person uses about five pairs of such chopsticks a day. Multiply this by a population of some 125 million, and the result is horrific. Forty acres of forest are clear-cut every day to supply wood for the chopstick industry.

Tokyo's most burning ecological problem is the disposal of used cars. No self-respecting Japanese would be seen driving a five-year-old car, as will be shown by the story of the battered seven-year-old Toyota which had faithfully served two Embassy families before I arrived. The Toyota very soon got on my neighbors' nerves because I parked it in the Royal Yoyogi's underground lot, between a shiny black Bentley and a silver Rolls-Royce. In the same row were parked several black Mercedes 560s with gold lights and panels, a fancy Porsche, a plain BMW 733, and two expensive Lotuses. The neighbors complained that anyone seeing my car would be appalled at the obvious poverty of its owner. In short, my car was well beneath my neighbors' dignity.

They poured out their wrath surreptitiously, late at night. They'd stop up the keyhole to the gas tank with chewing gum, smear dogshit on the handle, or simply give a passing kick at the already dented metalwork, in the hope that I would take the hint and get that pile of junk out of their parking lot. I was particularly offended by the dirty looks I got each morning from the uniformed, white-gloved chauffeurs as they stood waiting for their bosses.

After a war of attrition which lasted four years, I finally gave up and bought myself a newer and more respectable car. After all, one must remain on good terms with rich and irritable neighbors.

But then what was I to do with a used car? I went to Ogora, the Embassy's car dealer. Yes, he would be willing to dispose of the old crate for me, but I would have to pay him three hundred dollars for his trouble. A few phone calls by the Embassy's secretary saved me about one hundred dollars, and when they came to tow my Toyota away to the junkyard, at the cost of two hundred dollars, they let me know that they were doing me an enormous favor. My faithful old Toyota was mercilessly crushed.

Inconsiderate strangers, on leaving Japan, sometimes remove license plates and other identifying features from their cars and abandon them in some side street for the police to get rid of!

Gifts

The Japanese love to give gifts. And if you give a gift in Japan, you can be sure of receiving one in return, and if you want to receive a gift, you must first give one.

The gift you give in return must be better and more expensive and the gift you then receive will be more expensive than the one you gave. From a mathematical point of view, Japanese gift-giving increases geometrically. Luckily, we were able to escape from Japan in time; otherwise, we would have drowned in a sea of gifts. A French cartoonist living in Japan, once drew a couple of *gaijins* (foreigners) coming to visit their neighbors bearing a single flower. The neighbors return, bearing a little bonsai tree. The next visit sees them with a parcel, and the Japanese return with a larger parcel. And so on, until the last cartoon, when the foreigners are shown, despondently carrying on their backs a fancy gift-wrapped car, while the Japanese come to them with a yacht tied up with ribbons.

The first opportunity for gift-giving was on our first day in our new home in Tokyo. New neighbors are obliged to hand out gifts to the long-term residents and to apologize for the damage they have not yet had a chance to do. Thus, we found ourselves that same day, with a gigantic, carefully wrapped box of cookies, knocking on the door of our next-door neighbors, the Sasakis.

The door, which was held by a security chain, opened a crack to reveal the lady's worried and confused face. Worry, by the way, is the normal expression on the face of the average Japanese when approached by a stranger in the street or any other public place. This worry stems from the quite justifiable fear that he might not fully understand what the stranger wants and, therefore, be unable to help him.

Clutching the parcel in both hands, as we were instructed by the secretary, we presented it to our neighbor, muttering apologies for sins we had not yet committed. We apologized for the noise, the dust, the dirt, for disturbing the house's harmony, the peace and the quiet which we as new tenants would surely cost our neighbors, who would now have to suffer our presence for years to come.

The box of cookies was snatched from our hands through the crack left by the security chain, and a muttered *"Arigato-gozaimasu*—Thank you" was heard later from the depths of the dark apartment. Thus ended the first and most important stage in creating neighborly relations in our apartment block.

The next stage came the following day. A hesitant and unexpected knock on the door, and we, who were well trained in the Embassy's security precautions, jumped up to look through the peephole in the door. Mrs. Sasaki was standing there, hidden by a large and wondrous pot of orchids, wrapped and beribboned like a wedding cake. I had seen a pot just like this one in the flower shop next to the neighborhood railway station. It cost 480 dollars.

"I must apologize for the very cheap and poor quality flowers," whispered Mrs. Sasaki in embarrassment, and she pushed the heavy pot into our barren apartment. Thus ended the second stage in setting up neighborly relations.

I told the Embassy's secretary about the pot of orchids and she insisted vehemently, for the sake of our good name, that we go out and buy an even more expensive gift for our benefactor. Further consultations with Israeli friends who had lived in Tokyo a while and who had a lot of experience with this prevented a catastrophe—it was decided that we would not give a gift in return. Which was how we put an end to, in a forthright and somewhat unnatural way, the cycle of gift-giving in our apartment house.

But I never succeeded, no matter how hard I tried, not to be drawn into this gift-giving cycle to some extent. The Japanese have special days of the year when gifts are mandatory. On those days, all the big chain stores hold, literally, gift-giving festivals, putting aside whole floors for the purpose—during July, the time for summer gifts, and Christmas, which the Japanese were quick to adopt because of their love of giving gifts. The storeholders and factory owners have a heyday and, of course, so do those people lucky enough to receive gifts, who are also the ones giving gifts—in this Japanese orgy of consumer promotion.

What exactly do the Japanese give and receive on these special consumer holidays? Not a vase, or a painted plate, or a teapot, kitchen utensils or ornaments. They assume that you already have enough of these and anyway, your taste is not the same as theirs, and they wouldn't risk buying you something you wouldn't like. Also, since Japanese houses and apartments are usually small and overcrowded, any additional object would only cause headaches for the housewife, who would have trouble finding space for it. Which is why the Japanese invented perishable gifts, or edible gifts. For example: a Galia melon, presented in a fancy wooden box on a cushion of silk (150 dollars); a box of smoked duck (120 dollars); a frozen crab, on ice from an Antarctic iceberg, straight from the northern island of Hokkaido; a box of assorted teas, coffee, or oils; a parcel of jams, different-flavored butters; et cetera. A particularly original gift might be a container of hundreds of gallons of steamy, warm, and fragrant springwater, for filling the *ofuro* (Japanese bath). If the giver wishes to please a music lover, he might commission a small orchestra, who will play any tune for the modest sum of three hundred dollars. Some people might send an aquarium of live lobsters straight from Australia, at the cost of 150 dollars; fireflies, symbolizing the summer, which a young girl in a pretty cotton summer kimono will deliver to your home; and even statues made of ice in various sizes, which will be delivered to your doorstep by special deep-freeze trucks. Everything is acceptable and welcome, as long the principle of disposability is preserved. And all gifts are sent to your home wrapped in charming paper and tied with wide silk ribbons. Frozen gifts or perishables such as ice cream or chocolate, will be sent in dry ice in a special refrigerator truck.

Gift time means holiday time for the foreigners living in Japanese apartment blocks. This is when you can find elegant packages discarded in the apartment blocks' garbage rooms. Foreigners who are quick enough to pick up these discarded gifts can enjoy the full range of products offered by the fancy department stores. If the Japanese loathe or despise the bearer of the gift, they will not even open it, and thus save themselves the unpleasantness of enjoying it. Such a gift, wrapped and beribboned, will be thrown away. The recipients will be required to send a gift in return, of course, but this is merely *giri,* an unavoidable social obligation.

Then there is St. Valentine's Day, which in Japan is an all-chocolate gift day. This day was introduced into Japan during the 1960s by candy manufacturers, as a way of promoting chocolate sales. It has been a great success.

Unlike other countries where Valentine's Day greeting cards and gifts are exchanged, the Japanese use carved chocolate hearts wrapped in fancy paper as their main expression of affection on this particular holiday. On this day alone, chocolate sales can reach the sum of some $600 million. Only girls are allowed to give chocolate gifts to their boyfriends on Valentine's Day. Japanese sociologists explain that this gives young women in Japan a rare opportunity to take the initiative and form romantic connections with members of the opposite sex, within a society which does not usually encourage this kind of behavior. A young Japanese woman conducts her courtship of a man by baring her heart in a typically grave Japanese way. Unlike Westerners, who send anonymous Valentines to the objects of their affections, the young Japanese woman approaches her beloved quite openly and presents him with a gift of chocolate and an offer of friendship. By refusing to accept the gift, a young man shows clearly that he is not interested in a relationship.

St. Valentine's Day is most popular among high-school students. Large groups of girls, bearing carefully wrapped gifts of chocolate, crowd around the boys' schools, their eyes searching for the objects of their desire, who will soon pour out from the school gates. Since being adopted by the education authorities in recent years, this holiday has also become popular among all age groups, from elementary school to university.

The *"Giri-shoco,"* which can only be translated as "chocolate obligation," is another custom which takes place on this particular day. *"Giri-shoco"* is the chocolate gift a young woman is obliged to present to her male superior at work. While schoolgirls give chocolate gifts to the boys of their choice, working women have to offer such gifts to the young men with whom they work.

The Japanese male is given the chance to reciprocate a month later, on March 14. This day, known as the "white day," is an original Japanese idea, and was established by candy makers who, overcome by jealousy of the chocolate manufacturers' success, decided to create a day devoted entirely to men. This is the day on which men can return gifts of cookies, marshmallows, or any other kinds of sweet, so long as it is white. Any girl whose chocolate gift was received gratefully on Valentine's Day, and whose beloved gave her in return a gift of sugar cookies one month later, can safely begin sewing her wedding dress.

If you find yourself invited to a Japanese wedding, you are expected to bring with you a respectable check of at least $300, or an expensive, up-to-date electrical appliance. A gift will await you on your way out of the wedding. After all, you gave a gift, so you deserve one in return. Guests invited for the first time to a Japanese wedding find themselves somewhat embarrassed when they realize that the gift they receive is more valuable than the one they themselves gave. The kind of gift you might receive at a Japanese wedding might be a set of crystal glasses, an elegant hand-painted plate, a sophisticated wall clock bearing a photograph of the young couple, and all this is in addition to the large and expensive cake and fancy packaged trays of food.

And that's not all. If you are unfortunate enough to be invited to a Japanese funeral, you must bring with you an envelope containing a modest gift of money, perhaps $150. This is because a funeral costs a lot of money, albeit less than a wedding. The mourners must meet the heavy expenses of flowers, gifts to the priests, cremation, and payment for the hall. As you make your way out, with your head lowered in mourning, a gift will be pushed into your hand. You gave, therefore you must receive. This gift will be less fancy than the one given at a wedding, but then you did pay less this time. A funeral gift usually consists of a small tablecloth, or a few bottles of wine or a tray of sushi, all carefully wrapped and tied in white ribbon to signify mourning.

In receiving or giving gifts in Japan, one must follow the rules of presenting, receiving, and opening, and most important of all, wrapping. A person giving a gift must denigrate and devalue it as much as possible, and insist that it is no more than a bargain, bought at a cheap chain store (even if the gift is wrapped in "Wako" paper from Japan's most expensive store), altogether cheap and worthless. A good example is the gift I received from the wife of the president of a giant Japanese industrial concern: an unusual stand for a vase, made entirely of tiny pearls. When I expressed my delight, the giver waved her hand nonchalantly and insisted that it was cheap and that the pearls were paste.

A tip for the recipients: don't open the gift, unless you are specifically asked to do so. If you are asked, you must take the utmost care unwrapping it. You must not seem eager, or tear the ribbons, or, heaven forbid, the beautiful wrapping paper. The adhesive tape must be removed carefully, and the gift taken out gently. After looking at the gift and offering a thousand thanks and heaping praise on the giver for his excellent taste, the gift must be rewrapped, so that it may be taken home looking as if it had never been opened in the first place.

Every gift, even the simplest and cheapest, must be wrapped in attractive paper and tied with ribbons. Special care must be taken in choosing the quality of wrapping paper and the color of the ribbons, in order to avoid unfortunate mistakes, like the grave mistake I made when I gave a gift to my elderly friend. I chose the wrapping paper in the shop, and, of the large variety of ribbons available, I chose gold and silver, which I thought looked exceptionally beautiful against black wrapping paper. My friend paled as I ceremonially handed her the gift. It turned out later that gold and silver ribbons are used only for wedding gifts and my friend was an aging spinster.

You must be especially cautious with black and white ribbons, which are used only for wrapping funeral gifts. Green and red ribbons are used only on Christmas gifts.

When you're in Japan, you must also know what not to give as a gift. You must never give a gift containing fewer than ten articles, if they are of an even number. For instance, if you plan to give a coffee service as a gift, make sure the number of cups is uneven. An even number of cups spells bad luck, even death. Avoid, especially, presenting a gift containing four articles. The number four in Japanese, "*shi*," also means death. But you must also be careful of the number nine. In Japanese, nine—*kyu*—means devastation.

And as for flowers, act with caution. Flowers are customarily sent to a house of mourning, a hospital, and . . . when courting.

Cops and Yakuza

*T*he Japanese policeman at our doorstep bowed deeply and entered into a babble of apologies and questions in Japanese. *"Nihon go Vakarimasen.* I don't speak Japanese," I told him.

He hinted politely that he would like to come in, took off his highly polished shoes and, in snow-white stocking feet, padded his way reverently into our sitting room. From the polyethelene bag he was carrying, he pulled out a tattered, plastic-covered page written in English which began with apologies for wasting our precious time, for disturbing our privacy, and for the terrible inconvenience which awaited us. As soon as we returned the page to him, he pulled out a badly typed piece of paper containing a detailed questionnaire in English, requiring information on the size of our family, ages, country of origin, languages, pets, specific illnesses and problems, and all sorts of other weird and wonderful questions.

We later learned that, like all inhabitants of Japan, we had been honored by a visit by the neighborhood police officer. Our names and the other information he had gleaned were added to the list of all inhabitants of the Moto-Yoyogi suburb. This invaluable list is then kept in the police archives, at the *Koban*—the name given to the small, sparsely manned headquarters on the other side of the wide Yamata-Dori Road, which circles the city of Tokyo.

I had often seen this policeman patrolling the winding streets of our neighborhood on his bicycle. He made a habit of greeting me warmly, as if I were a close relation of his, asking at the top of his voice about my health and that of the rest of my family. That same Japanese policeman, whose name I never knew, became our own family policeman. All Japanese *koban* policemen are family policemen. They are supposed to be familiar with everyone who lives in their neighborhood, their families, their pets, and all their weaknesses. This proved to be very useful when we were expecting visitors who could not find their way to the little cul-de-sac where we lived. The *koban* police station is armed with detailed maps of the region, and the local policemen are always happy to come to the rescue.

"Ah, Horn-San," they called in relieved delight, as they recognized the name on the complex street map and led our wondering guest to our home.

Even when my son mislaid his school bag, or his gym clothes, the policeman would appear at the door and, with a ceremonious knock, present the lost objects. The policemen proved their exceptional efficiency when Shi-Shi, our rare Himalayan cat, was missing. On that occasion, the rest of the *koban* policemen were also called out, armed with torches, whistles, and a picture of the four-legged creature, who had disappeared while chasing a Japanese tabby in heat. Those same policemen would chastise me with motherly concern when they saw that I hadn't fastened the seat belts in my car, or call out over the *koban* loudspeakers if I neglected to follow the traffic rules. The policemen especially enjoyed accompanying my son, with the concern of a mother hen, when he crossed the street at the corner, calling after him, "*Aboonai*—Danger," and "*Kiyotskete*—Be careful."

The Japanese love to boast that their country is almost completely free of crime, and this is especially noticeable in the newspapers, travel guides, and the rest of the media. In fact, it was the first thing I read in my Japanese guidebooks.

Even the experts are unable to explain the "safe streets" phenomenon in the city of Tokyo. Is it because, or in spite of, the large number of policemen and police stations? Is the crime rate low because of the gentle and obedient nature of the Japanese people, or is it because of the many policemen constantly patrolling the streets and making their presence felt among the public?

One can walk through even the shadiest and seemingly suspect parts of Tokyo in relative safety. The drunks are not violent and don't attack you, and even in the terrible crush of the subway, you won't find any pickpockets (and if you do, they won't be Japanese). If you forget your purse or some other valuables in the street, the chances are you'll find them later on, lying where you left them, untouched. Either that, or waiting for you at the nearest police station.

Those who most appreciate this nonviolent society are Japan's foreign visitors. American women can breathe in relief at not having to serve as drivers and bodyguards to their teenagers returning home from late-night parties. They can also enjoy the luxury of wearing expensive jewelry or valuable fur coats in the street, without the fear of covetous eyes waiting to relieve them of their finery forcefully. In Tokyo, there are almost no burglars, no thieves, rapists, or even ordinary harassers. The Japanese enjoy watching such things in the movies, but not in their own homes.

The Japanese media enjoy boasting that the crime rate in Japan, which is already very low, gets lower every year. In Europe, for example, thirty-three times more people are robbed than are in Japan, and in the USA, the ratio is 274 times greater—or more. The already low percentage of break-ins in Japan gets lower by the year, while it rises steadily in the USA and Europe.

Japanese sociologists relate this to the Japanese educational system, which teaches its pupils docility and conformity. The low crime rate in Japan is due also to the long history of community policing and the neighborhood police station, the *Koban*, which was copied from the German police system and brought to Japan in 1888.

There are more than thirty thousand *koban* stations in Japan. These stations and their patrol system, whether pedestrian or on bicycles, permit constant police presence in the streets and accessibility to every place and event. At least once a year, the *koban* policemen pay a personal visit to all the inhabitants of their neighborhoods and take advantage of these visits to update themselves on all the latest gossip and to find out about any kind of strange activity which might be going on in any of the families. Occasionally, the policemen are called upon to admonish naughty children or quarreling neighbors or to investigate neighbors' complaints against each other. In smaller, more established neighborhoods, where everyone knows everyone else, the *koban* policemen use loudspeakers to wake up the inhabitants in the mornings, wish them a nice day, and offer them useful tips on how to behave during the day. And the public obeys.

We, the foreigners considered this blind obedience. People in Tokyo would never cross the road at a red light. Not even in a small side street and not if it was four o'clock in the morning and there had been no traffic on that road for hours. People in Tokyo obey the police even if they are being dispersed from fairgrounds and festival sites. Often, a police car drives up to a holiday site and a policeman preaches morality and good behavior for hours on end over a loudspeaker on the car's roof. As it starts getting late, the policeman, in the tone of a nursery-school teacher, tells the crowds that it's time to go home and to bed and the visitors, without protest and with perfect obedience, file out of the fairground in impeccable order.

Small towns and villages have their own local policeman, whose home is also the local police station. During the morning hours, the house serves as the police station, and in the afternoon, the policeman welcomes the local inhabitants, who come to dispense and hear the latest gossip. More than 250 Japanese policemen are employed "at home." Because of the negligible crime rate in these regions, the policemen are engaged mostly in keeping the peace between warring neighbors, looking for children who are late from some activity, and saving cats stuck in trees.

Policemen always arouse respect, mingled with some apprehension, among the general public. The Japanese police force knows how to make the most of this respect by placing policeman-shaped wood, plaster, or plastic statues at strategic points along the main highways. Sometimes, too, you can see a wood or plastic dummy police car stationed by the roadside. These full-uniform dummy policemen are cheaper to maintain than real flesh-and-blood policemen, but they are as effective in deterring crime. Coming across the dummy policeman or the shadow of a dummy police car, a law-abiding Japanese citizen will slow down and diligently follow traffic rules.

People in Japan receive constant reminders of the existence of the police force—in the form of their neighborhood *koban*, along the roads, the constantly patrolling traffic police, and of course, the dummy policemen. Thus the citizens of Japan are warned daily: the police are everywhere. Their eyes and ears are alert and open at all times. *Aboonai*—take care.

The Japanese respect for the law is probably based on the way in which the system originated. Following the Meiji revolution in 1868, a central government took over and the Feudal Lords lost all their power. The samurai were no longer allowed to carry swords in the street. It became necessary, therefore, to create a national police force. Toshiyoshi Kawaji, who was the first chief of the Tokyo police, defined the delegation of power between the government and the police force thus: "The government must serve as a parent to the Japanese people, while the job of the police force is as that of a governess."

The police in Japan have developed this rather nannylike image, so that when a citizen falls into their hands, the police will behave in a corrective and educational manner, pacifying and placating, just like a benevolent kindergarten teacher. A Japanese policeman usually contents himself with a reprimand when dealing with a citizen who has fallen afoul of the law, and releases him after a lengthy and exhausting sermon on morals. Naturally, the citizen is required to make a long series of apologies, groveling in the dust of repentance and a promise that he will never repeat his heinous crime.

Rarely do the police take stronger measures, more or less to set an example to the rest of society. The more drawn-out, profuse, and tearful the apologies, the more the police will see them as sincere and genuine. An apology accompanied by a long, heartrending confession causes the greatest satisfaction to the police, who see it as a successful fulfillment of their educational duty. This particular phenomenon is a staple of Japanese soap operas, which often depict a stern-faced policeman gradually softening and melting at the sight and sound of an endless apology delivered by a villain. The policeman stands there all the time sniffing back emotion and in the end, he packs the villain into a taxi and sends him safely home.

Quite a few foreigners making a lucrative living as street vendors or hostesses in Japan, and working without permits, fell into the hands of the police. They were also released after apologizing and promising that they would never repeat the crime. Of course, no sooner were they released than they were back along the sidewalk, or back in the bars.

All street vendors in Japan, whether foreigners or Japanese, are required to pay protection money to the Yakuza, the Japanese Mafia, who have taken over ownership of the country's sidewalks. This way they protect themselves from unpleasant confrontations with the police over street peddling, which is illegal in Japan.

Japan's police force has strong ties with Japan's organized crime. This organization consists of several gangs, whose members strut the streets, uninhibited and loudmouthed, dressed conspicuously in brightly colored outfits with wide flashy ties, their hair cut short to the roots or long and outlandishly curled.

The Yakuza organization, whose traditions go back hundreds of years, helps the Japanese police to curb the country's unorganized crime. It began under the Tokugawa shoguns who ruled Japan from 1603 to 1868. When Shogun Tokugawa's clerks decided that controlling organized crime was not in their power and they might as well recruit them to suppress the nonorganized crime in the country. So Yakuzas of old served to snuff out highway robbers and other small-time thieves and lowlifes who were not acting within a formal framework.

The Japanese Yakuza are full of professional pride. Each splinter gang has its own badge, slogan, and logo. The biggest gangsters flash their visiting cards, which are embellished with their gang's badge in exaggerated lettering. They also hand out gifts of magnetic telephone cards, bearing the gang's badge.

The Yakuza are convinced that they fulfill a very important social function. Were it not for their organization, they believe young people with antisocial tendencies would have nowhere to turn and Japan would have a high crime rate like the United States. The Yakuza gangs are among the very few organizations in Japan who accept members of the lower classes, as well as the "vile" Koreans into their ranks.

The Yakuza are often depicted in Japanese films as saviors of the persecuted. The Japanese film industry tends to throw a romantic light on the male solidarity and blood covenants within the various gangs belonging to the Yakuza and their stubborn adherence to ancient Japanese traditions. Television, too, devotes considerable time to them and allows gang leaders to explain to millions of viewers why no substitutes exist for the services only they can supply. When these gang leaders hold their periodic summit meetings in the best holiday resort hotels, heavily secured by hundreds of police, the organization makes sure the event is well publicized and receives plenty of media coverage.

The Yakuza also has its own internal newspaper, in which detailed reports appear of help given to the police in wiping out minor criminal activity, muggers, pickpockets, rapists, and kidnappers. The organization's unwritten rules say that the Yakuza are allowed to deal in the protection business, prostitution, protection against extortion, gambling, and pornography. The Yakuza are not allowed to deal in drugs (although changes have been seen here recently, since this is where the big money is. Still, in this field, the Yakuza prefer to keep their business outside of Japan). Furthermore, members of the organization are forbidden to conduct gang warfare in areas where innocent civilians might get hurt. Street signs have appeared recently, warning the public against the danger of gunfights in streets which belong to the Yakuza. These signs are put up by the police and recommend that the public bypass the streets in question rather than go through them.

This symbiotic relationship with the police may continue as long as the gang members do not deal drugs and no innocent blood is shed. In many cases, the gang leaders cooperate with the police by handing over members who overstep their own rules. These particular Yakuza members are then tried and thrown in jail, which gives them certain advantages and the chance to move up in the organization's hierarchy.

Despite its relaxed rapport and easy cooperation with the leaders of organized crime, the Japanese police force is always on the alert against attempts to merge all the various gangs within the Yakuza into a single national crime syndicate, which could easily endanger the delicate balance of power between the law and the Yakuza.

Every now and again, when the Yakuza raise their heads too high and become too conspicuous in society, voices are heard in Japan, calling to quash organized crime, once and for all. It is at such times that the Japanese police set about putting down the more fragmentary gangs, and help local groups quell the organization's activity in their neighborhoods, although these efforts are not really serious. The Japanese police are well aware that as soon as they do away with organized crime in Japan, they will be obliged to come to terms with unorganized crime, which might thrive in the land of the rising sun.

Recently, however, membership in the Yakuza has become less easy. A law passed by the Japanese Parliament in 1992 placed the organization firmly outside the law, thus ending the status quo which had always characterized the relationship between the organization and the establishment.

From now on, Yakuza members are not allowed even to hint that they belong to the organization. A person who looks as if he belongs to one of its gangs is in trouble. Admittedly, the law is not yet enforced, but many Yakuza members are now having plastic surgery to recreate chopped-off fingers, straightening hair previously permed into curls, and looking for lawful employment.

The organization's public relations have never been so good as they were in January 1995, when a disastrous earthquake struck Japan, destroying a good portion of the harbor town of Kobe and claiming some five thousand lives. More than three hundred thousand people were left homeless. The Yakuza revealed itself at its best. Thirty thousand members of the organization came from all corners of the country and took up positions on city streets armed with food, blankets, diapers, and milk for babies, at the order of Tashio Masaki, a henchman of Yoshinuri Watanaba, the leader of the Maguchi-Gumi organization. The Yakuza got some favorable coverage in the Japanese and international press, but it was short-lived.

Bathing Is a Community Affair

*C*onsidering her voluptuousness, Tova was surprisingly nimble as she peeled off her thick winter clothes impatiently. In no time at all she was naked, her heavy clothes stuffed into a small straw basket.

With her private parts covered only by a tiny towel and her bouncing bottom and majestic breasts exposed, Tova skipped to the baths, disdainfully ignoring the stark-naked middle-aged men busy scrubbing each other's backs. Try as they might, the Japanese men, famous for their discretion and champions of the sneak peek could not ignore her. It wasn't every day that the hot-water springs of the *onsen* were honored with a visit by a woman of such proportions, with such enormous breasts, and a redhead, too. The glances thrown in her direction were curious, wary, and amused, but held no lust. People go to the *onsen* baths solely to cleanse their bodies and purify their spirits. Flirting and sexual games are out of place and people do not go there to pick up partners.

Tova was oblivious to her audience as she slid into the bubbling pool of 45°C water, politely wishing the amazed bathers a polite and pleasant *"konichiwa"*—Good day. Within seconds the pool was empty of people. Tova floated on her back, thoroughly enjoying her privacy, her breasts resting on the surface of the water like two giant buoys. The Japanese bathers, who had beaten a hasty retreat, would have an impressive tale to tell at the bar or at the office when they got back from their vacation.

Tova surprised me, to tell the truth. We had been sharing a three-tatami-sized, horribly cold room. Room space in Japan is measured by the tatami, which is a three-foot-by-six-foot straw floor mat on which the futon is placed at night. In fact, it was the only room we could get at such short notice in the icy city of Sapporo on Japan's northern island of Hokkaido. The town was full of tourists because of the annual Festival of Ice. We had decided at the last moment to visit from Tokyo. Central heating was not included in the low price of the room. We had to sleep under several thick, cotton wool quilts to protect us from the cold, which was twenty-five degrees below outside. In the morning, after a restless night, red-nosed and stiff with cold, we got up to get dressed. Or at least I did. Tova insisted on getting dressed under her pile of quilts.

"Don't look," she ordered me. "I'm bashful. I don't want you to see how fat I am. I can't even look at myself." She was mumbling into the blankets as she went through complicated acrobatics trying to hook her bra. I looked away so as not to embarrass her. Later that day, after visiting all the fantasy buildings carved entirely out of ice, and freezing ourselves to the marrow, I suggested she come with me to an *onsen*.

"Are you crazy?" was her reply. "I've been living in Japan more than four years and I've never been to an *onsen*. I'm bashful. You know what Japanese women are like. They'll stare at me and then giggle behind their hands."

The cold, more powerful than even her bashfulness, finally led us to an elegant *onsen* not far from Sapporo. It was one of the most modern, well appointed and beautiful of all the *onsens* in Japan. "Don't worry," I told Tova, who was following me like a lost lamb. "This is a very modern *onsen*. I'm sure there'll be separate bathing for men and women."

I bought Tova a gigantic, garishly colored beach towel in a Sapporo department store. They couldn't understand why we wanted the largest towel they had in stock. Tova entered the water looking like a Moslem fundamentalist taking a dip in the sea, covered from head to toe in her enormous towel. The *onsen*'s warm water, relaxing atmosphere, and the sight of the Japanese ladies, wearing only a tiny towel for modesty's sake, soon thawed Tova's self-consciousness. After a few minutes she discarded her huge, soggy towel and dived naked into the pool of green tea. This was just one of the *onsen*'s several baths, each of which had a different water temperature, color, scent, and healing properties.

Her enthusiasm was undeterred by the presence of a few fully dressed male bath attendants, who made sure the baths were clean and unlittered. Men's baths, by the way, are usually staffed by women only.

By the following day, Tova was already getting dressed outside her pile of quilts. Encouraged by yesterday's pleasant experience, she urged me to go again to the *onsen*. We decided to try a different one, and I chose the classic, conservative *onsen* recommended to us by the hotel guidebook. I suspected that bathing in this particular *onsen* might be mixed-sex. I told Tova, and received a shy giggle in reply. We paid our token entrance fee and went into the changing room. It was a typical Japanese room: tatami-covered floor, straw baskets for storing clothes, and a wooden roof. Tova undressed quickly and hopped into the water. As I said, the surreptitious glances of the men all around did nothing to dampen her enjoyment. Tova, who had asked me just the day before to turn my back so as not to see her fat body, went freely from one bath to another under the probing and curious eyes of all the Japanese men present—and felt perfectly comfortable.

One outstanding characteristic of life in Japan is the national obsession with bathing. Anyone who's read *Shogun* remembers the thorough scrubbing the sailor undergoes after landing on the island.

The Japanese fascination with cleanliness is mentioned in Chinese history. The third-century Chinese described their primitive neighbors on the nearby island soaking and scalding their skin in hot baths. This feature of Japanese life was also noted by Christian missionaries and merchants from the sixteenth century. Foreigners don't understand this fascination until they actually experience the Japanese bath. Skeptical foreigners turn into devoted enthusiasts of hot baths, after emerging red-skinned, exhausted, and utterly relaxed.

Japan's many volcanoes and seismic regions supply hot spring-water to more than fifteen thousand baths all over the country. A Japanese bath is a delightful ritual. For some people, taking one is close to a religious experience. For others, it is purely physical, a healing cure for an ailing body and troubled soul. Few go to the baths solely to wash themselves and clean their bodies. In the West, bathing is an intimate act, carried out in the privacy of one's own home, but taking a bath in Japan is a public affair in which the whole family takes part, together with friends and business colleagues. Public baths in Japan have been an integral part of its communities for over four hundred years. Neighbors meet there to exchange the latest gossip. The hottest business deals are closed in the baths, and contracts are signed after lengthy and exhausting negotiations. People go to the baths to acquire new clients. Many choose to celebrate their birthdays in the baths, or their wedding anniversaries, or any other occasion worthy of a party.

The Japanese, who scrupulously avoid physical contact, can be seen at their best in the public baths, scrubbing each other's backs and, when asked, helping each other wash their hair. The bathrooms we are used to in the West are mostly small, sterile, and meant for one person at a time. Japanese bathrooms, on the other hand, are the most important room in the house. The rich, for whom the baths can be the center of household life, have their baths lavishly fashioned out of scented pine wood, with huge picture windows overlooking the landscape outside.

Like many foreigners in Tokyo, I soon became addicted to Japanese baths. After experiencing my first dip in the *onsen,* I tried them all, from the local neighborhood oforu, to the *onsen* and the open-air hot springs known as the Rotenburo.

They all have one thing in common: the bathing ritual itself. Each stage must be completed in a relaxed manner, and strictly according to the rules. This is crucial, and if you decide to skip any particular stage, you will be committing a serious breach of Japanese etiquette.

First you undress, slowly, calmly, taking care to fold your clothes and place them neatly in a basket provided for that purpose. Then remove your handkerchief-sized towel from its hermetically sealed packaging. This towel is meant to hide the genitals of the modest, to rub up a soapy foam on your body, or to place, soaked in cold water, on your forehead, to keep your head cool in the hot bath. You are supposed to wash and rinse yourself before entering the bath, using your small towel and the liquid soap provided beside all the taps. This is done in a kneeling position or seated on a small wooden or plastic stool, and bowls are used for pouring hot water over your soapy body. Heaven help the foreigner who dares climb into the bath before first washing himself thoroughly. This is unheard of and considered utterly filthy by the Japanese as well as extremely inconsiderate of other bathers.

After a dip in the bath, where the water is sometimes around 45°C, it is advisable to get out and scrub your body (or someone else's, while yours is being done for you) until you reach the boiled-red or purple color, typical of onsen bathers. Then out again, and in again, and so on. The climb into the water is slow and gradual and is a ritual in itself, especially if you are part of a large group of bathers. On entering the water, the Japanese make a point of loudly expressing their pleasure and discussing the quality of the water and the joys awaiting them. As they relax, they become gradually quieter and let their bodies enjoy the water, their eyes closed, and an expression of blissful oblivion on their faces.

It is difficult to explain the sublime feeling these baths engender. Stress vanishes, replaced by a relaxed feeling of harmony and happiness. All anger, tension, frustrations, and negative emotions disappear, and are supplanted by a complete and utter euphoria. The Japanese describe this sensation as that of a fetus in its mother's womb.

In private homes, the head of the family gets the privilege of taking the first bath, after which the children go in. Finally the wife gets her turn. The richer members of Japanese society have spacious bathrooms in their homes, and they tend to take their baths *en-famille,* helping each other get thoroughly clean. At the *onsen,* everyone, men and women and children, gets in together. Only the size of the pool dictates the number of people using it, and the larger pools can accommodate dozens of bathers at the same time. As far as the Japanese are concerned, a good wash is a communal one. Unlike Westerners, the Japanese have few taboos with respect to nakedness. They have always washed in groups. The traditional baths still have mixed bathing, although the more modern, Western-oriented baths tend to encourage separate-sex bathing. As soon as the clothes come off, the trappings of status and gender disappear. In a communal bath, everyone is equal.

Furthermore, a bath with friends, colleagues, and fellow students means that you develop a closer, more intimate relationship with them. *"Hadaka-no-tsukiai"* means "comrades-in-nakedness," and friends who have bathed together, so the saying goes, become closer than ever.

Bathing brings the Japanese back to nature. The bathroom in a Japanese house is inevitably built overlooking the pleasant view of a landscape, or a bush which grows close by, and baths in hotels are always decorated with natural-looking greenery, even if it is sometimes made of plastic.

Shinto, Japan's ancient religion, is also involved in bathing ritual. Tradition has it that the Sun God, the Moon God, and the God of Fertility and Agriculture were born in a bath used by the Isanagi (the Supreme God and father of all Gods) for washing himself. According to the Shinto religion, evil and immorality have always been identified with filth and iniquity, and these could be cleansed and purified by washing. In the Buddhist religion, too, Buddha celebrates his birthday in the bath. Statues of Buddha are transported from one place to another in mobile shrines, and washed in a rain of green Japanese tea, poured over them with a soup ladle made of bamboo. This washing is a gift to Buddha on his birthday.

My family, too, enjoyed the *onsen*, and we planned our tours of the Japanese islands to visit interesting baths on the way. There are plenty of them. We were always warmly welcomed, especially in the more remote places we visited, although once we were denied entry to a hilltop Rotenburo. After driving for hours and getting lost several times, we had finally reached these famous outdoor baths, set in charming scenery on the top of a hill. We sighed with relief, and went to pay our entrance fee, impatient to go in. To our great surprise, our entrance was politely but firmly blocked by the Mama-San in charge. With her arms crossed in front of her in a characteristic Japanese gesture of rejection, she made it quite clear that we could not enter and had best be on our way. We tried explaining to her that we had traveled far to get to her Rotenburo, whose tempting photograph was featured in the thick directory of *onsens*. But to no avail. Only when my desperately disappointed son burst into inconsolable tears did she give in grudgingly, drawing in her breath in a loud hiss. In Japan, when a child cries, you must let it have what it wants.

Happy and naked, we went straight to the steaming bath, politely wishing all the other bathers, *"Konichiwa*—Good day." The pleasant chatter which met our entry stopped abruptly and a tense and unexplained silence reigned. Not one of the bathers returned our greeting. We were watched with surprise and wonder by dozens of Japanese people scalding their flesh in hot water, but this was soon replaced by expressions of frustrated fury. They started stomping angrily out of the water, murmuring and muttering to themselves. It was only when we saw their naked, well-fleshed bodies that we understood why the Mama-San had tried to refuse us entry to the baths. The men's muscular, pot-bellied bodies were covered almost entirely with wonderful tattoos of dragons, guns, roses, and naked women. The women and children who followed them out of the water, also had pictures tattooed on their buttocks. We were especially taken by a beautiful tattoo of a brightly colored butterfly, on the shapely behind of one of the women. The butterfly seemed to fly with every step she took.

Our happiness at being allowed into the baths soon ended as we realized, horrified, that we had stumbled into a social gathering of the Japanese Mafia, the Yakuza. It was a closed event that no ordinary Japanese national had seen, or would ever see.

When we told the story to our Japanese friends on our return to Tokyo, we watched the blood drain from their faces. "You'd never have been allowed to leave alive," they told us in terror, "if you had been Japanese. Only the *baka-no-gaijin,* (the stupid foreigners, in other words) could get away with barging into a private party held by the Yakuza and live to tell the tale."

For us, the nicest kind of Japanese baths were the outdoor Roten-buros, and we were willing to travel for hours and brave traffic jams if we knew a special one waited at the end. Nothing compares with this kind of bathing. Anyone who has bathed under the skies, under a canopy of trees, on a starry night, knows the feeling of slipping calmly into the gentle harmony of his surroundings. Here, with your eyes closed, in a state of utter peace, you can hear the sounds of nature: the falling of autumn leaves on a bed of moss, the wind whistling through branches, and the soft bubbling of the scented water rising from the hot springs. This kind of bathing is extra special during the cold winter months, when the entire site is covered with a soft blanket of snow. With your head exposed to the freezing air, and your body deep in the hot bubbling water, bathing becomes a transcending experience. Climbing out of the hot water into the cold air outside is part of the pleasure. The heat accumulated in your bones stays with you all day.

An entire tourist industry has sprung up around the Rotenburo. TV programs and journals describe tours of Rotenburo sites all over the island. Some of the Rotenburo's "natural surrounds" are actually man-made. When we were there, the latest fashion was jungle bathing. Imagine a Rotenburo set in an artificial jungle, complete with plaster animals, tropical vegetation, piped birdsong, and the roar of wild animals, and to complete the jungle atmosphere, the attendants dressed in Tarzan outfits. A little more imagination and you believe that you are searing your flesh in an Amazonian rain forest.

The Japanese have devised other ways of dipping your body in hot liquid. For example, pools full of white oily water are reminiscent of the milk baths of the ancient Roman aristocrats—except for the huge plastic cow looking up at you from the water. There are mud baths, yellow baths full of dissolved sulfur, coffee baths, tea baths, baths full of Japanese rice wine, and baths where the bather is buried up to his neck in sand. Adventurous bathers skip from one kind of bath to another and wash themselves in clean water between each exotic dip. When it comes to the pleasures of bathing the Japanese know no bounds. Some baths have been carved out inside rivers, with plate glass instead of riverbeds. Bathers can watch fish swimming beneath them. Others are situated inside a moving cable car, and you can recline in the water at a height of sixty meters and watch the scenery moving slowly by. The cable car takes you to your final destination, which is a much larger bath, but this time, on solid land. The Kanaku Hotel, in Arito, has pools suspended between earth and sky. On the northern island of Hokkaido, there's a wooden bath fastened into a hole almost five feet wide drilled into the ice. That's the place to go when you fancy a sip of hot sake, while enjoying the frozen arctic landscape around you. The Japanese have also designed baths cast in gold, for those people who have plenty of ready cash. In Japan, when it come to bathing, anything goes.

There are baths in the wilds of the countryside, where you might find yourself sharing your water with creatures which are not of your own species. At the Rotenburo in Takaguwa, for instance, you'll have the pleasure of bathing with a few tame (or so you hope!) bears, belonging to the *onsen*'s owner. You might like to experience the Jigukodani onsen in the Nagano region, where you can bathe in the company of Japanese apes, who come down from the mountains to warm their frozen bones in the health-giving waters.

The culinary aspect is an integral part of the Japanese bathing experience. Hotels advertise their baths together with a vast array of dishes that their kitchens have prepared for your pleasure. Although menus are usually based on fish and fresh seafood, you can order any kind of meal you prefer.

The Japanese have also come up with a solution for people who can't afford, or have no time, to visit the onsen on a regular basis. *If* you cannot go to the onsen, the onsen will come to you. You can buy onsen salts in various shades, colors, and flavors, which you can mix into your own domestic bathwater and enjoy the pleasures of an onsen in your own home. You can even order the onsen container to come to your home where, for a pittance, warm, freshly drawn onsen water will be poured into your own private furo.

If faced with a choice between cooked food and no bath, Japanese people would use their precious coals to heat water, rather than cook food. They can live without hot meals, but not without their beloved hot baths.

The Throne Room

*O*ne of the things I dreaded most was a visit to the bathroom of a Japanese friend. Often I chose to suffer in silence, rather than use my host's bathroom. By holding it in, I spared myself unnecessary distress and humiliation. I would have done anything rather than go through a certain experience again. The memory of it makes me cringe in shame, even to this day.

Going to the bathroom in Japan can be a complicated business. Anyone wanting to use a modern Japanese bathroom should go through a special training course, because sometimes common sense may not be enough. A foreigner, unable to read Japanese, might well face disaster, humiliation, and disgrace.

I know, because it happened to me. When I was new in Tokyo, I was invited to a women-only lunch at the home of one of my new friends. The house itself, a typical Japanese home, old-fashioned and conservative, with low furniture and tatami-mat floors, offered no hint of the modern technological disaster to come.

I asked for the bathroom, and my hostess led me there herself, barely able to conceal her obvious pride. As I removed my soft carpet slippers and replaced them with a pair of special plastic bathroom slippers, I was overwhelmed by the modernity of the room. It looked like the inside of a spaceship. I made my way toward the toilet, which looked like the ejector seat in a fighter airplane, with dozens of buttons and switches arranged all around. I sat down with relief on the spotlessly clean seat, and jumped up again as if bitten by a snake. It was hot, scorchingly so, burning as if someone very fat had sat there for many hours before me, until a desired result had finally hatched. My bladder was insistent so I decided to hover some distance above the burning seat, to avoid scorching my poor bottom again.

I then looked for toilet paper and couldn't find any. I reconciled myself to this unfortunate fact, and decided to press the nearest button on the high-tech control board surrounding me. To my complete surprise, a small spout appeared from nowhere and sprayed me all over with a pleasant stream of water. If my bottom had still been in the vicinity, it would have enjoyed a very sophisticated bidet. Instead, I was soaked from head to toe. I tried the next button and immediately the small room was filled with deafening stereophonic music, which I didn't know how to turn off. Another button cooled the toilet seat and a fourth caused the seat to slam down; I was unable to reraise it. I point out in my defense that all the buttons were marked in Japanese, and had no translations of any kind for the benefit of guests from more primitive civilizations. No matter how hard I tried and the number of buttons I pushed, I was unable to find the one that flushed the toilet.

Shamed and embarrassed, I returned to the dining room, where twenty pairs of eyes awaited me, genuinely concerned at my delay. I walked up to them, soaked to the skin, my hair askew, still wearing the bathroom slippers and spreading unwanted germs all over the tatami floor.

In matters sanitary, the Japanese have come a long way in a short time. Until the Second World War, Japanese bathrooms, usually situated in an outhouse in the garden, were no more than a hole in the ground. The wealthier members of Japanese society had toilets made of fine porcelain, decorated with dainty blue motifs. Today, these antique toilets, which had to be flushed with a bucket of water, fetch hefty prices in many of Japan's outdoor flea markets. The Japanese themselves are shocked when they see these relics of their past in the homes of foreigners, used as plant pots or umbrella stands.

Until quite recently, the immaculate Japanese were appalled at the thought of the skin of their nether regions contacting a toilet seat that had previously seated someone else. Thus they invented the low toilet, which requires squatting. Japanese doctors insist that a squat is the healthiest one to empty the bowels. This is the most common sort of toilet in Japan's older homes and public buildings. A foreigner encountering one for the first time might be baffled as to which way he should face when squatting. One of my friends pinned a picture on the wrong wall of this important room, thus proving effectively that she was squatting in the wrong direction. It was only after I had pointed out her mistake that she knew that for all her years in Japan, she had squatted with her face, and not her back, to the door.

In Japan's past, public rest rooms were communal and still are in some places. I remember clearly my first visit to such a rest room, which was in the building where I taught a beginners' Hebrew class. I opened a door marked with a picture of a woman and a man, and found two of my elderly male students standing at the urinals. They greeted me with a pleasant nod of the head and didn't seem to understand my shock.

I ran out of there as fast as I could and made sure, throughout the lesson, not to look directly at them. I blamed myself, of course, for confusing the signs on the door. Later, during recess, I asked one of my female students to lead me to the ladies' rest room, and she took me back to the same place. She also told me that next to the men's urinals was a small door leading to a Japanese-style toilet for more solid needs and women's use. This kind of co-ed bathroom may still be found in Japanese institutions, restaurants, and railway stations. There's no point in waiting for the last Japanese gentleman to leave. The constant two-way traffic includes men and women alike.

Nowadays, Japanese bathrooms are the most sophisticated in the world, but the modernization of anything to do with the tender skin of the conservative Japanese bottom was difficult in the extreme. In May 1917, a company called To-To began to manufacture bathroom fixtures. This company was an offshoot of Noritake, famous for its beautiful porcelain dinner services. Introducing the porcelain commode into the Japanese market was not at all easy. Pamphlets were circulated and items were placed in the newspapers extolling the new kind of sanitary hygiene. The upper classes and hotels were finally persuaded of the advantages of porcelain receptacles over a plain old hole in the ground.

Following the Second World War, Western-style toilets became more popular. Provincial restaurants and hotels still have to put up notices explaining how to use these—where to place one's bottom and how to flush afterward. Since the bathroom is not heated in most Japanese homes, the Japanese have invented the electrically heated toilet seat. Those who cannot afford such a luxury, however, cover the seat with a piece of wool or flannel fabric.

The Japanese are world leaders in almost everything concerning toilets, urinals, and baths. In the heart of Japan's most expensive and prestigious business area, the Ginza, is the To-To Building: twelve stories featuring every kind of sanitary installation under the sun. Walk through this building and you will be exposed to the most unbelievable and imaginative ideas for toilets and bathrooms. For example, a digital medical toilet, perfect for the budding hypochondriac. Sit on this seat (with your pants down, of course), and it will take your temperature and blood pressure. The seat can also determine if there are traces of albumin, sugar, or blood in your urine, and will report this information on a computer monitor, placed above the toilet. Blood traces in the feces set off an alarm system, which will send you running to the nearest doctor.

Toilet seats of the kind I encountered at my friend's home are equipped with computer chips. They were first developed for use by the handicapped, and saved them the difficulty of using toilet paper, by automatically controlled washing and drying of the relevant area. However, they have become very popular among Japan's urban population and have replaced the old, traditional toilets in even the most conservative of homes.

Once again, the To-To Company used the same aggressive marketing methods it had perfected at the beginning of the century when it succeeded in persuading the Japanese to adopt the newfangled porcelain toilets. This time, however, it was to introduce the new toilet system into the market. By the end of 1992, the company had sold over four million such toilets, and Japan became the world leader in the system which is doing away with the need for toilet paper.

At the end of 1993, the To-To Company proudly reported a profit of 418.4 billion yen ($4.1 billion) and a staff numbering 11,640 workers. More than one-half of the country's toilets bear the trademark of the company which has so improved the lot of Japanese bottoms.

With all these innovations, the Japanese do not bother to repair a cracked toilet bowl or a broken seat. It is simpler to buy a newer, more modern model than to waste time with repairs.

An Israeli friend of mine, whose husband was the representative of a large company, had a broken toilet seat in her Tokyo house. Although it was an old-fashioned, plastic seat, it was of a particular aubergine color, which she was unable to replace. With the help of an interpreter, she managed to explain the problem to a technician, who arrived within an hour, dressed in a three-piece suit and white cotton gloves and carrying a leather briefcase. The toilet technician, or perhaps he was an engineer, was led to the bathroom. He studied the problem and puffed short rhythmic bursts of air through pursed lips—the Japanese way of expressing displeasure. On his way out he gave his diagnosis: a broken toilet seat.

"Yes, that's why I called you," my friend reminded him.

"I know," was his reply, "but I have to examine it and give a full professional diagnosis. I suggest you change the entire toilet. This one is an out-of-date model, at least five years old. It'll give you nothing but trouble from now on."

My friend refused his offer for quite understandable reasons, and the following day he returned with two more technicians, who carefully and professionally replaced the toilet seat. The price they demanded, and received, for changing a broken plastic toilet seat was $1,200.

Japan has also undergone a serious revolution with regard to public rest rooms. No more of those dank toilets of old. In 1985, an organization was formed called the J.T.A.—the Japanese Toilets Association. Among its members are doctors, engineers, architects, sculptors, and senior clerks, all trying to revamp the country's outmoded public toilets.

The association encourages local authorities and municipalities to construct public toilets which look like restaurants, bars, temples, churches, and space stations. In other words, any architectural style is fine. These new toilets have become a mecca for Japanese and foreign tourists, with taxi companies including them in their organized tours. Quite frequently, you come across exhausted tourists, wandering around a restaurant-style public toilet, who seem to be expecting waitresses and tables. Most of Japan's new public toilets are also equipped with large, well-appointed facilities for the handicapped, tiny toilets for children, as well as diaper tables. The association, almost fanatic in its concern for Japan's public toilets, even organized the first international congress on bathrooms. Sanitation experts from all over the world took part.

While we are on the subject, I might point out that the Japanese usually separate baths and toilets and when it comes to the bath—in Japan, the sky really is the limit! If you have enough money, you can buy a dream bath, which is enormous, and, of course, can turn into a Jacuzzi at the touch of a button. A color TV can be positioned near the bath to enliven bathing hours. If you prefer, you could listen to music on the sophisticated stereo system installed in the bath. Add a built-in telephone and computer console with which to turn on the oven to bake a cake or turn it off once the chicken is cooked. The TV screen also lets you know what is happening in the other rooms in the house. A touch of a digital button and you can change the temperature of the water and sweet-smelling bath salts will scent the water.

If you're thinking of buying such a bath, make sure you're getting your money's worth. Try it out first. All you need do is fix a date for a visit with the store's saleslady. You'll be presented with a new, soft and fluffy towel, slippers, and your favorite soap. You can now step into a bath full of steaming hot water, all yours to test for a few hours. The publicity people are confident that anyone who tries one, buys one.

A store specializing in special carved toilets imported from the West has found an original way of encouraging sales. It opened a coffee shop which overlooks Tokyo. Their customers are invited to sip coffee, nibble rich, cream-filled cakes, surrounded by toilets of all shapes and sizes—some elegant and shining and cast in gold or silver, some carved to look like the Venus de Milo or muscular Atlas, bearing a toilet bowl on his shoulders as if it were the world. They sell toilets made to look like genitalia, or supported by marble lions, and many, many others.

And finally, there's a gadget which has changed the water balance all over Japan. In recent years, Japan has suffered several droughts. The country faced a real danger of having her water reservoirs dry up completely. The result: the Japanese became acutely aware of water-preservation issues. Research carried out by the Fuji Bank on the water consumption habits of its workers, showed that Japanese women waste around twenty-five gallons of

water every day in flushing the toilet. They flush immediately before using the toilet; they then flush it during use, to drown out unavoidable noises. Then comes the final flush.

For $65, you can buy an interesting little Japanese invention
which makes a sound like a flushing toilet, without using any
water. This gadget has become very popular throughout Japan for
saving one out of three toilet flushes and a great deal of water in
the nation's reservoirs.

How Come the Japanese Don't Sweat in Summer?

*A*nyone traveling in a tightly packed subway in Japan on a sweltering August day when the temperature is high and humidity is around 100 percent, certainly must wonder why the Japanese (both men and women), buttoned up in their conservative suits, do not reek of perspiration. The train carriages are free of body odor. Nor is there a whiff of perfume of any kind, or of aftershave or even deodorant.

Indeed, it seems that the Japanese do not exude body smells, loathe them, try hard not to emit these in public, and do their best to dispose of obnoxious body odors and perspiration. The problem is especially serious among Japanese women. If a Japanese woman is ever accused of suffering from body odor, her chances of finding a decent husband are extremely slim.

Surgery is the most popular way of getting rid of one's repulsive body odor forever. For the meager sum of around $2,000, all your sweat glands can be removed in one operation. The most popular place for these operations is the Jojin Clinic at the Ginza.

The place looks like a beauty salon, with pink wallpaper and charming uniformed nurses, also in pink. As well as the popular operations for widening eyes and narrowing flat noses, the clinic deals largely with genital surgery. A circumcision costs around $1,000; for $1,200 you can have your hymen re-sewn; vaginal narrowing, for heightened friction and pleasure—around $1,300. The clinic doesn't really recommend stitching a pearl under the skin at the tip of the penis, but will do this operation if asked.

The Japanese don't like to hang their intimate laundry outside. Laundries in Tokyo have little cubbyholes which resemble safety deposit boxes in railway stations and airports, only these are used for intimate garments. For seven dollars, you get a key to your own private cubbyhole, into which you can shove all your dirty underwear. At the price of one hundred yen per object, you can come back the following day to find all your clothes waiting for you, clean, scented and immaculately folded.

These laundry deposit boxes are an ideal solution for those women who have fallen victim to underwear fetishists and various other perverts, willing to put their lives on the line and sneak up in the middle of the night to steal lingerie off clotheslines.

The Japanese have solutions to almost every problem. For instance, what if a child needs to go to the bathroom at a time and in a place totally unsuitable for this?

Simple. All you need is a little, elongated pocket-shaped rubber bag, which can be used for either sex and for any age (and in this case the Japanese make no distinction between male and female) to empty your bladder with utmost discretion. This portable potty may be attached to the body's nether regions and allows you to empty yourself quite surreptitiously. Not a single drop will escape and the product is almost accident-proof. After use, a chemical substance is added to the liquid, which turns the urine into a jelly which can be disposed of in the trash. A good solution for the bedridden as well.

Why do the Japanese wind a hot, thick cotton belt around their middles even in summer? This question always troubles foreigners to Japan, who first encounter this quirk of the local population when they share their communal bathing houses. There is a religious reason. The Japanese believe that, of all the body's organs, the soul, the *ki*, chose the stomach in which to reside. Since the soul is fragile and vulnerable, it must be protected from cold, blows, or any other mishaps. The belt keeps the *ki* dry and warm and serves as an excellent means of insulation in all seasons.

"In summer, it's especially important to keep the *ki* dry," I was once told by a naked Japanese man in a communal bath. "The soul has not yet had time to get used to the changing weather." He was deadly serious as he wound the lengthy bandage around his thick middle.Surgical masks covering the faces of many Japanese are also a commonplace sight in Japan. You can see them everywhere: in the train, in the office, in cinemas, and even in restaurants, where they are removed temporarily for easy access to the mouth. The masks are made of cotton and serve a double purpose: to protect the environment from the germs you might spread, and, at the same time, to protect you from all those fatal germs breathed out by inconsiderate people. Furthermore, the masks filter out the foul air prevalent in all the industrial cities of Japan. During the cold Japanese winters, the masks help warm up the air you breathe into your frozen nostrils. The Japanese, ever aware of the dictates of fashion, have recently manufactured surgical masks in various colors and designs. Now people can hide their faces behind brightly colored masks bearing the message *"Atishoo,"* or "Walking back to health."

A Japanese professor of medicine at the distinguished University of Tokyo has discovered that these simple cotton masks are very effective against common hay fever caused by plant pollen. The pollen count rises in the spring, when millions of Japanese suffer from chronic runny noses and red eyes. The professor exposed his students to air filled with some 15,000 units of pollen, and proved that the masks were able to block about 60 percent of the pollen. The masks become even more effective when first dipped in water and worn damp. Nearly 90 percent of the pollen was blocked.

Even Japanese chewing gum has special properties which supposedly promote health and hygiene. The Japanese do not chew gum merely for pleasure, or out of boredom. Each chewing gum has a different purpose, and one doesn't waste energy on idle chewing. The Japanese use chewing gum to learn about the state of their health, to improve their state of mind, and to enhance their concentration.

They have developed a special chewing gum for diagnosing a person's physical condition. "Chew for three minutes and check the color of the gum. If it's dark pink—you're healthy. Green—go straight to bed."

Chewing gum in Japan is produced for various other conditions. There's a special gum for life's more intimate moments, and for those who don't understand, the pink wrapping has a picture of a couple kissing; there's gum for swimmers; gum for tennis players; and there's even gum to chew before exams. You can buy gum to lift your morale and gum made especially for drivers, to keep them alert and safe on the roads.

Moving house in Japan is also done with maximum attention to hygiene. In addition to their meticulous packing, which treats your lowly bedroom slippers as if they were a priceless Ming Dynasty jar, the large removals firm, 0123, will handle your move with the greatest care possible. While you accompany your belongings in a giant container, which has a separate section for you and your family to sit in, and which looks for all the world like an average living room—with armchairs, a TV and VCR and videocassettes for you to watch on your way to your new home—all your worldly goods are undergoing a special process of sterilization against cockroaches, fleas, fungi, mildew, and many other evils. Your possessions, when unloaded in front of your new home, will be clean, sterilized, and free of all potential ills and pests.

And yet another unique Japanese service especially for those who suffer from the foul, polluted air in the industrial towns and who get dizzy from lack of oxygen: the Oxygen Bar.

This bar is usually situated in the sports departments of the large stores or in coffeehouses and offers an inhalation of 95 percent pure oxygen. The cost of a three-minute breathe-in is less than one dollar. If the customer wants some takeout oxygen for the wife and kids, he can buy a spray bottle of it for five dollars and breathe in fresh air in the comfort of his own home. With increased pollution in Tokyo, the demand for oxygen has grown enormously, and millions of yen have been rolling in for the company that invented the idea of air-to-go. Or would you like to breathe it here?

Unwelcome Guests

*O*n my return home one day, I confronted a tall, narrow, shiny, black-lacquered cabinet with carved golden studs.

"What do you think?" my husband asked me proudly, opening wide the doors of his first purchase in Tokyo, and showing me its insides. What I saw was incredibly beautiful. The cabinet contained an entire Japanese shrine carved in wood and painted in gold. Gold chains hung down from the roof of the shrine over a tiny golden altar, and miniature golden devotional objects, such as bells, boxes, and flowers, all made of black-and-gold lacquered wood, decorated the inside of the cabinet.

"What is it?" I asked. Of all the joys and wonders Japan had to offer, my husband was obsessed with collecting useless Japanese objets d'art. These gradually filled our home and left us barely enough space to move around.

"Can't you see?" he asked in reply. "It's a portable shrine. A real bargain."

I looked into the cabinet again. Despite the beauty of the shrine and the beautiful things inside it, I was overcome with an inexplicable and unpleasant foreboding. The following day, I stayed home with the cabinet. That was the day Maki, my ikebana (Japanese flower-arranging) teacher arrived. Maki, a fifty-year-old spinster with a high-pitched squeaky voice, was infamous for her un-inhibited bouts of hysteria.

She noticed the new acquisition as soon as she entered the apartment. With a cry of sheer terror, she turned on her heels and fled the house.

"What's the matter with you?" I followed her, worried.

"What's that thing doing in your apartment?" she asked in reply, her voice trembling.

"What 'thing'?" I asked.

"The *butsudan*" she whispered, as if afraid to say the word out loud.

"Oh, that cabinet. My husband bought it in the flea market," I tried to explain.

"*Dame, dame.* It's forbidden," she kept murmuring. "It's not good."

She asked that our next lesson take place elsewhere. In fact, following the incident with the family altar, she refused to set foot in our apartment ever again. So, I had my first and last lesson in the Japanese art of flower-arranging, a fact which made me practically the only foreign woman in the whole of Tokyo who never became practiced in it.

Similar responses, if more restrained and sometimes quite amusing, came from other Japanese people who visited our home. Every single one of them asked the same question: "What's a *butsudan* doing in your home?"

I discovered a similar cabinet when I went to Kazuko, my very first student of Hebrew. Kazuko was also learning Arabic, Persian, Greek, Russian, German, Egyptian-style belly-dancing and how to play the oud, a Middle Eastern stringed instrument. "It belongs to *Oba-san* —grandmother," she said, and pulled an ornate ceramic jar from out of the cabinet which could have been the twin of ours, and which had a place of honor, adorned with white plastic flowers, beside the TV in her room. The jar, she explained, held the ashes of her grandmother, who had died the month before.

With this revelation and fired by a spirit of mission, I returned home and demanded that we get rid of that coffin immediately.

"The Japanese will never visit our home," I threatened. "It is extremely tactless to use a coffin for interior decoration. How would you feel if you visited a family of foreigners who kept wine in a coffin or grew geraniums in a sarcophagus?" I asked my husband reproachfully.

But the cabinet did not leave the house even after I warned him that it was either it or me. The cabinet remained even when we encountered severe responses from businessmen who came to our apartment for a cocktail party and dinner.

Even when electric lightbulbs burned out with extraordinary frequency, the bathroom taps turned themselves on in the middle of the night and flooded the apartment, and strange grunts and groans could be heard from every corner, my husband remained adamant. The cabinet stayed.

Only after repeated arguments and for the sake of peace did he compromise and drag the cabinet to one of our smaller rooms. I hoped that this would solve the problem temporarily, but the poltergeists did not stop.

The Japanese secretaries at the Jewish Community Organization, which I managed during my stay in Japan, did not sound at all amused when I told them of my problem.

Even removing the cabinet from the apartment would not solve the issue of the *obaka,* the ghost of the mythological devil who dwells in cabinets of this kind, said Yamato with a deadly earnest expression on her face. "You'll have to call in the priest, who'll spray salt and holy water to exorcise the devil. In the meantime you have to mollify him. You're supposed to give the *obaka* a cup of tea and rice every day. The Japanese make a point of giving food to the butsudan before they sit down to eat. Otherwise, he will be angry. You've probably starved him half to death by now, and he's annoyed, which is why he turns on your taps and turns out the lights," she told me with a nervous and unpleasant giggle. Yamato also promised me that she would not set foot in my home unless I first got the priest to dispose of the *obaka.*

In desperation, I consulted with Mrs. Ono, an Irish woman with a great deal of humor and common sense, who had arrived in the country many years before and married a Japanese man, whom she had since divorced. Mrs. Ono insisted that Jewish blood flowed in her veins, and she never missed an event or celebration at the Community Building. She made her living by managing the International School in our neighborhood, and was famous for her partiality to her Israeli pupils.

Mrs. Ono was genuinely sympathetic and burst out laughing. "I bet you won't believe what happened to me when I first arrived in Japan as a young bride. I lived with my parents-in-law, of course. One day, my three-year-old son Stephen was playing with the ashes jar in the butsudan and all the ashes poured out on the floor, or rather the tatami mats. Since no one had told me what was in the jar, I quickly cleaned up the mess with a vacuum cleaner. You should have seen my parents-in-law and all the rest of the family having an emergency gathering after the tragedy. The contents of the vacuum cleaner were spread out on a white sheet and everyone was bending over with the fear of God in their eyes, trying to distinguish between *ogi-san*—grandfather, *oba-san*—grandmother, and ordinary dust.

"And as for the *obaka*"—she became suddenly serious—"I do believe in it. All sorts of strange things happened to me as well, and I was obliged to call in your rabbi, the minister from my church, and the local Shinto priest. I don't know which of them did the trick, but the fact is that the strange happenings did stop eventually," she said. Her earnestness sent a shudder down my spine.

Almost every Japanese I approached on the subject supplied me with their version of their experiences with the *obaka*. I got the impression that the entire island of Japan is alive with devils, ghosts, and all sorts of other ghouls, who delight in frightening the life out of us.

I was particularly upset by the story of Harada, a typical Japanese yuppie. I got to know Harada when she came to a reception I gave in my home, with her father, a Japanese businessman who had commercial ties with Israel. Harada, a journalist by profession, spoke fluent English, which she had picked up during her many travels around the world. She seemed to me the personification of the modern liberated Japanese woman. One evening she called me at home and asked urgently to meet me. The following day we met at the popular restaurant "Victoria Station" in the middle of Tokyo. I was already used to Japanese people I knew opening their hearts to me and telling me about their troubles and worries. It is always easier to confide in a stranger. I prepared myself for the usual "bride and mother-in-law" story that I expected to hear from Harada, who was about to get married to a young man she had met at the university.

"Every night," she began, without preamble, "an *obaka* appears before me in the form of a longhaired woman with blurred features. She sits at the foot of my futon. Only when I speak nicely to her does she disappear and get swallowed up in a dark corner of the room. Sometimes she even writes on an imaginary typewriter. I brought an expert on ghosts to the house, and she thinks the typewriter is a Remington model from the beginning of the century."

From the dark circles round her eyes and her drawn face, I could see that Harada was indeed in distress. The color and smile returned to her face several months later, when she moved away from her nightmare-filled apartment.

In Western folklore, troublesome ghosts tend to turn up with the wailing winter winds and the dry rustle of bare branches at the window. Japanese ghosts wander around freely throughout the hot and steamy summer evenings. The word *obaka* embraces a wide range of devils, ghosts, negative energies, dark forces, and haunted creatures. Tales are told of Oaiva, the beautiful young girl whose face was mutilated, and of the faceless Mojineh. There are also stories about Yoreh and Boreh, ghosts of the dead and hosts of devils and creatures of death, who play wicked tricks on humans. You simply cannot get away from ghosts in Japan. You find them in the comic books, in children's television cartoons, in adult entertainment programs, and especially in the imagination of the Japanese people.

Long before the invention of air-conditioning, the characters and ghosts of the Kabuki theater sent chills down the audience's spine, even on Tokyo's hot summer days. In July, so the legend goes, the lid is lifted off the cellars of *sheol* (netherworld of the dead) and the souls of the dead rise up to visit the living. The Japanese celebrate the arrival of the souls at a ceremony called the *obon*, when they visit the graves and ashes of ancestors and pay homage to them with offerings of white flowers—a food to which the dead are reputed to be particularly partial—and dances and fireworks. The trouble is that the souls of the loved ones are not the only ones to come up from those godforsaken cellars of hell. They are usually accompanied by repulsive, unwanted ghosts as well, all those unpleasant and frightening characters depicted in the Kabuki theaters, by famous Japanese artists, in much-admired movies, in children's animated cartoons, and in video games.

The Shinto religion in Japan believes that there is a ghost lurking behind every animal, vegetable, or mineral and is responsible for the animal stories. These include tales of the hairy, weasel-like *tanuki*, which takes on the shape of common household utensils and causes havoc in the homes of villagers; and the fox, which particularly likes to take refuge in a female body. Fox stories are very popular in Japan. If a little Japanese girl begins to be uncharacteristically naughty, to run wild in school, and cut off her classmate's braids, everyone will be quite sure that her body has been taken over by the soul of a fox.

Twentieth-century Japanese people, so modern and so technologically oriented, still make pilgrimages to Mount Osorezan, the mountain of terror. Crowds of photographers, journalists, the poor, and the prosperous climb to the highest point on the island of Honshu, the largest and most important of Japan's islands, to an ax-shaped peninsula in the Aomori region, sunk in the Pacific Ocean. This eerie, desolate, and dark region is the home of the wild Taiwan monkey, and is known for its long, harsh winters. The mysterious volcano Osorezan is thought to be the place where the living meet the dead. Dead trees grow on the edge of the abyss, which is surrounded by black granite rocks and malodorous sulfur lakes. The bubbling sounds from the bowels of the earth and the whispering sulfur steam which billows up from it are accompanied by the calls of the black ravens obscuring the skies.

Pilgrims come to the shrine for a meeting with the dead, to console children who were never born, and those who died at birth. People who come here behave seriously and with great respect, sincerely believing that one day they, too, will find their way to the mountain, but from the other side of the bridge, from the kingdom of death. The local priests insist that the sounds and images they see and hear are not of this world.

Mount Osorezan is used to put the fear of God into wayward children—that's where they'll end up if they don't behave themselves!

The Japanese are proud that Mount Osorezan is the most densely haunted place in the world. In their struggle against ghosts and ghouls, the sophisticated, modern-day Japanese recruit the help of Shinto priests, who exorcise the ghosts by waving tree branches and spraying water. Houses in Japan are built on dates predetermined by priests and all new houses and cars must first be cleansed and exorcised of the powers of evil. The sumo wrestlers spread salt around before each bout, and you can find little piles of salt at the entrance to restaurants and coffeehouses, which are meant to keep away unwelcome guests who might come and sip from the green tea and frighten the clients. Grave-faced men, wearing red, long-nosed masks, spread beans about in the homes of villagers to scare away evil spirits, and naughty children are warned that the *obaka* will come and punish them for their wickedness. Furthermore, the Japanese spend thousands every year on food, drink, and gifts for their dearly departed. Many of the spirits enjoy smoking expensive, imported cigarettes; others get whiskey poured out for them, and those ghosts who, in their life on earth, enjoyed the taste of exotic fruits, will continue to do so in the hereafter. The statues of the *mizu-ko* children—those who were never born—are treated especially well. Mothers, who are afraid of revenge by the fruit of their womb denied the chance to experience its current earthly incarnation, spoil it with toys, special clothing for summer and winter, candies, enriched milk, and children's books, so it won't get bored on its long sojourn until it is ready for reincarnation in the form of another child. This widespread belief in ghosts and dark powers has a negative effect on business and commerce. Despite the high cost of housing in Japan, you can sometimes find houses for sale at ridiculously low prices, if these houses happen to be situated near a cemetery, or were once the scene of a murder or a suicide. No sane Japanese would dream of buying a house like this, much less living in one, even if it were offered to him for free.

Nor are the *Gaijins*, or strangers in Japan, exempt from the stories of ghosts and spirits which fill Japanese folklore. A well-known story from the beginning of this century tells of a beautiful, young, but very poor, Japanese girl who was forced to marry a rich American. The spirit of her lost Japanese lover settled itself in the form of two rows of sharpened teeth inside her vagina. Her wedding night became a spine-chilling and castrating experience for her hot-blooded Yankee husband.

The spirits, it seems, like to go shopping, especially in Japan's more prestigious shops and department stores, as I learned from the window dressers at the Seibu department store in Shibuya. These women testified under oath in the newspapers that they noticed female ghosts trying on white kimonos (in Japan, white is the color of death). As soon as the lights went on, the ghosts were frightened off.

Many late night talk shows in Japan, especially on hot summer

evenings, invite people to the studio to discuss their intimate relationships with ghosts. These appearances are always accompanied
by films and photographs to support and give proof that these
sometimes quite horrible stories are absolutely true.

On one of those haunted summer nights in Tokyo, I was invited
to a birthday party at the home of a friend of Harada. The house,
which was decorated in pale pink and lilac, as befits a young unmarried girl, was full of soft furry toys, brightly colored balloons,
and other Japanese bric-a-brac. In spite of the good food, the exciting music, and the pleasant company, I didn't feel comfortable.
I couldn't explain why. Perhaps it was because I was the only foreigner there, or perhaps it was due to the dense cloud of cigarette
smoke which hung all around us.

When it was time for us to leave, Harada whispered in my ear:
"This used to be my house." The house that had given her such
nightmares gave me the willies, too.

As for the *butsudan* cabinet, it came back to Israel with us, only
to be given to a Japanese-born Israeli named Aaron, who was full
of nostalgia for Japan. He renovated the by-now battered cabinet
and filled it with Jewish talismans written in Japanese and other
pieces of Judaica which had originated in Japan. Aaron promised
to donate the *butsudan*, full of Jewish holy artifacts and a Japanese
obaka, to the Diaspora Museum in Tel Aviv. If the curators of the
museum agree to risk the *obaka*'s mischief, the *butsudan* will find a
permanent home there and serve the very respectable and responsible purpose of a Jewish-Japanese tabernacle.

A Dance with Death

*M*y first experience of a Japanese cemetery was a happy occasion. It was my first *sakura*—cherry-blosson ceremony—celebrated in a cemetery, among the tombstones.

Only when I overcame my fears, after freeing myself of my prejudices, my superstitions, and my strict upbringing concerning everything to do with honoring the dead, was I able to enjoy myself. I loved looking at the clouds of pink-and-white blossoms above the hundreds of cherry trees arching over the sprawling cemetery. It seemed to me to be the best place on earth for a mass picnic.

It was soon apparent to me that outings of this kind—life among the dead—were not only something perfectly acceptable but also most desirable. This picnic which marked my entry into the realm of the dead in Japan was held by the Japanese workers in our Jewish community in Tokyo. Thus I found myself marching with the Japanese, pulling behind me the huge tarpaulin on which we would sit, with packed *obento* containers, each holding an entire cold meal and several bottles of beer. We spread ourselves out on the tarp, beneath the cherry trees, while all around us, in silent vigilance, stood the black-marble gravestones, on which the names of the deceased were engraved in dull gold lettering. Our Japanese friends, who had noticed the terror which gripped me at the sight of the gravestones, tried to reassure me, explaining that by holding our festivities in the cemetery we were including the dead in the joy of the living, and that I should free myself of all my previous beliefs and Western conceptions regarding cemeteries.

"Just try to concentrate on the cherry trees, and you'll stop noticing that you're in the middle of a cemetery." I did. Within minutes I completely forgot where I was and my eyes filled with the sight of the blossoms. All around us we could hear other picknickers playing rock music, or traditional Japanese tunes on their stereos, some beer-happy couples could be seen groping each other among the tombstones.

The entire issue of death, which might shock strangers to the country, with our conservative, unenlightened, and deep-rooted prejudices, is dealt with quite naturally by the Japanese.

What could be more natural to life than death itself? The big cemetery in Tokyo, *Aoyamu*, where the *sakura* celebrations take place, is right in the middle of a huge park full of cherry trees, whose spring blossoming brings hundreds and thousands of visitors to sit barefoot on their blankets, drinking beer and eating sushi and exclaiming at the beauty of the flowers. Some get so drunk from beer and sake that they stretch out between the gravestones, and others, who came late and lost out on the better places for their picnics, are content to take over an anonymous gravestone and spread out their fare on it. Vendors, selling soy sausages, dried octopus, and beer and sake, wander freely among the stones announcing their wares at the tops of the voices.

It is not only at cherry-blossom time that the dead of Japan are honored with visits by the living. Twice a year, in spring and in autumn, on those days when night equals day in length, the peace and quiet of the Japanese cemeteries are disturbed and thousands of people pour in to visit the dead, bearing food and drink for the dead, and for the living. That's also the time the cemeteries are filled with the ring of the monks' bells and murmur of the sutra prayers. This particular festival of death is known as *Higan*, which means the Other Bank. On this Festival of the Dead, entire Japanese families flock in thousands to visit their deceased loved ones. Although the memorial services themselves are Buddhist in nature, and came originally from neighboring China, the actual holidays are a Japanese invention.

Celebrations in honor of the dead are always family-oriented.

The Japanese family arrives at the grave, well stocked with food, fresh flowers, tarps for placing on the ground, and a mobile stereo unit and tapes. After the plants on the grave are watered, the tombstone polished to high sheen, the flowers placed in a vase especially prepared for them, and the ashes of grandfather and grandmother have heard all the latest news and gossip, the family spreads out its picnic, which takes place on the gravestone, where this is possible or in the park around the cemetery.

The other holiday celebrated in honor of the dead is known as the *obon*. It is based on an ancient Buddhist legend, which tells how, on the fifteenth of the seventh month, one of Buddha's disciples offered a substantial sacrifice to save his mother from the tortures of hell. Nowadays, the *obon* is celebrated in the Tokyo region between July 13 and 15, and millions of families from all over the Japanese islands offer important gifts to the spirit of their loved ones. During the days of the *obon,* mass festivities are held in honor of the spirits and thousands sing, dance and play musical instruments in order to appease the spectral inhabitants of the dead.

But the Japanese, who so honor their dead, are well aware that their next life will be no less congested. If you live in Tokyo, and go through life jammed into a crowd of people, stuffed, like sardines, into a packed train by professional "packers," stand for hours in line for the movies or a department store and live in a modest little place which is known cynically as "a rabbit hutch," *you* know exactly what to expect in the life to come.

An inhabitant of Tokyo must bear in mind that his family will be able to visit his grave only on those days set aside each year for the worship of the spirits of the dead, and, of course, during the holidays. Daily or weekly visits are virtually impossible, since his future resting place will, by necessity, be several hours away from the city itself. Since many of the inhabitants of Tokyo do not own family burial plots near the city, and the cemeteries are full, they will be unable to be interred with their relatives, close to the city's entertainment and recreation centers.

Most of Japan's cemeteries belong to local authorities, religious organizations and nonprofit organizations. Private investors may also be involved, but they must first prove that their aims are totally altruistic, since undertaking in Japan is considered a religious affair, from which no financial profit may be made. There is little motivation for private entrepreneurs to buy burial spaces or turn land already in their possession into cemeteries.

This situation results in many families burying their loved ones outside of Tokyo. Sometimes the only available space for burial is the tops of hills. Since many of the people coming to visit these tombs find it difficult to climb up the mountain to the cemetery, it has become customary to construct a cable car, which goes up and down the hill, stopping at each level and giving the name of the station and the particular tomb number over an electronic vocal system.

It is forbidden in Japan to bury a corpse whole, unless the deceased was a foreigner, and then the funeral is held in special cemeteries (the Japanese Jewish community has its own cemetery near the port city of Yokohama). Almost everyone in Japan would like to have his cremated remains buried in the earth, at a proper funeral service, and to have an attractive marble tombstone erected over the grave. The best way to assure this, of course, is by buying a family tomb, since this ensures that one will lie forever next to one's parents, children, and other members of the family.

However, the spiraling price of land in Japan, and especially in Tokyo, as well as the shortage of land for building, has turned the issue of burial into a luxury. A decent burial, close to a religious temple, might cost as much as twenty to forty thousand dollars. And even then, not everyone who has this kind of money is able to find a decent burial plot, because of the dearth of available land in and around the city of Tokyo. A few years ago, a field containing space for 750 graves was auctioned among some seventeen thousand people.

These issues have fired the imagination of the Japanese, who are always trying to come up with new and original ideas for giving their dead a decent burial. A temple in the port city of Kobe turned its roof into a burial site, with each well-aired and sunny tomb going for a price of $4,000.

"There's a charming view, and some enterprising people have even suggested turning this site into a beer garden," jokes the Japanese priest. Indeed, in Japan's warm summer days, the large, flat roofs of department stores or movie houses would make lovely parks, where one could enjoy a cool glass of beer and a refreshing breeze. Anyway, the priest managed to resist temptation, and the temple decided to stick to undertaking.

Another solution to the problem of burying the dead is gaining popularity in Japan. I came upon it during the last year of my stay in the country.

"I must show you a very strange place indeed," said my Israeli friend Batya, who knew Tokyo well.

As we drove in the direction of her home in the Meguru neighborhood, she told me that she had come across the place by chance.

"You'll see what I mean when we get there," she said mysteriously. We turned off a crowded side road and made our way down a narrow street lined with high-rise buildings. We parked by a gray seven-story building, which looked no different from any of the other buildings on the block.

Batya pushed open the wrought-iron gate and motioned for me to follow her up a staircase which looked like any other staircase. Batya took her shoes off at the first floor door and walked in. The room was dimly lit.

Once my eyes became accustomed to the dim light, I saw that the large hall I was standing in was sectioned off by metal cabinets, as tall as an average man. The cabinets were lined up closely beside each other, much like book cabinets in a giant library, or luggage lockers in a railway station.

"What is this place?" I whispered. I had a strong feeling that I was trespassing.

"Come and have a look," Batya called from the other end of the hall.

She opened the door of one of the cabinets, and a bright light flooded its inside. The inside of the cabinet held a small synthetic Japanese shrine which contained a jar of ashes, a picture of the deceased, incense sticks, a bell for calling up the dead person's spirit, and some offerings. It seems that the deceased, when still alive, had enjoyed smoking American cigarettes and the Japanese beer, Asahi Dry. The cabinet next door, which belonged to a lady, contained expensive fruits, exotic flowers, small furry toys, and pictures of the deceased standing alongside a canal in Venice. Another cabinet contained cash offerings, a bottle of imported whiskey, and a miniature game of Mah-jongg, which is so popular in Japan.

"There are cabinets like these in all seven stories of this building, thousands of them," said Batya. "It's a skyscraper cemetery."

In Japan, this kind of cemetery is called Nokotsu-do, which

means literally "room for storing bones," and it contains thousands of cabinets holding human remains. But the Japanese prefer to have their remains interred in the earth. In order to reassure the potentially deceased and to encourage them to request this compact form of burial, the country's priests insist that it is perfectly correct religiously, so long as all the rules are followed. These require that the burial ceremony include wood (although flowers may be used as a substitute), stone (the altar), and water (an offering of tea), all of which must be placed by the dead person's ashes.

There are plenty of undertakers in Japan ready and willing to take care of all your funeral arrangements. These undertakers tempt potential customers with colorful brochures, videos, scaled-down samples of headstones, pictures of flower arrangements, seating arrangements in the funeral parlor, and topographical maps of the grave site. You can choose, at your leisure, the exact kind of funeral you would like long before it actually takes place.

Of course, nothing is complete in Japan without the wonders of technology, and the life-after-death industry is no exception. The communications and electronics company Mitsui, together with the largest Buddhist undertaking firm in Japan, has begun selling to Japan's cemeteries a special truck equipped with a communications satellite. This vehicle is able to transmit a live commentary on the entire funeral procession, the cremation of the body, and the faces of the mourners, to any place you choose, such as the office where the deceased used to work, for the benefit of his colleagues who were unable to take part in the funeral, or to family members who live too far away or are too sick to make the journey to the funeral. Viewers can feel as if they, too, are taking part in the funeral. Proponents of this funeral satellite service suggest that viewers place their TV sets next to the family shrine, light incense, and cover it with white flowers. At the time of writing, however, this form of funeral-by-satellite is not widespread in Japan, since people are unused to this novel idea. The Mitsui Company has already practiced the method by transmitting the funeral of their former chairman, Mitsui Mizukami, who died in 1989.

What does one wear to a funeral? Here, the rules are rigid: a black suit and a black tie for a man and either a black suit or a black funeral kimono for a woman. Women may wear a necklace of white pearls, but no other jewelry.

You can send mourning wreaths of white flowers to the home

of the deceased. These are much appreciated. Some are made of plastic or paper and are enormous. They are usually decorated with black mourning ribbon and can be seen from far off, propped up against the fence where the deceased used to live.

As for the deceased themselves, it seems that in Japan, while you can live well, you can actually die a millionaire. A 1988 survey shows that the Japanese bequeathed an average of 264 million yen each—$2.64 million in cash, bonds, real estate, and other kinds of taxable assets. Although this particular year showed a decrease in deaths, the total value of posthumous property increased by 16.8 percent, reaching around 9.6 billion yen.

The Japanese tax authorities collected some 1.5 billion yen in death duties. This makes Japan perhaps the only country in the world where you can bequeath a fortune on your death, yet be obliged to have your remains buried in a metal cabinet in a high-rise apartment building, or in a remote cemetery, miles away from home.

Why Do They Sleep Outdoors?

*Y*oshi is the name we gave to our adopted homeless man. He turned up one day and settled under the pedestrian bridge near the the busy highway which separated the Royal Yoyogi's Garden and the stadium which hosted the Olympics in the sixties. The Royal Garden contains the modern Temple of the Emperor Meiji, grandfather of Hirohito, who was the first emperor to open Japan to foreigners.

Yoshi was one of thousands of homeless people in Japan who spend their lives out of doors, sleeping under the stars. For us he was unique. Without his knowing it, we became involved in Yoshi's life. We saw him every day when we drove to work. Yoshi was a true individualist. Other homeless people tended to flock together for protection, for company, and to discuss the local garbage situation, but Yoshi guarded his independence jealously. He set up his cardboard home under the bridge, always considerate of tourists and passersby and other people using the area. He laundered his white socks in the park's taps, looked for food in the garbage cans, where he probably found the Walkman which took care of his cultural needs. There were always plenty of old newspapers, magazines, and books, discarded by Tokyo's better-off citizens, which he read to his heart's content. Yoshi was a bookworm, emerging from time to time to take in a breath of fresh air. His "home" was surrounded with piles of books and newspapers, which he went through at a feverish pace. In complete peace and quiet, oblivious of the hustle and bustle of life surrounding him, Yoshi managed to read anything and everything he could lay his hands on.

During the second week in his new "home," he pasted the walls of his cardboard house with pictures of Swiss landscapes: plump cows grazing in a green field and sloping, snow-covered roofs. A vase on a makeshift table contained beautifully arranged flowers.

On the first day of December snow, we came to make sure that everything was all right. We had adopted him, although he didn't know it. Under the bridge, surrounded by tall piles of sheltering snow, he was warm and dry. He had hung up his underwear and socks to dry on nearby tree branches and he was blissfully listening to music and reading a book. Even the screeching black ravens trying to snatch the rice cake he was eating could not disturb the tranquillity of his perpetual picnic.

Spring Sundays supplied Yoshi with free outdoor concerts. The road was closed to traffic on those days. All of Japan's freaks and weirdos got together in their outlandish outfits and teased, colored, and sprayed hairdos, or stiff, black, Elvis Presley pompadours to play their own particular brand of music. None of these gatherings was complete without the tinkling voices of the round-faced Japanese girls, with stiff black braids on either side of their heads. During the week, Yoshi would be entertained by frustrated musicians, who were not allowed to practice at home. They flocked to the garden, where they could play drums, cymbals, and French horns to their hearts' content, without upsetting the peaceful harmony of their neighborhoods. Unfortunately, our friend's private concert often turned into an earsplitting cacophony when more than one group of players practiced.

Yoshi disappeared one day, as suddenly as he had arrived. We found his cardboard house discarded in a nearby garbage truck. We had no way of knowing what had happened to him, nor was there anyone we could ask. The Japanese are not romantic about their homeless population.

You can't avoid the homeless in Japan. They are everywhere. They settle in public parks and sleep in the subways, especially in Shinjuku Station. You can see them sprawled across the entrance to Tokyo's most prestigious store, Wako, in the expensive Ginza area, forcing the elegant shoppers to step over them. They hang around the food cellars in the city's fanciest department stores, helping themselves to a taste of everything they see. They are easy to spot, dressed in threadbare suits and carrying plastic bags that contain all their worldly goods. Sometimes they sleep in improvised tent cities between trees, on the city's sidewalks and subways. Many have long, matted hair, which has not been washed or cut for years and their faces are filthy. They crowd the doors to the 7-Eleven in the early hours of the morning, patiently waiting to collect their *obento*. When this prepackaged Japanese lunch has passed its "sell-by" date, it is handed out free to the homeless, instead of being thrown away.

Japan, the richest country in the world, is unable to cope with her homeless, and the problem is increasing as the country develops and grows wealthier. Local authorities try to sweep this unpleasant issue under the tatami mat and refuse to divulge the real number of Japan's homeless population. Perhaps they really don't know. The problem of the homeless remains the problem of the homeless themselves.

Christian missionary sources who work within the homeless community claim that their number reaches several thousand in the Tokyo region alone. In Tokyo's Sanya neighborhood, the number of homeless counted by the missionaries exceeds eight thousand. Most are over fifty years old. This is the city's working-class area, where the descendants of the *eta* or *burakumin* live—the caste of untouchables who are traditionally employed in work the Japanese consider unclean, such as butchery, leather tanning, cremation, and all those professions which contradict the laws of Buddhism. The others are impoverished members of the loathed and despised minority groups of foreign nationals, such as Koreans. Still others are poor villagers who came to the big city to look for jobs. Like their counterparts all over the world, the homeless in Japan are often alcoholics and drug addicts, and many suffer from mental illness and various chronic diseases. In Japan's harsh winters, many of them die.

Since begging is against the law in Japan, the homeless sell empty cartons, glass bottles, or recyclable paper. They are also recruited for menial labor by the Yakuza. Others simply rummage in the city's garbage cans for food and castoffs.

The garbage rooms in the city's apartment blocks supply the

homeless with virtually all their worldly needs, from bedding and clothing to household utensils and battery-operated electrical goods.

Recently, churches have been successfully pressuring the local authorities to set up temporary shelters for the homeless. These relatively luxurious shelters offer baths, medical clinics, and dining rooms, but there are few of them and they are unbearably crowded. Government welfare clinics are not prepared to treat the great number of homeless, and stories abound in Tokyo about dying people turned away from hospitals which had met their quota of homeless patients for the day. As Father Gerim of the Franciscan Church says of the homeless he helps, "The Japanese simply don't see the people living in the streets." So long as they don't constitute a public menace or a health hazard, the homeless can be ignored. Elegantly dressed pedestrians step genteelly over the dozens of homeless people occupying the busy Shinjuku railway station, and not even see them. Lovers can sit on the edge of one bench in the giant Ueno Park and take no notice of the disheveled homeless person sprawled across the adjoining bench, fast asleep and snoring so loudly that the branches above their heads shake. The homeless in Japan simply are not seen as human. They make no contribution to society or to the national economy, and they pay no taxes. They belong to a different category of creatures that the authorities choose to ignore, as if they do not exist.

"In Japan you don't get a second chance. The little fish who got away through the hole in the net, won't ever be allowed back in," say the foreign volunteers who work with the country's homeless population. "The homeless problem in Japan, in comparison with the USA and Europe, is marginal and could be easily overcome with the help of the authorities. But unless the public takes some kind of action on the issue, the problem will only get worse."

The United Nations declared an International Year of the Homeless, which was approximately translated into Japanese as: "The International Year for Housing," since, officially, the problem does not exist in Japan. Anyway, the Japanese feel that the homeless are responsible for their fate since they themselves chose it. They chose a life of freedom; they wanted no commitment to family, to work, or to a mortgage. They obviously enjoy getting drunk and betting—living out of doors is just a part of this package. Furthermore, according to the rationale of Japanese society, most of the country's homeless are people on the run from creditors, or criminals hiding from the law, or alcoholics who don't belong in any kind of social framework anyway.

Japan's homeless are not really concerned with appearances or keeping up their good name, or with what the neighbors think of them. Their lives are mostly aimless, a mere existence; they fight for their food, and don't ask too many questions. Some of them are clever and some are drunk, some are healthy and some sick, some are crazy and others quite normal. For a more extensive survey on Japan's homeless population, there is enough serious material around to fill volumes and enough pathetic stories for any sentimental soap opera. Just open your eyes and ask a few questions.

A Dog's Life

"*W*hat kind of funeral were you thinking of?" the Cohens were asked politely. "Buddhist, Christian, Shinto, or something else, perhaps? Would you like to keep the ashes in a ceramic or metal jar? Where would you like to keep the jar? In your home, or at our temple?" The Cohens were also told that a company representative could call on them at home and present their color catalogue, which gives a comprehensive outline of the funerals available, as well as details about headstones and urns for ashes.

They were in deep mourning for Titus, the beloved cat who had come with them all the way from Israel to Tokyo two years before, and who had managed to overcome language difficulties and bloodthirsty fights over territory with the local, tailless (genetically, not from mutilation) Yakuza cats. But the Cohens couldn't help laughing.

"You are obliged to report the death of a family pet to the authorities," the Cohens were told by the Japanese Secretary for Integration at the Israeli Embassy in Tokyo, where they worked. A phone call to City Hall resulted in a visit by the municipal veterinarian, who made out an official death certificate, declaring that the cat Titus had died in his sleep of kidney failure. The visit was followed by telephone calls from several of the local animal undertakers. "We deal with all sorts of animals, from horses to goldfish," they were told by one company. Another offered to stuff the beloved cat, so that it would remain forever with the family, and not reduced to ashes, or a sad burial in some cold, distant graveyard.

Animal cemeteries were all the rage. The Gi Temple, which belongs to the Buddhist Judu Shinshu sect, was the first to offer burial services for pets, when a demand arose for elegant funerals for animals. Other temples followed suit, and made sure to include a morgue, where the family can part from its faithful friend, a crematorium, and a cemetery for those who prefer a more conservative form of burial. The pets' headstones are decorated with pictures of the deceased, flowers, and fancy collars. On memorial days, the families visit the cemeteries, bringing offerings of bones, the deceased's favorite food, bowls of milk and toys, so that their dearly departed will not be bored or hungry on its long journey to the next world.

Hachiko is a Japanese dog which became famous posthumously. Anyone who arrives at the Shibuya Center railway station in Tokyo will find thousands of young people crowding around the bronze statue of a dog. This is Hachiko, loyal legend, a symbol of the faithfulness of a dog for its human master. The town square bearing its name is one of the largest meeting places in the world. The real Hachiko, who lived in the forties, was an ordinary, everyday Japanese dog. Every morning he would go with his master to the railway station at Shibuya, and every evening, he would be there, waiting for his master to get home from work. One day, Hachiko's master went the way of all flesh, but the faithful dog still went each evening to the railway station, hoping against hope to meet him on his way home from work. The dog waited, in good weather and bad; and the kind people who lived nearby made sure he needed nothing, until he himself finally died of old age. His stuffed body, a symbol of faithfulness to his master, has a place of honor in the Museum of Science and Natural History at the Ueno Center. Dozens of books have been written about him, drawings and paintings have been done of him from every possible angle, and several Japanese films have been made of his life. For the Japanese, Hachiko will remain forever a symbol of blind devotion.

In Japan, however, a person who has lost his pet need not mourn for long, providing that he has made appropriate arrangements in time—and insured it with the animal insurance company. This company does not pay out money when the pet dies, but gives out compensation in kind. If your beloved dog dies, you will be reimbursed with a younger model of the exact breed, gender, and color.

The insurance premium costs between eighty and three hundred dollars, depending on the type of animal, its age, and the state of its health. The insurance company assures itself that the animal is in a good home and that its pedigree papers are in order. Stray dogs and cats are not, of course, included in the arrangement—perfectly in keeping with the rigid class system in Japanese society.

Any animal taken in by a Japanese family may consider itself fortunate indeed, and later, when its time comes to go a better world, the family will continue to take care of all its immediate needs.

Japanese pets are treated as part of the family. The dog or cat, which is usually bought in a pet boutique, will never feel neglected, not for a moment. If the family's little girl is given a new kimono for the *Shichi-go-san* holiday—a special celebration for seven-, five- and three-year-olds—the family will make sure its female dog is also decked out in a new pink silk kimono of its own. At Festival time during the summer, the streets of Tokyo are full of dogs dressed in cotton *yukatas,* pink for a bitch and blue for a male. Tokyo's cold winters are a perfect excuse to take your pet to the animal boutique (every department store has one on the top floor), and buy it a hooded raincoat, or a pure camelhair duffle coat, or, if you love it very much, a white mink coat. Fashion collections for dogs also include matching underwear, plain white cotton for the male dog and frilly lace for the bitch, and well-cut trousers with a fly for him, or a flower-print silk dress for her. You can also buy Wellington boots for rainy days and white socks and slippers for cosy evenings at home around the TV. Your dog might like a wool hat, or a flowery straw boater for spring days. You can buy a hat to prevent the dog's pompadour from getting mussed up when it goes out to play in the sand pit. Unfortunately, dog clothes are available only in small sizes. Larger dogs walk the streets of Tokyo naked, even in the freezing cold of winter. This favoritism stems from the fact that most pet dogs have to be tiny and compact, to fit into small urban apartments. It's difficult to keep a Great Dane, St. Bernard, or even an ordinary German shepherd in an apartment whose total size, including the kitchen, is no more than thirty square yards—and make room for a child or two as well.

Which is why the Japanese developed the Bonsai breeds of dogs—named after the miniature bonsai trees. These dogs are quite delightfully tiny, and I have never seen anything like them anywhere else in the world.

There are other weird and wonderful toys, games and accessories to make your pet's life more enjoyable. It is fashionable to take your animal for psychological counseling if it is suffering from loneliness, cramped living conditions, or for any other condition. Veterinarians explain that the stressful lifestyle in Japan often has an adverse effect on sensitive cats and dogs. One solution might be "Music for Healthy Pets." This was developed by a record company called Nippon Crown, which also produces relaxing music for human beings, and was composed and played by professional musicians especially for household pets. Nippon Crown, which has sold thousands of these records, explained that animals nod their heads to the peaceful sound of the music and even fall into a deep sleep. Sony has produced a recording of relaxing sounds for cats, including the buzzing of flies, and Hungarian dance melodies, combined with cat-calls.

Pet stores also supply small warming cushions for kittens or puppies who get cold at night, diapers for dogs who cannot be taken out or who are incontinent. These diapers are also useful for bitches in heat. There are shampoos and conditioners for dry or oily fur, various kinds of powders, deodorant sprays, medicines and vitamins, toys, hair clips, and ribbons. The cage and kennel department of these stores is especially fascinating. There are cages made from bamboo, wood, plastic, or metal. One model, a high-tech kennel, developed by the Japanese electronics company Matsushita, won a prize and was advertised all over Japan. The kennel looks like a two-story cottage with an additional sunroom and balcony. It has an area of about three square yards and is 1.5 yards high. The kennel's living room is equipped with a color TV and cassette radio, which are button-operated by the dog itself. An electronic chimney vents dog odor to the outside of the kennel, whose entrance is blocked by a curtain of air currents to keep out biting bugs or other uninvited guests. The kennel's roof and floor are both removable and the entire construction can be expanded. This luxury home for your four-legged friend costs $9,000. At a press conference, the Matsushita spokesman insisted that a dog will indeed make good use of a sunroom leading off its living room, and it also enjoys watching TV as much as any other member of the family. Other essential accessories are scented paper tissues and a pooper-scooper. Heaven help any dog owner who lets his dog leave a mess in public. Passersby would very likely call the police and the unpleasantness, and the fine, would turn the matter into a traumatic experience both emotionally and financially. If your dog has inadvertently fouled a Japanese street, the matter is easily taken care of with the help of a pooper-scooper, after which the dog's bottom can be wiped clean with specially scented tissues.

Japan also has elegant veterinary hospitals supplying medical and dental treatment to animals. Some have pink-wallpapered beauty parlors, where each pet customer is tended by about five uniformed beauticians, dressed to match the wallpaper. One deals with the animal's fur, one brushes its teeth, another clips its nails, a fourth does the drying, and a fifth supervises.

Pet pampering would be incomplete without a highly developed gourmet pet-food industry catering to your pet's sophisticated palate. Supermarket shelves are stacked with pet entrees: pâté de fois gras, caviar, creamed lobster, turtle soup or plain chicken or rabbit stew. Every few months Tokyo hosts an animal festival, at which your pet can sample, free of charge, all kinds of pet food.

Unfortunately, these expensive gourmet foods have adverse long-term effects on pet health. Japanese dogs, used to eating highly processed and preserved food, tasty, delicate, and melt-in-the-mouth, lose the use of their mouth's most basic and natural activity. They don't need to chew and develop cavities and severe gum disease. Many of Japan's dogs suffer from chronic gum disorders, and bacterial infections which enter the bloodstream, causing heart attacks and renal failure. Japanese dogs are regular patients at veterinary dentists—to have plaque removed, to have their teeth polished, or to have their gums treated and brushed. The market is full of canine dental-hygiene products, such as toothbrushes and chicken liver-flavored toothpaste, chewable toys which massage the dog's infected gums, and toy balls containing disinfectant creams.

The same medical treatments are used on animals and humans; if it's good enough for us, it's just as good for our four-legged friends. The Japanese, of course, use many of Eastern therapies, such as acupuncture. Vets believe that if it helps humans, it won't harm horses. Almost all of Japan's racehorses receive regular professional acupuncture sessions, where they are treated by the ancient Chinese system which uses needles to soothe painful muscles. The horses seem to enjoy it.

The needles used on horses are more than twice the size of those used on humans, nearly four inches long and almost a quarter inch in diameter. The horse's acupuncture diagram has some 120 points. In order to make the treatment even more effective, the vets use mild electric current treatment as well and burn herbs near the surface of the horse's silky skin.

Not everyone in Japan can afford the time or the expense involved in keeping a household pet. Some are content with keeping seasonal substitutes, giant phosphorescent beetles, for example, which look like the horned helmets of the samurai warriors. These beetles, ridiculously inexpensive to buy in department stores or at summer fairs, survive happily in a small plastic aquarium, with just a slice of cucumber or eggplant for food. Others buy fireflies for seven nights of illuminated pleasure. Pet shops also stock alarming-looking centipedes, black or yellow scorpions and giant spiders imported from the jungles of the Amazon. And those who can't afford to buy a bug make do with goldfish, which can be won all summer long at fairs and festivals. For fifty cents, you get a miniature net with which to fish out your own goldfish from a bath full of sickly creatures too weary to swim away. If you net one, it's yours. It might even stay alive in the bag of water in which you take it home. And if it does get home safely, it might even stay alive for a few days more!

The rich of Japan, fortunate enough to live in large houses with gardens and water fountains, keep beautiful carp known as koi, distant relatives of our own gefilte fish. And instead of the familiar, boring gray, the lucky Japanese carp comes in gold, orange, yellow, red, and pink. There are also tiger-striped hybrids or fish with giraffelike markings. Some have bulging eyes or overdeveloped fins, which give the fish the look of a lion—the result of many years of diligent genetic engineering. Needless to say, none of these fish is ever eaten.

These fish can be bought on the top floors of department stores at prices which range from several hundred dollars for a mundane specimen to thirty thousand dollars and more for an unusual one, the rare result of generations of breeding. Koi are found in rich people's ponds, ponds belonging to religious temples, and ponds used in interior decoration in fancy restaurants. At entrances to public parks you can buy special fish food and then watch the pond water churn and foam as dozens of carp fight over each crumb, making loud slapping noises every time they open or close their mouths. It is an unforgettable experience.

Koi will swim up to you if you clap your hands, so don't be surprised if you see Japanese people enthusiastically clapping their hands near pools of water. They are not performing ritual applause—just getting the fishes' attention.

Not all animals in Japan are so fortunate. Some not adopted by the right family might easily end their days in an "animal disposal unit." This is a large metal garbage can with a pop-up lid, into which are placed those animals whose owners are tired of them, old or sick animals, or those who cannot move with their owners because pets are not allowed in many of the city's apartment blocks. The municipality takes care of them, either by poisoning them or gassing them to death.

These in-house disposal units were still in operation in 1986 in the town of Kitami on the northern island of Hokkaido. As a result of a news item on the subject and a barrage of letters, the Japanese prime minister issued the following statement: "If these details are true, we do not approve of this system, especially since the killing is done in a public place and can be observed by passersby. It is especially grave that children are allowed to witness this spectacle." This single-minded declaration resulted in the cans being removed to the municipal garbage dump. Japanese children can continue throwing away their pets, so long as they are not allowed to watch the slaughter.

Tokyo street cats receive special consideration. Besides their dangerous role as fish tasters in Tokyo's famous Tsukiji fish market, they, or rather their skins, have the dubious honor of being in great demand by the Japanese music industry. If these cats survive the country's kamikaze drivers, they might fall prey to cat catchers, who trap their innocent victims by using *matatabi*, a special herb which gives the cat a moment of unwary ecstasy. The poor cats are captured, slaughtered, and their skins used for shamisens, string instruments used by Tokyo's geishas. Unfortunately, catskin tears easily, and the shamisen must be re-covered every few weeks. It is the fate of many Japanese cats, therefore, to end their lives under the tender fingers of white-faced geishas. The geisha's feline nickname is Neko—which means cat, although this refers to their high-pitched singing.

Stray dogs caught in the streets suffer a fate similar to that of the cats, but the skins of dogs are stretched over drums.

Compared with the cats and dogs who finish their lives as drums or shamisens, animals who die for the sake of scientific research meet a miserable end. Take, for example, the Japanese monkeys who are used by the Japanese Institute for Car Research in simulated traffic accidents.

These simulations are carried out in the science and technology town of Tsukuba, although using monkeys as drivers in simulated traffic accidents was first done at the University of Tokyo Medical School. The monkey is fastened to the driver's seat, using a metal frame and thick leather straps, and the car is driven, by remote control at very high speed, straight into a concrete wall. Changes in the monkey's behavior and reflexes up to the moment of its death are measured with the help of medical instruments. Any monkey unfortunate enough to survive the first impact, is left to die in agony or made to experience other accidents again and again until it finally dies.

Japan has no laws restricting the use of animals for research, and each year thousands are slaughtered in the name of science, or community-sanctioned euthanasia. In one year alone, 545,000 dogs and 240,000 cats were slaughtered by municipal authorities and various private research organizations.

In Japan, as in other countries, the animal issue is a function of the people's culture, belief, and economy. If the fifth shogun of Japan, Tokugawa Tsunayoshi, (1680–1709) were alive today, dogs would be revered. This shogun was born, to the joy of the dogs of that period, in the year of the Dog. Thus Tokugawa promulgated animal rights in general and canine rights in particular. With admirable fanaticism, he passed laws for the protection of animals. The most famous of these stated: "We shall not be dissatisfied if dogs walk freely in the streets of our country." Dogs were brought together by official government appointed "matchmakers" and dozens of samurai were obliged to commit ritual suicide for killing a troublesome mosquito or for hurting a dog. The shogun went so far as to prohibit the eating of certain kinds of eggs or fish within the confines of his palace, and devoted 10 percent of his national budget to the needs of the canine population, which grew and reproduced at an alarming rate during his reign. The shogun also had two giant parks built for dogs, in Tokyo's Nakano and Okobo regions, where, in three hundred kennels, the city's dogs bred and reproduced to their hearts' content.

The most popular and beloved animal in all of Japan is a giant female panda. Millions of Japanese children cuddle a stuffed version to sleep each night, and her picture appears on posters, cartoons, and children's books. She can also be eaten in the form of a marzipan candy or a lollipop.

She, of course, is the Chinese panda Huan-Huan, brought to Tokyo's Ueno Zoo as a gift from the people of China to the people of Japan.

At the age of thirteen, Huan-Huan finally became pregnant by artificial insemination. She and the happy father, Fi-Fi, fought whenever they were together. The zookeepers were obliged to keep them apart. Fi-Fi was brought to the operating table and, under general anesthetic, provided the sperm used to impregnate his mate. When the little cub was finally born, after 160 days of healthy pregnancy, the Japanese people were delirious with joy. Stores sold out of toy pandas, and cake shops did a brisk business in panda-shaped marzipan. Pictures of the happy mother holding her little cub filled the newspapers, and little Japanese children went about with panda hats on their heads, sucking on panda lollipops. Adults spent hours discussing the health of the mother panda and the daily weight gain of the new baby. The Japanese telephone company, NTT, offered its customers a special recorded bulletin on the cub's physical condition and development. This report was accompanied by strange crying, sucking, and burping sounds allegedly made by the cub. This service was so successful that it eventually caused disturbances on the line. The company spokesman informed the press that more than 200,000 people per day had called the service. According to the company's accountant, the service earned some two million yen a day (about 20,000 dollars) since its inception.

The cub grew up and Huan-Huan has given birth to its brother. While Huan-Huan continues to nibble at her favorite bamboo shoots, in her elegant, specially built glass cage at Ueno Zoo in Tokyo, the panda fever shows no sign of abating.

Pleasures of the Table

The Japanese like their food fresh, the fresher the better, best of all, alive. No self-respecting restaurant is without an aquarium containing a representative selection of fish and other creatures of the sea. The fish, or whatever other creature must give its life for gastronomy, is drawn out of the aquarium and placed directly on the plate. If you can't stick the whole thing in your mouth in one go, you can always cut it up and dress it with soy sauce. On more than one occasion I found myself eye to eye with a fish thrashing around on my fellow diner's plate, desperately trying to get oxygen into its gills. The Japanese are mostly indifferent to the fish's efforts to remain alive, and like to stick a finger into its mouth, or a sliver of its own flesh, or a flower from the table's centerpiece.

We were once served a dish of locusts for dessert (dead, fortunately). "They're full of calcium," coaxed our hosts. They popped whole locusts, including innards, bony legs, and plump stomachs into their mouths. An Israeli friend was invited to the meal with us, and pretended to enjoy the crunch of locusts between his teeth. He was given a tin of grasshopper preserves as a parting gift. The picture on the tin showed a smiling grasshopper perching on a green blade of rice. A shake of the tin produced the same sound as the rattles we made in kindergarten from used tins of shoe polish filled with dried beans.

The descendants of the samurai enjoy culinary adventures with a hint of danger. For example, the famous Japanese delicacy, the fugu fish (a blowfish with a highly poisonous liver). Anyone who eats it risks death, since this delicacy kills several people in Japan every year.

Any chef who cuts this fish must first undergo a special training program, lasting several years, until he is proficient enough to identify and dispose of all the poisonous parts. He must then take a stringent examination before being granted the necessary license for a restaurant serving this fish. A truly conscientious chef, who wants to remove all trace of doubt from the heart of his customer, would take the trouble of tasting the delicacy himself before serving it.

But even the strictest safety precautions are not foolproof, and every year reports are published in the Japanese press of fugu aficionados who have died with their mouths full.

Fugu is not the only food in Japan which represents a serious health hazard to the lives of those who eat it. There are inocuous-looking rice cakes, known as *Mochi,* customarily served on happy occasions, such New Year's Eve, weddings, holidays, and festivals. These cakes are made of cooked sticky rice, kneaded inside a huge wooden crater with the help of a heavy wooden hammer. The rice is beaten into a sticky paste and rolled into a tasteless, rubbery cake. These can be dangerous, especially to the toothless. Anyone lacking premolars can't bite a piece off. Even those with the usual complement of teeth find it difficult to chew. Chunks of *Mochi* can easily slip down the throat and lodge in the esophagus, or even worse, in the windpipe. Every year, especially during the holidays, dozens of old gluttons breathe their last while eating rice cakes.

Though decidedly adventurous in culinary matters, the Japanese are well aware that not every creature in the sea is edible.

All kinds of weird and wonderful sea animals find their way to the famous Japanese fish market, Tsukiji; some of them have never been seen before, let alone eaten. The market, therefore, employs tasters, specially qualified to sample any suspicious or unidentifiable fish. These tasters, who are willing to sacrifice one of their nine lives each time they fulfill their professional responsibility, are the market's cats, and are kept in bamboo cages. The Japanese believe that any sea creature not venomous enough to kill a cat is suitable for human consumption. I was unable to find out from the market's management exactly how many of the cats ate their last meal on earth as a favor to the human race.

The Japanese are very fond of the sea and this is evident in their movies and TV programs. TV photographers love location shoots on fishing boats. One photogenic television announcer is often seen, buttoned up to her ears in a pink Chanel suit, bobbing on the sea near some obscure island, in the company of uncouth, uncomunnicative fishermen. The next shot is usually of her alone, beside herself with excitement, still dressed in her pink suit, standing alongside the catch of fish flopping on the deck. The camera zooms in on her, yelping with delight as she grabs hold of a giant octopus, which is purple with righteous indignation. Gurgling with pleasure, the woman places one of the octopus's wriggling tentacles into her mouth and bites off a piece. She continues to express her enjoyment, "*Oyshi*—How delicious this is!," as the seven remaining tentacles are also swallowed alive. The head is thrown away, and the Chanel suit dives once again into the throbbing mass, and resurfaces with some new booty in her hand.

Some people like to hear their food sing before it reaches their mouths. Musical meals of this kind are served in restaurants known as "The Sadistic Kitchen," and are quite popular on the southeast coast of the island of Honshu, which is the main and the largest of the Japanese islands. In these restaurants, live oysters, known fondly as *A-Pa-Pa*, are pulled out of the water and placed straight on a grill of sizzling, red-hot coals in front of the diners.

As they are grilled, the oysters open and close and make sounds reminiscent of their Japanese nickname. Prawns, fish, and lobsters are also grilled alive, and their every move, jump, sigh, or groan is met with joyous applause from the diners.

Another way to see live fish tortured to death is a dish called Tofu Hell. A bowl of boiling, clear soup, resting upon a base of flames, is served. Into the bubbling soup goes a big cube of cold tofu, followed immediately by tiny, live, fish, which look like underdeveloped eels. Shocked by the heat, the fish take refuge from the boiling soup by boring into the cold tofu and digging into it from every direction until it, too, becomes unbearably hot and the fish cook inside it. By now the tofu looks like a piece of Swiss cheese, studded with tiny fish, dead and gone to Tofu Hell. This is considered a great delicacy.

Although the Japanese favor seafood and eat meat, they are also quite fond of the fruits (and vegetables) of the earth. Anything that bears leaves, branches, roots, or flowers is considered edible. Walk into the vegetable department of an average food store in Japan, and find, beside the round lettuces and the huge Japanese radishes, shelves upon shelves of flowers. These are not for vases or traditional ikebana arrangements, since they have no stems. These flowers are meant for the human digestive system. Thus, for example, the yellow chrysanthemum is served with sushi, while sweet pea flowers are delicious with meat.

At elegant receptions, too, brightly colored edible flowers abound. Fresh petals of every shape, size, and shade imaginable cover the food buffet, and it's all natural and good for you. As for flavor, that's a matter of taste!

When it comes to flavors and food combination, the Japanese are original and imaginative. I still remember the taste of an innocuous-looking cake I bought at the Kyoto railway station. The sweet pastry was filled with a hot curry sauce and, buried in its center, were strawberries and slices of pineapple. Another delicacy I don't think I'll forget was served at a dinner for the diplomatic corps on one of the Emperor's estates, which grow organic vegetables especially for the Emperor's table. This particular offering was a huge crystal bowl, overflowing with huge strawberries. A waiter handed me a big bowl of strawberries, and asked if I wanted cream. I nodded yes and my plate was piled with dollops of yellowish whipped cream. I returned to my seat, and began filling my mouth with the delicious fruit. Within seconds, I spat it out into a napkin monogrammed with the initials of the royal house of Japan. The whipped cream so generously piled on my strawberries was hot Japanese mayonnaise.

Only in Japan can you find ice cream tasting of sweet potatoes, sharp cheese, and green horseradish, tomatoes, eggplants, sweet beans, basil, or parsley—to name but a few of the many flavors offered by any ice-cream shop in Japan.

From a Vegetarian Point of View

Once in Japan, I vowed to begin the diet I'd been putting off for so long back home. As a devout vegetarian, my gastronomic path in Japan had been rocky at first.

I became a vegetarian more than three decades ago, on the day a live carp was placed in our bathtub before being made into Saturday's gefilte fish. I adopted it and watched over it until the moment it was lifted out of the bath, hit over the head, and its throbbing intestines spilled out for all to see.

Next came Kuki, a fluffy yellow chick, bought for next to nothing. I sheltered him in my bed. Kuki, who grew into a large white cockerel, was slaughtered and served to us on a plate for lunch. I have never understood such callous cruelty, nor have I tasted meat since.

From a vegetarian's point of view, Japan seems to be a place where a lust for meat and seafood prevails.

In Tokyo's restaurants, of which there may be more than a million, it is virtually impossible to find a dish not decorated with pink prawns or fish scales. Meat, tuna, fish, and sea creatures inhabit every pizza, salad, omelette or even perfectly innocent-looking sandwiches.

After several frustrating visits to Japanese restaurants, where I looked on helplessly as a poor openmouthed fish floundered for dear life on a plate, I concluded that it would be best to eat at home. Anything put on my plate was gobbled up by those sitting beside me, while I had to make do with plate decorations: a radish masquerading as a rose, or a blade of celery carved into a comb.

I worried about accepting invitations from Japanese friends. In their efforts to impress, they would usually choose exotic restaurants, which served food fresh enough to walk across your table, spraying water in every direction or trying desperately to attach its suction pads to your chopsticks. I was particularly alarmed by the lobsters, which were boiled alive, and the long-spined sea urchins, which awakened atavistic hunting instincts in my fellow diners.

It is almost impossible to explain to the Japanese that a fellow human being can choose not to eat meat or fish: they are unable to grasp the idea. Surely meat can't be unhealthy, it's absolutely illogical. I explained away my aversion to still-live food, by saying that I was allergic to seafood, and couldn't eat meat because high cholesterol runs in my family.

It seemed I was destined to survive eating only gummy rice cakes and chocolates, until the day my faithful students, the Suzukis, invited me to a meal in a restaurant.

I decided to be honest and explain my delicate situation. I hoped this would kill the issue, but I miscalculated their determination, because a month later the invitation was reissued.

"We want to invite you to a kosher vegetarian restaurant," Mrs. Suzuki said to me in Hebrew over the phone.

"The only kosher restaurant is in the Jewish community," I said to her.

"There is also a kosher restaurant for Japanese," she repeated, and entered into a long and detailed description of the Buddhist religion, which preaches the morality of vegetarianism. She stressed that there were still a few Buddhist restaurants in Tokyo, where one could be served only vegetable food.

We set a date for the meal and met at the restaurant, situated in a typically Japanese wooden house, surrounded by a pool of goldfish. A pleasant swishing sound came from a large waterwheel which poured water into the narrow canals separating the rooms from each other.

We removed our shoes at the entrance, and followed the smiling, gold-toothed hostess, who pattered ahead of us on feet covered with *tabi* (white glove socks) to the private dining room reserved especially for us.

We sat on silk cushions, legs folded beneath us in a typical Japanese position, which foreigners are usually unable to hold for longer than ten minutes.

After exchanging polite words with the hostess, offering exaggerated compliments on the location, gushing over the beauty of the restaurant, its decor, and the size of the goldfish in the pool, our first course arrived, borne by five elderly waitresses in kimonos.

Bowing at the entrance to the room, the waitresses entered one after the other, carrying black-lacquered trays, which they laid on small stools beside us. According to Japanese custom, the men are served first, then the children, and finally the women.

The tray before me contained the most beautiful arrangement of food I had ever seen. A number of small plates, each with a different, tiny piece of food, in colors that mixed and blended in exquisite harmony.

The black porcelain plate, no longer than a bottle cork, contained a single purple *umeboshi*, a salted and pickled plum—merely an appetizer. On the plate next to it, in a translucent yellow pumpkin flower, sat a lone green soybean. A larger, square plate held a polished black pebble, which had been heated over coals. On it lay a tiny piece of tofu, skewered on a large pine needle. The tray itself was decorated with red maple leaves to remind us that we were in the middle of autumn.

The disappointment I saw on my husband's face was mixed with amusement at the size of the portions, while my son sat there silently, suspiciously examining everything that was set before him as if we were trying to poison him. I soon finished off everything on my own tray, and then my son's, which he passed to me surreptitiously.

The second course arrived inside a miniature bamboo grasshopper cage, which contained a sliver of gelatin the size of a thumbnail, with a few herb leaves suspended in it. Then came small slices of cooked vegetables, laid inside a carved snow igloo, lit up from inside by a tiny lightbulb connected to a digital battery at its base.

We counted more than forty different miniature dishes at that meal, which lasted about four hours, all beautifully garnished, and placed before us one after the other at intervals of a few minutes.

I understood from the look on his face that my son, who had not put a thing in his mouth throughout the meal, was waiting impatiently for his dessert, which we knew was imminent when rice was served. In Japan rice is eaten only at the end of the meal. Japanese rice is very sticky. It is almost impossible to make out any of the original grains—they stick together like a complex molecular formation. Rice has to be eaten just as it is. No salt may be added, or vegetables, or even a drop of soy sauce. The addition of sauce to white rice is considered bad manners in Japan and an insult to the cook.

Cheered by the idea that dessert was on its way, my starving son polished off the one familiar food he had so far been served, and I found his chopsticks invading and fishing around in my own bowl of rice.

Once the rice bowls were cleared, we stretched ourselves out on our cushions in anticipation of the promised dessert. The thin, rice-paper Shoji doors slid open and our five costumed waitresses brought in our desserts.

We were served grapes. Each of the red-lacquered plates laid before us contained three large, green, shining grapes, arranged in a perfect equilateral triangle. I noticed later that the plate had three small equidistant depressions, perfectly suited to the size of the grapes. With our three grapes we were each given a thick bamboo toothpick and a tiny wooden knife.

Why three grapes and not four? The Japanese, like the Chinese, believe that even numbers are unlucky. If you count the number of stories in a Japanese pagoda, you'll see that there are either five or seven. Stores sell sets of crockery for five servings only and cutlery for five people only. You must never give a bouquet of flowers containing an even number of flowers. It's *"dame,"* taboo. The worst number of all is four—because the Japanese word for four is *"shi,"* which also means death. Superstitious people would never live in a house whose number is four, would avoid buying four tomatoes in a shop, and would rather use the neutral word *yon* to express the number four.

Back to our dessert. I looked at our son, whose face had brightened considerably at the sight of the grapes. He shoved one into his mouth, sank his teeth into it, caressed it with his tongue, and rolled his lips to keep in every drop of juice. When he'd finished the grape, he spit out the pips. My husband hesitated for a moment, but succumbed finally and devoured the grapes, totally ignoring the knife and toothpick on his plate.

I decided to wait and see what Mrs. Suzuki would do with her grapes. She had been pointedly ignoring my family's appalling table manners so as not to embarrass them. Her eyes turned politely to her own plate. She carefully picked up the grape at the top of the triangle, and laid it delicately in the palm of her hand. Her manicured nails slowly and methodically peeled away the transparent skin. Skinned and naked, the pink-veined grape was placed in the top depression of the red-lacquered plate. Using the tiny wooden knife, she cut the grape into equal halves, which were then cut into quarters. There they lay, like the four leaves of a lucky clover, each precisely like the other as if they had been dissected by a computer-operated laser beam. The pips stuck out annoyingly from the green juicy flesh. These were removed gently with the help of the knife, as in a surgical operation to remove a malignant growth.

After a brief break, Mrs. Suzuki speared a piece of grape with the toothpick, slowly and expertly, as if fearing to squirt so much as a drop of the precious juice. The peeled, de-pipped quarter grape was presented cautiously to her mouth, while the palm of her other hand was sent under her chin to catch any unwanted drips. The quarter grape was demolished in three delicate bites.

I watched her helplessly. There was no point in attempting, as patiently, calmly and cleanly, the ceremony taking place before my very eyes. She had at least fifty years of experience in eating grapes. In a final act of despair and reconciliation, I popped the grape, peel, pips and all into my mouth.

With my stomach pleasantly full of the delights of the kosher Japanese kitchen, and full of appreciation for our hosts, I looked smugly at the harrowed faces of my husband and son. Surely now they understood how I felt, eating nothing in the slaughterhouses they called "restaurants."

We stretched our atrophied legs and massaged the blood back into circulation after four hours of unaccustomed sitting on cushions. "I'm dying for a hamburger," said my husband, as we put on our shoes. "Me too," squeaked my son. "I'm starving."

After a long ritual of farewells, bowing, thanks, and praise for the wonderful food in the restaurant, we parted from the hostess and made our way to the car. The Suzukis insisted on leading the way, at least until we reached a familiar street. We followed them a short way, until my family, by now crazed with hunger, demanded that I signal to our benefactors that we could manage on our own.

The car screeched to a halt at the first McDonald's we saw and my starving men tore out toward the counter, leaving the doors gaping open behind them. I found them later, bent over Big Macs, bags of greasy french fries, and giant cups of cola and milk shakes. Grunting with joy and relief, they sank their teeth gratefully into the oily, cholesterol-filled hamburgers.

Back in the car, my son sighed in contentment, and, patting his stomachful of junk food, declared: "That was the best hamburger I've ever eaten in my life."

A Land of Plenty

"**W**hy is everyone looking at our shopping cart?" we asked each other on our first visit to the local supermarket. It was a strange feeling. Dozens of pairs of eyes peered inquisitively at what we were buying.

Everything in the cart was absolutely Japanese, including the tofu, which we had picked up by mistake because it looked exactly like a piece of white cheese. Only when we reached the checkout, and dared take a reciprocal peep into the carts of those scrutinizing us, did we realize what all the fuss was about. The Japanese have different shopping habits from our own, and the difference is quantitative. Our cart was piled high with sacks of onions, potatoes, loaves of bread, three chickens, and all the goods of the earth. But a Japanese family's cart would contain one tomato, half a cucumber (theirs are very long), a couple of onions and four slices of bread. This gastronomic extravagance might be augmented by a fresh fish or half a lobster and a small bunch of sprouts. We soon concluded that our purchases would fill the carts of about six Japanese shoppers. The guiding principle in a Japanese household is freshness and frugality. The Japanese housewife prefers to shop three times a day, rather than buy large quantities of food which need to be stored and might spoil and have to be thrown away. The average Japanese homemaker buys food for breakfast in the morning, and goes out again in the afternoon to buy food for supper. There are plenty of food stores, most open for long hours and sometimes even around the clock, seven days a week. The funeral of Emperor Hirohito caused quite a problem with the 7-Eleven convenience stores, which are open 'round the clock and year round. By national decree, all places of business had to close for the day, but how could you close something which has no doors or locks?

It is virtually impossible to hoard food in Japan. Houses are small and usually overcrowded, the kitchens are no larger than a sink and cooker, and the fridges are barely large enough to store ingredients for one meal.

We made sure our future food-shopping excursions were Japanese-style.

One visit to a Japanese supermarket convinces anyone that Japan is indeed a land of plenty. You can find anything, from prickly pears imported from Mexico, packed and handled as if they were valuable pieces of crystal, to rare and exotic fruits from the Pacific Islands. In Japan, you can get strawberries all year, fresh coconuts, African breadfruit, figs the size of small oranges, and all sorts of fruits and berries from the forests of Europe. Every self-respecting grocery does its best to copy God's Garden of Eden in its boundless choice of fruit and vegetables—a joy to the eye and a delight to the palate.

As far as I was concerned, however, the fruit and vegetables in the Japanese supermarkets were there to look at but not to eat. They were always arranged in orderly piles, decorated with greens or fresh flowers, wrapped in crinkly cellophane or transparent plastic, packed and diapered in small wooden crates, or fixed stylishly upon an autumn leaf. Sometimes the fruit was tied with colorful silk ribbons, like the long hair of a little Japanese girl.

In Japan, it is *dame*—absolutely forbidden—to touch the fruit, feel it, or, heaven forbid, taste it before buying. And if you gave in to temptation, and drilled a tiny hole in the plastic wrap to sample a single grape, it's the end of the world! The shopkeepers, who follow your every movement with seven eyes, will humiliate and demean you in public. They will declare loudly that the bunch of grapes you have just desecrated is now damaged beyond repair, unfit for sale, since who would pay good money for a bunch of grapes with one missing?

What's more, when you shop in the fruit and vegetable section of the supermarket, you might as well leave your sense of smell at home. You won't need it. All the charming little parcels are wrapped and sealed in such a way that even an experienced police dog, who makes its living from its nose, could not scent them. Not a single whiff of odor escapes to whet your appetite.

The prices are astonishing. Who can afford to buy a sweet Yubari melon for $100? True, the melon is round and perfectly formed and grown in the fresh air and not on the ground; and the melon is packaged in a padded wooden box on a cushion of silk, and its tiny stalk is tied with a pink ribbon. It's only half-price if the stalk is off. But even if you feel you must have a melon, wouldn't you think twice before investing so much cash in a single one?

The highest-priced melon ever recorded in the crazy history of Japanese fruit prices, was on May 26, 1994. At an auction in the Sapporo wholesale fruit and vegetable market, a single melon sold for a record price of 130,000 yen (about $1,300!). Actually, the Japanese also felt that this exorbitant price was a little exaggerated. A photograph of the winning melon, enclosed in a wooden box, hardly suitable to the most expensive fruit in the world, let alone Japan, was printed the following day in every one of Japan's newspapers. The captions added that fifty-seven such melons had been auctioned off within five minutes of being offered.

Add to the list a slice of watermelon, which costs seven dollars, an apple, with the words "I love you" (or any other message) written on it in Japanese, prepared by the farmer especially for you, which costs $15, or even a pair of Matzutakeh mushrooms, which cost $180 dollars in season.

How can anyone afford a fruit salad in Japan?

We made do with bananas, which are cheap for some reason, and plentiful, and the fruit of the Mikan, which resemble mandarin oranges, and are soft to the touch and bland to the taste, and strawberries in season.

The most fascinating section in any Japanese supermarket is always the fish and seafood department, a real treat for lovers of bugs and eaters of creepy crawlies. This is where you can get fresh or smoked eels, shells of every type and color, crabs and lobsters, frogs' legs, all kinds of fish and other rare and interesting sea creatures, whose pictures illustrate books on marine biology. There they lie, cheap and fresh, in mile-long refrigerators, just like the milk products in Israeli supermarkets. And while we're on the subject of milk products: the job of finding plain, white cream cheese turned into a great challenge. As in the rest of the East, milk products are unpopular in Japan. Their milk is tasteless, the cream stiff, and their cream cheese, which tastes like moistened ground plaster, is sold as a medication, in small thimblelike packages. To bake a cheesecake, tour all the grocery shops for miles around and beg them for their entire stock of cream cheese. Even then you might be unpleasantly surprised, when the cheese you've spent so long collecting has gone moldy from so long on the shelf. As for milk, you don't have to compromise in Japan. You can get milk as good and fresh as any back home, if you're willing to pay the cost of the flight as well. This milk is flown in first-class especially from the northern Japanese island of Hokkaido and definitely does justify the cost of the plane ticket. And stop at the meat counter, where you can get the famous Kobe beef reared on beer and massage, which makes it melt in your mouth and very easy to digest. It can cost as much as one thousand dollars a kilo.

Our shopping excursions to the local supermarket were always an adventure. Our first tofu, which we mistook for white cheese, was soon joined by many other packages, bearing only Japanese lettering, with labels which had nothing to do with their contents. For example: spaghetti sauce turned out to be fish sauce; cooking oil was really vinegar; bitter Chinese tea called oolong masqueraded as orange juice; apple juice was really vinegar; the fish gelatin which we bought for dessert and so forth. All these goods were left in our fridge until they became moldy and were thrown away.

Even today, my five years of constant searching for reasonably priced and edible food products in Japanese stores affects my behavior. On my first day back in Israel I paid a visit to an Israeli food store, and was told off roundly by my friend.

"What *is* the matter with you?" she said, reproachfully. "You're behaving like a refugee from the Third World."

And indeed, I was in shock at the huge variety of colors, scents, and sheer plenty on the shelves. With considerable respect and fearing to get too close, I looked over the cantaloupes and watermelons and sniffed at the air around the mangoes and the grapes. The prices seemed unbelievably cheap.

After a few moments of spiritual intoxication, I started filling up my shopping cart, my hands trembling, with everything that caught my eye and captured my heart—for the first time in five years.

Festive Sounds

Kanamara's Big Day

The Japanese do things in a big way, and their timing is always perfect. When spring arrives and the cherry trees blossom and the air is filled with the sounds of mating cats, that's when the Japanese nation proves that the great Japanese erection is still in top form. Nowhere is it more evident than at the Festival for the Fertility God, Kanamara.

Ask a Japanese about the festival, and he would probably shrug his shoulders. He's never heard of it, or seen it. Tourist guidebooks offer information on the dozens of spring festivals all over the country: the *sakura*—cherry blossom festival, Buddha's birthday, the Nō Theater Festival, and many others. But a festival for the God Kanamara? No such thing. The traditional Kanamara Festival, celebrated in Japan for hundreds of years, is now swept away in shame under the tatami mats.

Foreigners who have heard of the event soon discover that, apart from themselves and the Japanese priests conducting the ceremony, few Japanese people participate in the Kanamara Festival. What was once a popular folk festival in Japan has, with the years, become something to be ashamed of.

Half an hour from Tokyo in the town of Kawasaki stands the Temple of Kanamara—close to the flashing red neon lights of the Horinouchi, the city's famous brothel. Kanamara is the god of hunting, fishing, and rice fields, but is mainly concerned with fertility, in all its forms: on land, sea, and air; in plants, animals, and human beings. This god takes life very seriously. He has no interest in the afterlife, or reincarnation; he is concerned only with existing life on earth, and the sexual relationships that create life.

It is a fact of life that our sexual powers sometimes disappoint, and we need help. The god Kanamara exists for just such needs. He is visited by impotent men and frigid women, people suffering from sexually transmitted disease or broken hearts, abandoned wives, cuckolded husbands, and many, many childless couples.

Being the god of fertility, Kanamara is also traditionally responsible for the inhabitants of the red-light districts. Indeed, before people became ashamed of him, the Horinouchi whores came to pay homage to him at cherry blossom time, and he would receive wonderful phallic gifts carved in wood, stone, or metal. He in return did his best to fulfill worshipers' requests for a well-heeled flow of regular clients. As a god of fertility, it is easy enough to guess what statue adorns his temple. It stands tall, firm, stiff, and festive—the biggest penis imaginable, almost seven feet high, cast in metal and painted a bright red. At its base lie offerings brought by its worshipers: phallic symbols in every shape, size, and material, made of clay, wood, and there is even a daikon, the giant, tubular Japanese radish. The temple's ceiling is decorated with painted tiles depicting the seven Japanese gods of fortune. Each god has only one eye, and they are rowing calmly toward a large human vagina, which is equipped, for some reason, with a set of pointed, castrating teeth. The temple is lit by upright, penis-shaped candles.

Outside the temple, dozens of foreigners, drunk on beer or sake, are waiting eagerly to celebrate the holiday. Nervous-looking Japanese transvestites and a group of locals stand shyly to the side, anxiously waiting to bare their problems to the god Kanamara.

Some foreigners are dressed in macho-looking samurai outfits and others have donned tall stiff papier-mâché hats shaped like erect penises, complete with testicles. If they were curious to know what it would feel like to own the world's largest penis, all they would have to do be to remove their hats and tie them to their loins.

The temple's yard is full of large carved-wood phalluses, fixed at a slight angle to the ground. Giggling Japanese schoolgirls and foreign women ride them as they might a horse. These carvings are especially favored by the transvestites, who seem to get great pleasure from riding them.

Other transvestites wander around in the temple's gardens, with small carved penises strapped to them like infants. Groups of men carry small shrines containing carved penises, swinging between them in regular rhythm.

A turn around the nearby erotic market reveals red, long-nosed masks, small ivory dolls in various positions of fornication, phalluses in every shape and size known, or unknown, to man, and Japanese Shunga drawings, ancient woodcuts depicting sexual poses. Other stalls offer more radishes carved into the shape of male and female sexual organs. Vendors with a sense of humor sometimes place a special flower arrangement inside the gaping radish vagina.

As the festivities heat up, groups of muscular young men burst into the temple's yard, dressed in *happi* coats—short Japanese cotton kimonos worn especially at festivals—and shouldering a portable shrine containing a perfectly proportioned image of the god Kanamara. The god, or rather the penis, is fixed to the floor of the shrine, so as not to fall off during its journey. To the beating of drums and the rhythmic cries of the men, who by now are in a state of semitrance, the little shrine sways up and down, right and left.

The festival reaches its high point in the evening, when Kanamara's priests wheel the god out to the yard. Burning coals and logs are piled all around him. The fire burns under the cast-metal penis until it turns a bright red color. Only then, to the wild beating of the drums and wild cries of the spectators, will the red-hot penis be thrust into a gaping, toothed vagina, whose ring of sharp pointed teeth can do absolutely nothing to deter the god Kanamara in his burning determination.

This exhilarating day comes to a close with a meal at which the visitors are seated on straw mats inside the temple. As might be expected, the food is in keeping with Kanamara's earthly manifestation and you can't miss the visual allusions of thrusting bamboo shoots, green asparagus spears, and stiff baby carrots.

The Great Kite War

*K*ite-flying in Japan is anything but a kid's game. Only macho descendants of the samurai, or other tough guys, involve themselves in this kind of work. Kites and kite-flying are out of bounds to women and children, because flying kites in Japan is not merely a pastime. It can be a declaration of war.

Four hundred years ago in Hamamatsu, a coastal town near the large town of Nagoya, a son was born to Lord Hikoma. As a token of his pleasure and in thanks to the gods, the distinguished lord had a giant kite flown in the sky, bearing the name of the newborn prince.

Ever since, the fifth of May has been set aside to celebrate the births of boy babies. Hundreds of men gather in Hamamatsu to fly their kites, at the biggest kite-flying event in the world. The town's population of half a million welcomes a further two million tourists from all over Japan.

The giant kites, each weighing around twenty-two pounds, with ribs measuring about thirteen feet, bear the names of babies born during the previous year in Japan. The entire cost of constructing and flying the giant kites is borne by the proud parents. When it comes to kites, the Japanese make no compromises on price, which can be sky-high. Besides the cost of the giant handmade kite, a team of flyers (which can be as many as thirty-five men) is hired and dressed and their salaries and living expenses paid during the long and arduous training period. Then there are the parties given for all the neighbors and the flyers themselves on the first evening of the three-day festival. Flying a kite on this special occasion could cost as much as $25,000.

This is considered a worthwhile investment in Japan. Nothing could satisfy a parent more than seeing his child's name gently soaring high in the sky on a kite.

Gently? No. Kite-flying in Hamamatsu can be, as I have said, a declaration of war. Any kite flying gently in the sky is in mortal danger, and chances are that it will end up crashing unceremoniously into the ground with thundering sounds of splitting bamboo, tearing paper, and the raucous cheering of the opposite team. As soon as the kites are sent up into the air they become instruments of destruction. Each kite is equipped with a weapon: a sharp hook designed to latch on to an opponent's kite and bring it down, after an elegant and exciting dogfight in the air.

Kite-fighting requires quick thinking and excellent reflexes as well as considerable physical strength on the part of the operating team. On kite-flying day, the enormous field at Hamamatsu looks like a battlefield, filled with hundreds of thousands of spectators crowding around the kite strings, which resemble large rolls of telephone cable. The teams must be constantly aware of changes in the wind direction and the movement of the other kites. A group of thirty muscular, tough kite-flyers, together with a few hundred supporters, often change course suddenly, and charge off to the other end of the field. The music and noise of war fill the air; drums, trumpets, and whistles resound. Often one team will get entangled with another and, balance lost, find themselves slipping and sliding in the mud, while the enormous cable spool rolls off on its own into the crowd.

In serene contrast to the hysteria and commotion down on the ground, the kites, bearing the names of newborn sons, float peacefully up in the sky—until they are forced down.

The great festival ends on the evening of the third day, by which time everyone is exhausted. It is then that the town's population of half a million is joined in the streets by the two million visitors, dressed in team colors. The masses pack the main streets, straining to watch a procession of colossal temples, with rich carvings of gods and monsters, which are pulled along on thick ropes by the crowds. Groups of musicians sit in the shrines, playing traditional Japanese musical instruments.

The kite-flyers and their supporters march proudly in front of the chariots, calling out team slogans and blowing on horns. Everyone participating in the festival carries a Japanese paper lantern with a burning candle inside, as well as miniature versions of their team flags.

After midnight, the families of the newborn sons prepare to be visited by hordes of well-wishers. We were swept along with the crowds right into the home of the Yamagi family, one of the town's wealthiest, whose celebration was twofold. The previous year, Mrs. Yamagi had given birth to twin boys, and this required the flying of two kites. The Yamagi flying team was necessarily the largest. It won the kite-flying battle, and this, of course, ensures a rosy future for the twin boys.

The narrow road leading to the Yamagi house had been cordoned off and long tables, laden with beer, sake, and a large assortment of seafood, awaited the kite-flyers and friends from the neighborhood. Sounds of the approaching teams could be heard from a distance, and they soon arrived in the team colors, proudly representing the family. The noise they made with trumpets and whistles and waving, flickering paper lanterns, was deafening.

The sleepy, mewling Yamagi twins were taken out of their cribs, so they could see the vast mass of humanity cheering ecstatically in their honor. The family home was circled several times in a wild, euphoric scramble by the kite-flying team, until their leader let out an almighty roar. The time had come to open the barrels of beer.

With trays cleared away and the last drop of sake drunk, the proud father was raised in the air, firmly grasping his twin sons. We were amazed at how coolly the two babies took all the noise, the flashing lights, and the strange, excited faces. During the entire six hours of noisy revels all around them, they neither cried nor seemed in the least bit frightened.

Early the following morning, the streets were clean and swept, as if nothing at all had happened.

The defeated kites lay smashed against the sands at Hamamatsu.

There's a Japanese song that says a kite is like a shadow that disappears in the afternoon and returns with the setting sun. The kite is not dead. It is merely waiting to be repaired and repainted and have its strings untangled. Then it will be reborn when the winds of spring return and it is called once again to the skies.

Walking on Hot Coals

The crowd around the huge bonfire seemed to be in a deep trance. All around the raised wooden platform stood priests, dressed in ornate white, gold, purple, or green robes, according to their professional status. With a flurry of axes and a barrage of arrows to banish evil spirits and whispered prayers to the God of Fire, the platform, piled high with dry firewood and branches of Japanese maple, was set alight.

For two hours, the flames licked at the wooden platform, and the priests changed monotonous Buddhist sutras, accompanying themselves with ringing bells and rhythmic banging on drums. Several of the priests blew on giant conches, with mouthpieces made of gilded metal. The sounds emanating from the conches, seemed to us Israelis just like the blowing of the shofar (ram's horn) and made us think of the Day of Atonement. The fire, which burned noisily, was fed with slivers of wood bearing the names and birth dates of believers, together with their special prayers. The Japanese believe that the piece of wood should be rubbed over the part of the body that hurts, before it is thrown into the fire. The smoke from the burning wood takes the prayer to the heavens, and the pain will disappear as if it never was. All around, we saw the faces of thousands of Japanese people, animated by the heat of the giant bonfire and the excitement. The heat around the fire was so fierce as to scorch the skin of those standing nearby.

As soon as the fire died down to a pile of red-hot coals, the high priest turned to the stage, and, whispering a few fortifying sutras, made his way barefoot over the burning scarlet embers. Because of his high standing, the high priest was afforded the greatest respect. He was the first to cross and feel the fire at its fiercest—a heat that could singe an eyebrow from a distance of two yards. The priest seemed to float above the coals, and his footsteps left a sizzling path of low fire behind them. When he'd finished his solo crossing, other priests followed him. I looked at their faces, calm and peaceful, as if they were about to take a quiet walk in the park. There was no sign of pain on their faces; nor was there any ambulance waiting around the corner to take away burn victims.

When the priests completed their march, a shudder of anticipation passed through the crowd. Within seconds, thousands of shoes and socks had been removed and the crowds started flowing in perfect order toward the burning coals. Suddenly my son, who was then nine years old, freed himself of my anxious grasp, took off his shoes and socks, and went to join the martyrs waiting to singe their feet on the burning coals. His turn arrived within seconds and, encouraged by the cries of the crowd, he ran across the platform. His little feet sent up clouds of thick gray ash and his entire body was surrounded by a heavy cloud of smoke. At the end of the agonizing journey, which lasted a few minutes but seemed like eternity to me, he stepped off the bed of coals and strode calmly over the layer of salt which had been laid nearby. He walked up to the High Priest, who patted him on the head and murmured a few words of blessing.

"How was it?" I ran to him breathlessly.

"Like walking on hot sand," he explained impatiently, and hurried off to the end of the line to do it again.

He wasn't the only foreigner to try this experience.

"If you can walk on fire, you can do anything," murmured an American tourist near me. He also took off his shoes and socks, folded up his trousers, and started hopping and skipping over the red-hot coals.

After my son's third walk, I went up and pulled him forcibly off the coals. The soles of his feet looked like potatoes which had blackened in a bonfire. After careful washing, I was unable to find any blister or lesion on the soles of his feet.

The firewalking ceremony is indeed a trial. The Japanese believe that the coals are not hot for good people, but will burn the soles of the bad ones. For others, the ceremony constitutes a test of tenacity. For everyone who tries it, walking on hot coals is certainly a test of courage.

Yet the original aims of the Hiwatari Festival were different. Walking on fire, the priests believe, cleanses the soul and ensures protection against road accidents and other dangers. "Cleanse your soul and the God of Fire will devour your sins and free you of the blemish of your mistakes." For anyone locked in a material prison, a walk on burning coals can bring an uplifting of the spirit, which transcends carnal desire and temptation and the agony of pain.

The burning mountain is also visited by people in trouble: families of the terminally ill, children who have failed their school exams, young couples about to be married. All of them are offered a walk over hot coals as a remedy for the soul.

The Hiwatari ceremony, practiced in Japan since the year 744, was a secret ceremony meant for the priesthood only. Laymen were forbidden to take part, and it was only in the year 1950, when it was opened to the public, that other people were encouraged to take part in the exhilarating experience of walking on fire.

The priests spend the day before the firewalk fasting, and the night in isolation offering up prayers to Buddha to give them strength in their legs. They continue to do this throughout the two hours when the fire devours each sliver of wood thrown into it. They walk around the burning wooden platform, humming sutras and looking like zombies.

Kaji Yamada the high priest of the monastery, whose feet encounter the first, hottest fire, claims that he doesn't feel a thing. He feels no pain or burning in his feet, because his soul is pure. As he walks over the fire, he thinks of water.

Water is another test for the priesthood of Shugenedo. Priests must go through several tests to achieve enlightenment: the *Chi* test—earth; the *Sui* test—water; the *Kah* test—fire; the *Fu* test—the test of the wind; and the test of *Ku*—the sky. The water test consists of a winter wash under a frozen waterfall and the earth test consists of a hike over several miles at a murderous speed.

The priests believe that only those who pass all the tests achieve superhuman strength and acquire supernatural powers, which will lead them to Nirvana.

How to Make Love in Japan

The Most Married Nation on Earth

"**A** woman who has never married," laugh the Japanese, "is like a Christmas cake after the twenty-fifth of December," hinting at the age, twenty-five, after which a woman's marriageability is reduced considerably. There is a word in Japanese, *tekireiki*, which means the right age for marriage: below twenty-five for a woman and above twenty-five for a man. Three years is considered an ideal age difference between a man and a woman.

Today a woman does not necessarily turn into a stale, unwanted Christmas cake after the age of twenty-five. In fact, statistics now show that the average marrying age in Japan, both for men and women, is creeping upward. The sociologists pin this change on Masaka Owada, the career-woman wife of Crown Prince Naruhito. The same Masaka, who before her marriage worked as a diplomat in Japan's Foreign Service, married the Emperor's firstborn son in 1993; and at the advanced age of twenty-nine, no less. Just as English girls imitated Princess Diana, Japanese girls were quick to adopt Masaka's personal style, taste, and fashion sense. Since Masaka met the Crown Prince, the sales of pearl necklaces have soared, Toyota Corolla II cars have been selling like crazy and a certain kind of German-made raincoat has disappeared from the retail shelves. Young Japanese women started dressing like her, keeping her breed of dog, wearing pearl necklaces like hers, and most important of all, receiving approval to raise the age at which they marry. They now may marry at twenty-eight or twenty-nine, and no one dares raise an eyebrow. Men, too, received an extension. The Crown Prince married at the age of thirty-three, after his younger brother. And if it's all right for the Crown Prince, it's all right for the rest of the country.

In twentieth-century Japan, they don't believe in being single. The Japanese are the most married nation on earth. In fact, only four percent of the population of Japan are still single in their forties.

But men, not women, are under the most social pressure to get married. A single man is usually considered gay, impotent, or simply unsuccessful. His chances of promotion are slim, since, in his private life, he has not proved himself to be a mature and serious-minded adult. On the other hand, when a man marries, he is very likely to receive a generous gift from his employers as well as immediate promotion. An employer expects a man to be married and taken care of, rather than spending his time and energies looking for a wife.

It's altogether different for single women. A woman who chooses to remain single and develop her career can't be categorized with the rest of womankind. The sexes in Japan are divided into three: male, female, and career-woman, a combination of the two.

The most desirable kind of marriage in Japan is called *ren'ai*, or love match. The couple meet at college or at work, fall in love, and get married.

However, things are not always so simple in Japan. There are some 8,500,000 single men in Japan aged between twenty and thirty-nine, as compared with only 5,200,000 single women.

The unbalanced ratio of men to women in Japan begins in the cradle. All over the world, 2.5 percent more boys are born than girls, but the rate of male infant mortality is slightly higher, creating a 50:50 ratio of male to female infants. Since infant mortality in Japan is virtually nil (or so I was told), the ratio of males to females stays the same: males outnumber females. It presents a significant hurdle for Japanese men looking for brides.

Despite modernization, widely available higher education, and the fact that more and more women work, it is still very difficult for the average young Japanese to find a suitable partner for marriage. Meetings between the sexes are still restricted. The Japanese in general, and Japanese men in particular, are shy and inhibited and often not very good at communicating with members of the opposite sex.

Japanese boys attend government-run single-sex schools, and see girls only as unobtainable objects beyond the school gates. And there's the Japanese mother, spoiling and pampering her son, taking him everywhere: to school, to the playground, to visit his friends, and even to college. That same mother, if she yearns for grandchildren, is later obliged to accompany her son to a matchmaking agency as well. Altogether, women in Japan are a desirable commodity. So much so that Japanese men, eager to compete for their favors, often attend special schools for bachelors like the one which has opened in Osaka. The school teaches the basics of catching a bride. Its five commandments are: do not humble yourself before a woman; do not patronize her; be understanding; be self-confident; and be open.

The Osaka school was founded in the early nineties and has become extremely popular. Even parents who are sure that their son is a real catch are interested in its services.

The school's principal justifies the necessity for his institution by pointing out that there is an enormous surplus of unmarried men in Japan. He insists, moreover, that Japanese bachelors do not know how to communicate with women. The school has set itself the task of helping young men in Japan find soul mates.

Another problem is the long working day, which leaves little time for a Japanese man to search for the ideal partner, let alone court her. Furthermore, Japanese factories often supply dormitory-style housing for their unmarried workers. An average factory worker shares a room with two or three others. These rooms are so small that the men stretch a rope on the ceiling to hang their clothes on; the only closet is stuffed with futons and bedding. A TV, video, and computer take up the rest of the room. Women are forbidden to enter these bachelor quarters and romantic interaction between male and female workers in the same factory is severely frowned upon.

Only, or oldest, sons are the most seriously afflicted. A Japanese woman usually prefers not to marry an only son or the oldest son in a family. The wife of such a man automatically becomes responsible for the care of his parents. Furthermore, as the wife of the oldest son, it is her job to invite every member of her husband's family to her house on all of Japan's national and religious holidays. And what bride would agree to such conditions, even if her potential bridegroom is the best man on earth?

Unmarried Japanese women often live with their parents until a suitable match is found for them. Many of those who work are known by the English initials, OL, for Office Lady. One out of three working women in Japan works in an office. Her job usually involves answering the telephone, making tea, welcoming clients, and running various errands.

Office Ladies are considered fortunate and happy people. Much is written about these young, single women in the press: An editorial in the paper *Asahi Shimbun* once claimed that "Japan is the only place in the world where young women are so fortunate and such a source of envy to their peers."

Young, unmarried Japanese women are free, in a world full of obligations. An OL is obviously a very happy young lady. She lives with her parents, and has no demanding career to advance. She is not required to work overtime. She is free to decide what to do with her salary, which she usually spends on clothes, cosmetics, restaurants, golf, and movies. She is free to travel, and does so, making frequent trips abroad, usually to Hawaii, Guam, the United States, and Europe. Most important of all, she is free of all home and family responsibilities, since she is not yet married. Of course, as soon as she does get married, her life will change completely. Still, the average Japanese woman is interested in marriage, but only to a man who can fulfill all her requirements.

Dazzled by the large supply of single men, young, unmarried Japanese women insist on their potential bridegrooms meeting three basic qualifications: he must be a university graduate, preferably from one of the more prestigious institutions of higher education, such as the University of Tokyo; he must have a high salary, or be employed by a prestigious company; and he must be tall, by Japanese standards—at least five-foot-eight. A man below average height, or one whose salary leaves something to be desired, is a poor marriage prospect. Such a man will have to make do with a women of lower social standing than his own, or one who is not very good-looking, or even one who is older than he is.

How then, with all these obstacles and hardships, did the Japanese become the most married nation? How are matches made?

The traditional and surest way of ensuring a match between a man and a woman is known as *omi'ai*—the ancient system of matchmaking.

In the days of the shoguns and the samurai, matchmaking played an important role in the institution of marriage. In fact, it was the only way to get married. Marriage was then more a matter of politics than one of family. Marriage ties were formed as a way of increasing the power of a family, its property and capital, its political standing, and its clan unity. Couples often met for the first time on the bridal night—they had no choice.

Surprisingly for one of the most advanced and modern countries in the world, the concept of arranged marriage is still going strong in Japan, but with one difference. Today, the young man or woman is allowed to disqualify an unappealing candidate. However, this must be done carefully, or they will get a reputation for being too choosy, or for having unrealistic expectations. And if a disqualified marriage candidate was introduced to you by a family member or close friend, that person most certainly will be deeply offended. Many Japanese young people are very happy to have a match made for them. This way they make their parents happy and avoid choosing a partner who does not live up to their family's expectations.

The matchmaker makes a thorough study of the families of the future couple, making a special point of examining their social background and their income. People using their services can be sure that they are not matched up with a member of the tribe of untouchables, the *burakumin;* someone of Korean origin; or even a descendant of an atom-bomb victim from Hiroshima. Preliminary analysis also prevents involvement with families with a history of mental illness, genetic disorders or suicide.

The matchmakers like to conduct their activity in the lobbies of Japan's luxury hotels. If you find yourself in Tokyo's Okora or New-Otani hotels, you might spot an elderly *nakodo*—matchmaker—sitting with a horribly embarrassed, red-faced, young couple. After a few minutes, the matchmaker gets up discreetly and leaves the couple on their own. If the match succeeds, she will receive expensive gifts from the couple's parents.

No statistical data exist in Japan on the percentage of arranged marriages. Some claim that it is no higher than 20 percent of all marriages; others believe the figure is more than 60 percent. This discrepancy might be because many couples who met through the *omi'ai* method claim that they actually married for *renai* (love), since they really did fall in love before they got married. Love matches are considered more modern. They are also more risky, since the divorce rate is higher between couples who married for love.

The giant commercial concerns in Japan also fill the role of traditional matchmaker. Since they keep thousands of files containing the most intimate details on their employees, these companies are in an ideal position to introduce their loyal male workers to women who can be devoted wives and mothers and make their husbands' lives easier. Once he has found his mate, the worker can stop wasting time and energy searching for and courting a potential marriage partner, and devote himself to his work.

Large economic and industrial concerns make use of institutions known as "Family Clubs." One of the biggest matchmaking institutions in Japan is called "The Diamond Family Club," and represents over thirty companies. The club has successfully helped thousands of Japanese couples find marital bliss.

The clubs make use of computer data for matchmaking and do not offer their services free of charge, since in Japan anything that has not been paid for is considered worthless and unreliable. However, only a token sum is charged at registration, and the cost of a successful match is miniscule by Japanese standards. Most of the candidates bring their mothers along when they fill in the registration form. This can contain as many as 755 questions, and is usually filled in by the candidate's mother, who yearns for grandchildren. The meeting with the potential marital candidate then takes place in the clubhouse itself, often under the watchful eye of the young man's mother.

Most Japanese companies are especially considerate of a newly married employee, although once the first child is born, usually a year or two after the wedding, the company expects its employee to devote most of his time and energy to his work.

From the moment he gets married, the Japanese male divides his loyalty between his place of work, and his family. Every year results are published in Japanese newspapers of surveys in which new employees list their priorities: the companies which employ them or their families. In recent years Japanese men are more inclined toward their families than their place of employment, a trend which has been given an Anglo/Japanese nickname: *My-home-o-shugi*—I prefer my home. However, other surveys claim that when conflict of interests exists between the employer and the family, it's the family that pays the price.

Other singles try their luck at one of the fashionable match-making parties, like those organized by the highly experienced Tokyo company, "For-U." Another veteran matchmaking company, Altman, organizes over three hundred such parties each year. Single women pay only $50 each for these parties, while men pay the full $100.

There are also specialist matchmakers. Do you hanker for a doctor? Or an engineer? A computer expert? You can be introduced to any kind of professional you like, when you apply to the company dealing with each specific commodity.

The men who go to these matchmaking parties look as if they are in dire need of counseling, to the tune of "Getting To Know You." They cluster in groups in the corners of the room, staring, bewildered, at the girls around them. The more courageous might try to strike up a conversation, but in most cases they just shrug their shoulders and turn their backs. The organizers try to help the baffled gentlemen by handing out a list of pertinent questions or witty remarks with which to amuse girls. There are prizes for couples who pair up during the evening—a luxury boat ride in Tokyo Bay, a romantic dinner for two, or a visit to Tokyo's Disneyland. The last is very popular, because the girl can cling to her gallant partner every time the roller coaster takes a dangerous dip—another way to the Japanese male heart.

It is especially difficult for a man to find a wife in Japan's rural regions, where every local girl tries to escape the fate of her mother, a bent-backed farmer's wife, old before her time from hard work in the rice fields. As soon as they can, rural girls leave to try their luck in the big cities, leaving the menfolk in solitary misery on the farm. No town girl would agree to marry a farmer with rough callused hands and coarse dark skin. Japanese farmers are obliged to import brides, chiefly from China and the Phillipines. A Filipino bride can be bought from her parents for a meager sum (though it is enough to support an entire Filipino family for several years), and sent to live and work on a Japanese farm. The Filipino women are friendly, accustomed to poverty, don't balk at hard work, and are considered by the young farmers' Japanese parents to be very suitable wives for their sons. However, trouble starts with the arrival of children, when the obvious cultural gap between Japanese and Filipino turns into a real burden. The young Filipino bride, usually cheerful and full of vitality, finds it hard to get used to the stern, conservative mentality of the Japanese farmer.

Japanese newspapers often print tragic stories of Filipino women escaping from their homes in the country and leaving their children behind them, or committing suicide, and many others who go on living on the thin line between sanity and madness.

The problems of their menfolk scarcely concern the merry potential wives of Japan. On the contrary. The more the matter is discussed, and the harder it becomes for Japanese men to find brides, the easier it is for Japanese women to become choosy and demanding, with their expectations for their potential bridegroom ever on the rise. The men themselves become irritable and lose confidence in their ability to find brides suitable for their families and for themselves—in this order, of course.

But as sociologist Mariko Bandu says, "Today, it is no longer necessary for a woman to marry for financial reasons, or be dependent on a man, as it was in previous generations."

The women of Japan are no longer in a hurry to marry.

And what about love?

It took me four years of living in Japan to realize that I didn't know the Japanese words for that old, hackneyed and most banal of all expressions, "I love you," a sentence I learned almost as soon as I landed in any new country on my travels around the world.

I discussed this puzzle with my close friend Akiko one afternoon, over a cup of coffee in a nice café. I simply asked her how to say "I love you" in Japanese. Akiko blushed daintily, and whispered, so the other customers wouldn't hear: *"Aishite iru."*

"I've lived more than four years in Japan and I've never heard this important sentence. How come?" I asked.

"Because the Japanese don't make a habit of saying it."

"How do people know that they love each other?" I asked her.

"They know without saying it," she insisted. "Anyway, the Japanese are not demonstrative people."

"Has your husband ever told you he loves you?" I asked her impudently.

"Why should he?" she asked in reply. "We're married, aren't

we?" Akiko lodged a counterattack. "Anyway, you Westerners are always saying it to each other. Perhaps you're not really sure of your love, or of your partner's."
I decided to change the subject.

Once the Japanese decide to get married, they begin planning a complicated production composed of laser beams, helicopters or gondolas, transparent elevators, Rolls-Royce rides, and a great many fluffy, dry-ice clouds and boring speeches.
Around 700,000 people get married in Japan every year. One could say that every forty-five seconds, a wedding is taking place somewhere in Japan. About 40 percent of the weddings take place at Wedding Palaces, while another 30 percent prefer large halls belonging to the luxury hotels. Others marry in church, to the romantic music of an organ (even if they are not Christian), or in Hawaii, as part of a package deal, which includes a fancy wedding and round-trip plane tickets for the guests.
A Japanese wedding can become a gigantic production, in which dozens and sometimes even hundreds of workers are involved. After all, most Japanese marry just once.
The bride and groom might alight from a white helicopter or a giant gondola flying down from the ceiling of the huge wedding hall. More modest couples might arrive in a Rolls-Royce or a Bentley, and as they do, the hall fills with the sound of the "Wedding March" and multicolored laser beams and white clouds of dry ice. The domed ceiling sparkles suddenly with thousands of stars and turns into a magic planetarium, highlighting the happy couple's zodiac signs, with a detailed explanation of the potentially successful marriage and the wonderful life awaiting them. Then the ceiling opens up and showers hundreds of brightly colored, heart-shaped balloons on the guests.
All these pyrotechnic delights are usually accompanied by loud cries of amazement and enthusiasm, and the louder these are, the more successful the wedding.
A Japanese wedding can take up most of a day. This is when the bride plays the role of princess, and the groom is her fairy-tale prince. The bride changes her clothes at least four times during the wedding festivities, at a special ceremony known as *oironaoishi*. She first enters the wedding hall in the traditional Japanese bridal costume of large, ornate wig, and a heavy silk, gold-and-silver-

embroidered kimono. Her face is powdered white and she wears a large boat-shaped hat on her head. This is the costume she wears to the temple for the Shinto wedding ceremony. Once everyone has seen her, she rushes off, and, aided by a team of ladies-in-waiting, changes into a white, Western-style wedding dress, with a long, flowing train. Later, she will make another change or two into evening dresses, usually reminiscent of Cinderella's ball gown. Since each of these dresses is accompanied by appropriate makeup and hairstyle, the bride is absent from the festivities for an hour or two whenever the time comes for a change.

A self-respecting bride actually buys all these clothes for her wedding, although she knows she will never wear any of them again. The financial outlay is enormous. For example, the majestic *junihitoe* kimono consists of twelve layers, the top one of thick, padded, embroidered silk. It weighs around one hundred pounds, and is often heavier than the bride herself. The Japanese princesses wear similar kimonos on their wedding day and a specially trained lady-in-waiting stands by to discreetly wipe away sweat from the heavily madeup face, without disturbing the white powder. No Japanese girl, budget permitting, would miss the chance of being a princess for a day. It costs two million yen to rent a kimono like this for a day—or $20,000.

The bridegroom, too, takes advantage of the day to put on a traditional male kimono, which bears his official family crest. He wears this *hakamu* to the marriage ceremony at the temple. Later, he will change into a velvet or shiny silk tuxedo. The guests, too, come dressed in their nicest clothes. The ladies wear kimonos in every color under the sun and the men come in tuxedos and white silk ties. The outfits are often rented.

The highlight of the evening is the wedding cake—huge and impressive, with an uneven number of tiers, of course. It is wheeled into the hall on a large platform, and is often as tall as the couple getting married, so they must climb a small ladder to cut it. But a Japanese wedding cake is a cake only in the region which the knife cuts. The rest of the construction is made of polystyrene and cardboard, suitably decorated in wedding colors. The slices of cake which arrive in the hall soon afterward come from the kitchen and not the wedding cake.

Speeches play a significant role at a Japanese wedding. The first to speak is always the most illustrious guest, who gives exaggerated and flowery descriptions of the bride and the groom. He is followed by family members, parents, and the bride and groom themselves, who thank their parents in emotion-filled speeches for all they have done for them. Japanese weddings are often poignant, sentimental events, with the guests sniffing and wiping away tears at the end of every speech. Some of the speeches are amusing and witty, and there are even guests who sing to the bride and groom.

The wedding program sometimes includes a slide or video show, in which the happy and romantic couple is shown in various embarrassing moments, as babies perhaps lying naked on a bearskin rug. The show always draws exclamations of fellow feeling and excited cries from the audience.

As for gifts, the guests don't spend sleepless nights wondering what to buy the young couple. At a Japanese wedding you give money. This helps cover the cost of the wedding—and the guests know exactly how much that was, by the hall in which it was held—with a nice, fat addition to smooth the young couple's path to marital bliss. In return, each guest receives a gift from the young couple. This might be a set of crystal champagne flutes, a dinner service, a fancy watch, or . . . food.

The cost of a wedding, including clothes for the bride and groom, artistic photography, video, gifts for the guests, flowers, pyrotechnics, and meals, can add up to four million yen, or $40,000, for a modest wedding. The cost of hiring a hotel hall $100,000, which is divided equally between both sets of parents. Bear in mind that the average Japanese earns around $45,000 a year.

But the Japanese don't pinch pennies at weddings, and anyway, who wouldn't jump at a once-in-a-lifetime chance to play the romantic role of prince and princess at the Royal Court?

According to the country's sociologists, the astronomical costs of weddings in Japan serve as a psychological block to divorce. You can't consider getting divorced after your parents have laid out a fortune on a wedding. What's more, the guests have given generous sums of money to help make the marriage a success. However you look at it, the question of divorce in Japan is a very uncomfortable one.

Once the wedding is over, the guests disperse, the waiters and kitchen workers clear away the remainders of the meal, and the young couple drive off in a Rolls-Royce supplied by the management of the wedding hall. The luxurious car brings the tired but happy couple to the entrance of the nearest railway station.

The royal act is over and they return to everyday routine, to the kitchen in their tiny apartment, and to a world where princes and princesses are found only in fairy tales.

And What About the Morning After?

I am devoting this part of the book to romantic men who fantasize about an ideal woman, believing that she exists in the shape of a dainty Japanese lady, soft and gentle and kimono-clad, submissive and obedient. In other words, a geisha. Other, more dramatic men might like to recall the lovely and tragic Madame Butterfly, who sacrificed herself on the altar of her love.

Sorry, fellows. Your masculine illusions are about to be shattered. Once the wedding is over, real life in the Japanese home is not the way you wish it were. The submissive Japanese wife has ceased to exist.

It is only fifty years since Japanese women, their heads lowered, holding on to the ends of their kimono, would pick their way a few tiny steps behind their husbands. Tiny? Their tight and narrow kimono restricted their movement. Today this is seen mostly in villages and remote regions of Japan, and in the private quarters of the Emperor of Japan, since tradition dictates custom in the Royal Household.

The modern Japanese woman walks beside her husband, dressed in an elegant Chanel suit, or well-fitting designer jeans. The kimono is kept in the closet for special occasions.

Still, even today, a Japanese wife will pour out her husband's drink, light his cigarette, and stay awake for him until late at night (unless he lets her know that she can go to bed) with food kept hot in the oven and a *furo* full of hot water for his bath, just as her mother did for her father.

Japanese women refer to themselves as "supporters," and this is also the way they contribute to the country's flourishing economy. They are considered the other half of the Japanese economic miracle. It is they who free their husbands from day-to-day problems like paying bills, bringing up the children, shopping—leaving the men free to devote all their attention to their jobs. The word "wife" in Japanese means "inside person." Her responsibility for all aspects of the household, and the exaggerated care she lavishes on the children, confers an immensely powerful status for a Japanese wife within her own home. In return for his freedom from minor and major irritations of home and family, the husband must, according to Japanese convention, hand over his entire salary, in cash, to his wife. She knows best what to do with it. For his own needs—train fare, lunches, newspapers, and cigarettes—he gets pocket money. How much of his salary does the Japanese man receive from his wife? The answers are easy enough to find. Every year, Japanese papers publish articles with lengthy titles like: How Much Pocket Money Will the Japanese Male Receive This Year, Considering Inflation and the Rising Cost of Living Index. Both men and women in Japan are amazingly candid on the issue of pocket money for the husband. Naomi, a plump forty-year-old waitress who loved diamonds and well-cut suits, often told me that Japanese men were *kwa'iso*. I had heard this expression used by other Japanese women friends, so I asked Naomi what it meant. She answered with a giggle, hand upraised to hide her mouth.

"*Kwa'iso* means poor devil. All our husbands are poor devils."

"Why?"

"Take my husband for example. He works hard from morning 'til night. At the end of the month he gives me all his money, and I decide what to do with it, If I feel like it, I buy myself jewelry or a new suit and not long ago, I changed my car."

"And what does he live on?"

Another giggle. "I give him pocket money, $350 a month. It's up to him to make do with it."

"What if he feels like buying himself a new shirt?"

More giggling. "He can save up and buy one. And now do you see what I mean when I say that they are *kwa'iso?*"

My neighbor, Hiroko, proudly showed me a nice cashmere jacket she had bought for her husband on sale.

"I'll tell him it cost me more, so I can take it off his pocket money for the next three months," she said with a sly grin.

Yet the men in Japan don't look pathetic. They enjoy themselves after work, they go to fancy restaurants and dress in expensive suits. Where, then, does the money come from?

I met the well-dressed managing director of a giant Japanese concern at an elegant celebration dinner. I looked admiringly at his silk suit and complimented him on it.

He pulled open his jacket and showed me the label: Christian Dior.

"It cost $4,500," he whispered in my ear.

I almost choked on my soup and stuttered: "How can you afford to buy such a suit? Did you save your pocket money for a year?"

The gentleman burst out laughing as he gave me his answer. "I get the money for my suits from my mother."

And where does the money come from to pay for their entertainment?

A survey taken not long ago showed that the Japanese spend more on entertainment than on the country's entire defense budget. The average Japanese man does not go home after work. He would rather go to a bar for a drink or a karaoke singalong with his colleagues, or for an elegant meal, or he might choose to spend the evening with a pretty little hostess on either arm, who amuses him and gives him the feeling that he is the most desirable man in the world. A glass of whiskey diluted with water and a chat with a professional hostess can easily cost $400 an evening and a good meal at a fancy restaurant can cost more than $1,000 a head. That's not pocket money, doled out by wives.

Men get it from their employers. Vast sums of money are allocated and spent on what is called "Making friends and getting to know people." This includes entertaining potential clients, hosting business associates, tightening interpersonal relations within the workforce, and occasionally, industrial espionage. Money is given to employees in the form of vouchers. In many cases, the restaurant sends the bill directly to the employers. And if the husband is only a minor employee, is not a candidate for frequent promotion, and is not given money to "make friends," still he will not rush home as soon as his day's work is over. Home for him is a tiny apartment most of the Japanese refer to as their "rabbit hutch"—stifling in summer and freezing in winter, full of whining children and a demanding wife, and worst of all, the neighbor—what would the neighbor say if she saw him coming straight home from work? She'll think he's a failure and spread the gossip all over the neighborhood. A salaryman prefers to spend time with his friends over a plate of hot steamy ramen (noodle soup), or to sit for hours on end at noisy pachinko machines, shooting little metal balls through a maze.

The later her husband comes home and the more time he spends out, the better, as far as the Japanese woman is concerned. It's a sure sign that he is doing well at work, and with promotion comes money. Above all, Japanese wives believe their husbands should be "healthy and absent"—a perfect foundation for the ideal Japanese household.

There are about 500,000 Japanese women who never see their husbands even at night. These husbands have been sent by their employers to work in another city or another country. Children in Japan come first, so that if the schools at the husband's new posting are not good enough, or worse, no Japanese schools exist where their father is working, their mother stays behind with the children and avoids any unnecessary upheavals which might ultimately affect their higher education. Anyway, employers prefer to save the costs of transferring the family, since they only distract the man and prevent him from concentrating wholeheartedly on his job. The family usually reunites on national holidays or once a year during the summer vacation.

You can learn a lot about the way a Japanese husband treats his wife from the way she complains about him. We had a business meeting at the coastal town of Hamamatsu with a Japanese businessman, who suggested we go out together for dinner. I asked that he bring his wife, whom I had never met, so that I would have some female company.

He arrived with Kiako, an elegant Japanese woman of about forty, who was happy to talk about her children, her work, and her hobbies. Our conversation changed character as she began to discuss her husband. Her face took on a sour expression as she confided in me. "My husband is a typical Japanese male. We did marry for love, after having known each other briefly at university, but he soon started behaving toward me just as his father had behaved to his mother and my father to my mother. His daily conversation moves around the same four nouns: newspaper, sleep, food, and bath. Or what we Japanese call *Mi No Mawari*, which means to do with the body. We hardly ever go out, and I haven't seen a movie since our courting days."

What she was saying somehow didn't ring true.

"And how many nouns has he used today?" I asked her.

"None. And if he does, it will probably be one of the usual four."

"That's impossible," I said. "He must have said something else in order to bring you here. He'd have had to explain that we were visiting and he wanted you to join us." I was embarrassed by her reaction. Kiako burst out laughing and covered her mouth with an upraised hand. She pointed at our host. "He's not my husband, he's my lover."

There's nothing extraordinary in having a lover in Japan. One of the first questions I was asked at a reception given in my honor by my female neighbors was "Have you got yourself a Japanese lover yet? Or are you seeing a foreign lover?"

My closest friend, Kinoshta, who was always a welcome guest at our home together with her husband, the managing director of an important government office, called me one day in response to our invitation for dinner and drinks.

"My husband is busy that evening. Will it be all right if I bring along my man friend?" she asked.

I began to flounder.

"Well, yes, but everyone else who has been invited knows you . . ."

Her reply was a short giggle and she turned up at the reception with a smiling, elegantly dressed man, whom she introduced to the other guests as her closest friend.

Away from home, a Japanese wife will never disagree with her husband, never interrupt him when he is talking, nor ever contradict him. It is considered terribly bad manners. But it's very different at home, as shown in the evening TV soap operas, known locally as "home dramas." Japanese husbands laugh their heads off in sympathy with their TV counterparts, at a complete loss when it comes to anything to do with the home and absolutely penniless, while his wife has him wrapped around her little finger. "You just need to know which strings to pull," say the Japanese women.

The Japanese wife ostentatiously fusses, and goes to great lengths to make her husband happy. She prepares his meals, lays out clean clothes for him to put on in the morning, pushes a handkerchief into his breast pocket—or a condom into his suitcase, if he is going on a business trip—and gives him his pocket money. She waits up for him when he returns, even if it is very late at night, with his futon spread out and a hot bath awaiting. She will even scrub his back for him.

She takes care of him exactly as his mother did before his marriage. But with all this mothering, he loses sexual interest in his wife and finds emotional excitement in the company of bar hostesses, or an occasional call girl, or in the arms of another married woman, whose husband has lost interest in her.

The crisis comes when the man reaches retirement age. Until then the couple usually keeps the relationship going for the sake of the children. Retirement age in Japan is low in comparison with life expectancy, and in recent years, with the economic crisis in Japan, men retire at sixty, fifty-five, and even fifty years of age. According to a report by the World Health Organization in Geneva, Japanese men and women enjoy the longest life expectancy in the world. A Japanese man can expect to live for 76.3 years, while his wife might live to the age of eighty-three or more. Thus, if a man retires at fifty, his wife has more than twenty-five years left to live with him, and this is the crux of the problem. A Japanese woman has formed her own circle of friends, has gone to school and enriched her education, has a closet full of beautiful clothes, and a nice bank account added to over the years. All of a sudden her life is invaded by her retired husband, bored, helpless, and penniless. He, who has never had to look after himself, be responsible for his clothes, or even brew himself a cup of tea; he, who has no outside interests because of his commitment to his work, nor any social ties not connected with his work; and worst of all, he who has been pampered all his life, first by his mother and then by his wife, now finds himself totally dependent on her. It's at this stage in his life that his name changes from *kawa'iso* (poor devil) to *sudai-gumi*—the name for dry garbage, like old appliances. And that's exactly how the Japanese man feels—a useless old nuisance, helpless and underfoot: *sudai-gumi.*

It is not uncommon in Japan to see a couple of old-timers, the wife, who always kept her mouth respectfully shut while her husband was employed, yelling like a fishwife at the poor, trembling old man.

This is when a Japanese marriage is most likely to end in divorce. The term "retirement divorce" came into use because of the large number of women who divorce their husbands once their working life is over. In her book *The Japanese Women—Traditional Image and Changing Reality*, Sumiko Ewao, professor of psychology at Keio University, tells of a woman who spent the last ten years of her husband's working life preparing for the day she would inform him that she was divorcing him. As he returned home from his retirement party after thirty-two years with the same firm, her suitcases were packed and ready by the door. She had rented herself an apartment two months before and removed most of her belongings from the family home, without her husband even noticing. Often the packed suitcase waiting by the door belongs to the husband, who is then thrown to the streets, tired and penniless.

"See all the people living in cardboard boxes?" asked Suzuki, my guide during my last visit to Japan, as we walked through the tunnels under the Shinjuko railway station and reviewed the rows of cardboard boxes prepared by the Tokyo municipality for its homeless. "Many of them are men who have been thrown out of their homes once they retired from work." Worried, he added that he had another five years to go until retirement and that he had already bought himself an instruction book telling men how to retire wisely and avoid getting thrown in the street.

The women of Japan finally achieve peace and quiet when the ashes of their husbands are placed in the family butsudans. This is the ornate domestic shrine usually placed in the living room, next to the TV set, which contains the ashes of the family's loved ones. It receives daily offerings of plastic flowers, as well as cups of tea and bowls of rice. From time to time a widow might remember her husband with tears in her eyes, but her life becomes much calmer and pleasanter once her husband is no longer with her.

Thus, surrounded by her children and grandchildren and cared for by the wife of her oldest son, whom she can tyrannize as she herself was tyrannized by her own mother-in-law, the Japanese woman can end her life in peaceful tranquillity.

Divorce Japanese-Style

"**Y**ou can't trust Ishi," the Embassy secretary whispered in my ear.

"What's wrong with Ishi?" I asked her, surprised.

"You can't trust him," she repeated. "He's not reliable."

"But Nuriko-San, why do you say that?"

Nuriko, a fifty-year-old spinster, whispered her terrible secret in my ear: "Didn't you know? Ishi is divorced."

"Surely not," I said confidently. "We've been to his home several times. I know his wife well, and she's always there when we're invited. Anyway, even if he were divorced, that's no reason for him to be unreliable." I decided to put an end to this wicked gossip.

I recalled fondly the pleasant evening my family spent with Ishi and his family on New Year's Eve. Ishi's late father had been a member of the Diet, the Japanese Parliament, and well-known for his unreserved admiration of the State of Israel. His son, a close friend of ours, did all he could to promote business relations between Japan and Israel. His cosmopolitan education resulted in a perfect command of the English language, which he spoke with a wonderful British accent. We were surprised to receive his invitation to spend New Year's Eve with him and his family. Ever since General MacArthur's social reforms after the Second World War, New Year's Eve has been a holiday in Japan; a time for the immediate family to gather for an intimate celebration. Apart from anything else, an invitation to a Japanese home is extremely rare. The Japanese tend to be ashamed of their small, cramped homes and avoid inviting foreigners, unless they can offer what they consider to be suitable hospitality.

Ishi, who lived in a small town on the outskirts of Tokyo, picked us up at the railway station. His wife, Yoko, was waiting for us at the door, with a pleasant, welcoming smile on her face.

As soon as we had changed into warm winter slippers, we were introduced to the other members of the family: Ishi's old mother and his teenage children.

We spent several hours at his home that day, passing the time away pleasantly, eating, drinking sake, and listening to the old mother's memories of her late husband's adventures in World War II.

Yoko made sure we were well fed. Ishi himself was obviously proud of his wife, a former beauty queen, and praised her frequently. As far as he was concerned, she was the best mother in the world, a wonderful wife, an excellent cook, and of course, a career woman. Unlike other Japanese men we had met, Ishi seemed to support his wife's career.

And while he was singing her praises, Yoko sat there, like a good, obedient Japanese wife, with lowered eyes and a light blush on her cheeks.

"Ishi-San is the first real gentleman I've met in Japan," I declared firmly on our way home.

I visited Ishi's home several times more that year. He asked that I record his mother's memories of his father's adventures and ties with Israel. All day, as I worked with the old woman, Yoko fussed around me, plying me with dozens of specially prepared vegetarian dishes. So as not to disturb my interviews with her mother-in-law, Yoko busied herself in the kitchen, cleaning, tidying, and ironing her husband's shirts. Actually, I wondered what she was doing at home since her business was in Tokyo, but I held my tongue and didn't ask.

The close friendship which developed between Ishi's family and our own brought them to our home several times. The relationship between him and his wife always seemed close, warm, and very pleasant.

Until the day the bomb fell.

"You're not going to believe what I just saw." This was the sentence that opened almost every conversation in our house since our arrival in Japan. "I met Ishi at the Technology Fair," my husband informed me, with a strange look on his face.

"What's so surprising about that?" I asked.

"He was there with another woman."

"Probably his secretary," I said dismissively, "and don't gossip," I warned.

"That's not all," he added. "He was with a three-year-old girl, whom he introduced as his daughter."

"It's quite common for Japanese men to have children by more than one wife," I pointed out, shocked that this was the case with Ishi.

"And that's still not all," my husband added. "He introduced the woman with him, who was half his age, as his wife."

"So. Plenty of Japanese men have more than one wife," I said, Nuriko's words churning over in my mind.

"No, it's his only wife. He's been divorced from Yoko for over ten years."

"If that's the case, why was she there when we visited him?"

"I've no idea," said my husband, a puzzled look on his face.

I came across several more stories similar to Ishi's during my stay in Japan. I would hear "secretly" from the Japanese secretaries that the gentleman who invited us to his house was divorced, yet the welcome we received from the woman of the house was inevitably warm and pleasant. At the reciprocal visit they behaved like a married couple in every sense of the word.

The institution of marriage is of supreme importance in Japan. But this does not mean that a husband must forgo the pleasures of other women, or that a wife must deny herself the warm and loving companionship of another man; but to break up a family and cause suffering to the children, Heaven forbid!

Moreover, in Japan, divorce is seen as failure. A man who has divorced his wife is not trustworthy and not stable. If he is unable to hold his marriage together, he won't be trusted with a good job. It is extremely difficult for a divorced man to get a promotion at work.

Thus, a Japanese couple would hide their divorce, especially from colleagues at work, and pretend to be part of a happy, stable family, at parties and official luncheons. A Japanese woman knows that it is in her interest to cooperate in this charade. If he is not promoted, her alimony, small enough as it is, will become smaller still. At pretending that everything is all right, the Japanese have no equals. Which explained why Yoko took time off work all those days I was at her home, just to give me the impression that the family was intact.

The lot of Japan's divorced women nowadays is far better than that of their nineteenth-century predecessors. In feudal times, a decision to divorce was in the hands of the husband only, and he was permitted to divorce his wife if she were barren; immoral; argumentative and didn't get on with her mother-in-law; talkative; dishonest; jealous; or sick. All he had to do was write a letter saying: "You are not compatible with the customs of this family, you are not needed, and you are free to seek happiness elsewhere."

The only option for a woman who wanted to leave her husband because of his mistreatment was to escape to a Buddhist temple or a convent, known as a *kakekomi-dera,* or sanctuary. If she succeeded in getting there before her husband and throwing her shoes over the fence, she was admitted, and after two years was declared divorced.

Most Japanese men of long ago would not take such a crude blow to their masculine pride and formed posses to seize the wayward wife and drag her back home. The posse, consisting of the husband's close friends and relations, would celebrate their successful hunt at the local restaurant, while the wife, still tied up, lay where she had been thrown, on the dirty kitchen floor.

Japanese women were granted civil rights only after the Second World War, although they were given the right to divorce their husbands in 1898 during the Meiji period. Women who wanted divorces made the most of this law, although had to contend with two serious problems. First, a divorced woman had to support herself, then virtually impossible. Women did not work outside the home in those days and were unable to learn a profession. Second, children were removed from the mother's custody. Her former husband's family retained custody of her children and, as a wayward wife, she was refused access to them. Thus, many Japanese women went on with a life of *gaman,* or no choice. Things are different in contemporary Japan. Nearly 75 percent of all divorce suits are filed by women. There are divorce mediators in Tokyo and a telephone hotline offering advice on divorce. Statistics published by the Japanese Ministry of Health show that divorce figures have doubled over the last twenty years. Still, compared with the U.S. and other Western countries, Japanese divorce rates are among the lowest in the world. Less than twenty percent of marriages end in divorce, compared with fifty percent in the U.S., and forty percent in England and Sweden.

In spite of everything, the Japanese remain married—for the sake of the children and their education and for economic reasons. Japanese mothers, who devote their lives to their children are convinced that healthy, happy youngsters can only be brought up within an intact marriage. They feel that divorce will harm their children's chances of success in school and deny them the financial support they need. Furthermore, as I was told by a close Japanese friend with whom I discussed the subject, "If I divorce my husband, his career will be ruined. I don't have the guts to ruin a man's career. His firm will think that if he isn't capable of organizing his personal and home life, he will be incapable of handling problems at work. Furthermore, although I could easily be granted a divorce, we Japanese women have been conditioned to be patient." She added, "It might be that we are in no hurry to get divorced because of the shame and humiliation involved. What will the neighbors say? And, how can we get divorced if everyone we know came to the wedding, and what shall we do with all the wedding gifts we were given?" she said, half-jokingly.

She could not ask her tyrannical husband for a divorce. The fact remains that divorce is considered a social failure in Japan, where tolerance and self-discipline are supreme values.

What reasons do people give to obtain divorces in Japan?

One of the greatest problems facing the Japanese wife, especially if she is married to an oldest son, is her responsibility for the care of her husband's elderly parents, especially his mother. This is every bride's unwritten obligation, even if she and her mother-in-law don't get on. The old woman who tyrannizes her poor daughter-in-law, as she herself was tyrannized by her own mother-in-law when a young bride, is a stock character in Japanese soap operas. In Japanese, if you join the word *yume* (bride) with the word *shutome* (mother-in-law) you get a word meaning fight, or struggle. Although fewer couples live with their parents in modern Japan, many Japanese men still suffer from *maza kon*—a mother complex.

Maza kon is especially common among firstborn sons, whose future wives will eventually have to take care of their mothers-in-law. Most Japanese women prefer not to marry a firstborn or only son. Japanese mothers-in-law have the habit of making surprise calls and looking into pots and pans, to make sure their daughters-in-law are feeding the sons the right kinds of food. It's a serious matter when the son compares his mother's cooking to his wife's, or compares their taste in clothes, or their ability to run the financial affairs of the household.

If the son does suffer from *maza kon*, or mother complex, the mother controls everything that goes on in her son's household. He might even call her on his honeymoon to ask for advice.

Domestic violence is also grounds for divorce. Since this usually occurs behind the locked doors of the family's home, the problem is looked upon in Japan as a private matter. A survey by the Domestic Violence Research Group points out that violence against women is widespread in Japan and occurs in all socioeconomic groups. In the survey, five thousand women filled in (anonymously) questionnaires handed out by women's organizations, lawyers, counselors, and various welfare institutions. The results showed that wife-beating takes place in the homes of Parliament members, senior officials, university professors, journalists, and others, and demonstrated that the social position of the batterer does not inhibit domestic violence.

About one-half of the women stressed that they had been beaten or sexually assaulted by their husbands. About three hundred of them had been hospitalized because of serious injuries inflicted on them by their husbands. Nonetheless, not one of these women lodged a complaint with the police against her violent husband.

From a list of thirteen possible reasons for divorce, a Japanese couple almost always choose incompatibility. The Japanese, who value calm and harmony, try to avoid lengthy, bitter divorce suits, and sort out their problems as quietly as possible.

"Education for women is the root of this evil." So says a noted Japanese sociologist. "It's why Japanese women have such small families and it also explains the high divorce rate in recent years."

Once property, custody, and child-support issues are settled, all a couple needs to get divorced is to visit the nearest branch of the Ministry of the Interior, fill in and sign a one-page form, and that's all. Easy.

If one spouse or both disagree over any issue, they are required to go to court. A conservative judge usually leans toward the husband's version and asks the wife to capitulate to his demands, to be tolerant, and continue living with him, always assuming that she, herself, has no valid grounds for wanting the divorce.

Most divorces take place between couples who have been married less than three years. Some marriages are even shorter and are known as Narita divorces, named for Tokyo's international airport, for those couples who marry, fly off for their honeymoon, and divorce upon their return. Usually the wife claims incompatibility, especially if the marriage was arranged, and the couple had met each other less than a dozen times before the actual wedding.

Japanese divorcées find themselves facing a tough employment market, and many Japanese firms avoid hiring them. A lot of divorced women are obliged to take jobs well below their capabilities: supermarket checkout clerks, shop assistants, or waitresses. Others even find themselves working as hostesses in bars or as prostitutes.

The divorce settlement usually includes a single payment of between $7,000 and $40,000. Often the agreement makes no mention of alimony or child support and the wife and children receive no more money from the husband. This is an echo of feudal times, when a divorced woman returned to her parents' home, where all her needs were taken care of. Indeed, the word for divorcée in Japanese combines the word *demodori*—to leave—and *memodori*—to return.

Children usually remain in the mother's custody, in at least 80 percent of Japanese divorce cases. The judge bases his decision on two factors: the age of the children and the mother's financial position. If the child is more than ten years old, his father can demand, and often is, granted custody. This is usually true in the case of sons.

The minute sole custody reverts to the mothers, children are considered fatherless. They rarely see their fathers and spend all the rest of childhood with the mothers. The Japanese truly believe that a child cannot have divided loyalties. This might prove harmful, they assert, and cause the child severe confusion. According to this theory, joint custody might cause children irreparable emotional damage.

Some women choose another way out. Those who dare not ask their husbands for a divorce, or who fear social ostracism, financial hardship, and what the neighbors will say, sometimes choose suicide, which often includes killing their children as well. If they are no longer around, who will look after their children? To be an orphan in Japan is a fate worse than death, since the child's entire future is affected. A child with no mother through these critical years would be better off dead.

A great number of Japanese women are dissatisfied with their marriages, but they would rather live a life of *"gaman"*—silent suffering. After all, they were brought up to be obedient and tolerant, and this is their reward.

Kawaii, Kawaii!

*K*awaii! A word heard often in Tokyo, usually from the mouth of a longhaired Japanese teenage girl, dressed in ridiculous clothes more suited to a six-year-old.

It was repeated wherever I went with my nine-year-old son, and I figured that it had something to do with children.

I heard the word *kawaii* used to describe a large, fluffy stuffed panda in Kiddyland, Tokyo's largest toy store, where customers can play with any toy they like. Girls peeping in through the window looked hungrily at a red sweater with embroidered cat appliques and squealed the word at the tops of their voices.

Kawaii is a modern Japanese expression, commonly used by Japanese girls. It means cute and sweet. The cuter a thing is, or sweeter, or more desirable, the more *kawaii* it becomes.

Kawaii denotes the little Japanese girls themselves. It is their duty to be cute. It is also the greatest compliment you can give a Japanese girl. A junior high or high school, or even college student, will go to great lengths to look, sound, and act *kawaii*. This word connotes innocence, naïveté and childishness, traits considered alluring and attractive in young ladies. Unlike female students all over the world, who want to be thought of as women, a Japanese student prefers to be seen as an innocent little maiden. The *kawaii* syndrome appeared when singer Seiko Matsuda became popular. She appeared in childish gingham skirts and lace blouses, acted virginal, innocent, and naive onstage; and she made sure to include a soft toy and a teddy bear or two in all her photographs.

She, and similar female pop stars, were the forerunners of the *kawaii* craze in Japan. In a desperate attempt to look cute, a Japanese girl will wear sweet little shoes with smiling Mickey Mouse faces on the front. She'll wear a full, childish-looking checked skirt, fix her hair in fetching braids, tied in pretty ribbons, on either side of her face; and stand with her toes pointing in, showing off her knock-knees to their best advantage. These girls carry small, soft toys with them wherever they go and Snoopy books, and visit Disneyland wearing Mickey Mouse or Donald Duck hats on their heads, even if they are twenty years old. They let out high-pitched giggles behind their upraised hands, and earsplitting screeches whenever they see a butterfly, moth, or innocent fly, come to endanger their existence. Thus they seem more feminine, helpless, and worthy of protection, and, of course, cute. Japanese boys find this act attractive, but it looks ridiculous to foreigners.

Japanese women feel that being cute comes quite naturally to a Japanese girl and is not an act. Possibly. But it is next to impossible for Westerners to accept this behavior as natural, or cute.

To be *kawaii*, according to the male sex in Japan, a girl must have knock-knees and crooked, buckteeth. In the sixties, girls who had their teeth straightened had trouble finding a bridegroom. They were no longer *kawaii*.

Japanese women will play the childish game of *kawaii* right up to the day of their wedding. Only then will these women turn into *shakaijin*—mature, sensible, and responsible members of Japanese society.

Kawaii is also a purely commercial concept which brings in vast sums of money. Anything cute is snatched up by Japanese girls, and a whole industry of cute and worthless things has filled stores, stalls, and homes in Japan.

Cuteness can be codified. I found this official list of ten characteristics in a Japanese newspaper:

1. It must be small. Anything small, or a miniature version of something large, is considered cute. Especially cute are tiny

versions of huge, ugly animals like the hippopotamus, rhinoceros, or giant Galapagos Islands turtle.

2. It must be soft. Small, horny Japanese beetles are not cute, despite their size, because they have a hard shell. The Japanese will cuddle only creatures which are soft and fluffy, like rabbits, kittens, puppies, and baby koala bears (the dream of every Japanese girl on a trip to Australia).
3. It must be childish. Youth in Japan holds a monopoly on cuteness. Babies, infants, and especially little foreign children are considered cute.
4. It must be warm-blooded. The tarantula spider is small and furry, but it's not cute, because it is not warm-blooded and is not a mammal. On the other hand, any small, young, furry mammal is definitely cute.
5. It should be round. Take, for example, Tokyo children's fashions. Babies and infants are dressed in wide harem pants, which make them look like a walking ball. That's cute.
6. The smoother and less cluttered, the better, without any repulsive bumps.
7. Androgynous. Cute means having no sexual definition.
8. Having no bodily orifices—mouth, ears, or genitalia.
9. Dumb. Mouthless creatures are cute because they don't speak or argue.
10. It is cute to be helpless and defenseless, and in need of adult protection.

Add to this list pastel colors, especially pink.

Even cars can be cute. If you want a Nissan BE-1 car, prepare for a long wait, because the Nissan BE-1 is small, round, comes in pink and therefore is very popular. It costs about 2.5 million yen (about $25,000), an enormous amount for a car of this sort. Mazda has also produced a car which they tout as "small, soft, rounded, and comfortable, a cute little companion, just like a puppy." A buyer of this model, which has broken sales records in Japan, is at a loss to know what to do first, drive it or cuddle it.

Nissan's new model, named Es-car-go, is designed especially for young people. The little car's name comes from the French word for snails, a delicacy in Japan.

Food products are also marketed as *kawaii*. Soft, round, innocuous McDonald's hamburgers are cute, as are many other kinds of junk food, all made to sound *kawaii* by perky cartoon figures with cute voices.

There are cute houses, too, painted pink and built to look like cream cakes. There's a cute bank called Tomato, with a logo in the shape of a round, red tomato, where you "deposit the lettuce and draw out the carrot," as promised in their advertisements. This bank attracts cute young girls who deposit their adorable money and is considered a great Japanese success story. Others, like the large Fuji Bank with its serious image, have adopted winsome mascots like Paddington Bear and his friends. Paddington Bears are handed out to delighted new customers, and a giant version of the bear decorates the bank's front window, dressed in a green trench coat and checked cap.

And of course, cute clothes. It is difficult to find a children's hat without rabbit ears, or an infant's ski suit without a piggy-wiggy tail. Clothes often come covered with cute (and soft) dinosaur scales and elephant tails.

Domestic appliances also are designed to look cute and sweet. It is hard to find a vacuum cleaner that doesn't look like a pink ball, or plain toaster, or an unwhimsical washing machine.

Even the stern Japanese traffic police publish cute pamphlets, with smiley policemen parading the streets disguised as pink bunny rabbits.

Many Japanese couples prefer to get married in a cute church. About one-third of the weddings in Japan take place in churches, although Shinto and Buddhism are the major religions in Japan. The wedding, inevitably pink and kitschy, ends with the bride and groom driving off to a life of happiness in a replica of Cinderella's carriage.

There is no end and no limit to *kawaii.* Every second of the day a Japanese genius invents another version of *kawaii,* so that cute little girls everywhere will have something new to buy. Hundreds and thousands of tiny, pink objects are bought every day for the simple reason that they are cute. Every supermarket, corner shop, department store, and street stall are full of things that people buy for a moment's pleasure, tire of, and go off looking for more.

Little Geniuses

My calm friend Juri had been looking worried and preoccupied. She wasn't phoning me as often as usual, was uncharacteristically short-tempered, and took to lashing out against her husband. I missed our outings into town, our heart-to-heart talks and her year-old son Kiku, who came with us wherever we went.

"You're a foreigner. You'll never understand what I've been going through in the last couple of months," she told me, when I tried to find out the reason for her misery.

"Please confide in me. I might be able to help," I told her, fearing the the worst.

"I'm going through hell at home," she said, through her tears. "Kiku is about to take his school-entrance exams, and I'm afraid he won't pass. He's too immature." She almost choked.

I thought I wasn't hearing her correctly. "You mean exam hell?" I asked. "He's only a year old. Surely he's got plenty of time for that."

"I knew you wouldn't understand," she interrupted. "He's got to take the exams next month and he's not ready. If he fails, he won't be accepted to this school, and the only other school is much less good. And what about his professional future? It'll ruin his whole life. He won't even marry well." She was sobbing bitterly.

I drove, uninvited, to her house. The small room in the cramped apartment was full of wooden blocks, balls, and colored paper boxes. Kiku sat in the midst of the upheaval and smiled at me with his two teeth. Juri looked troubled and exhausted, with dark circles around her eyes from sleepless nights.

A month later, Juri announced that Kiku had passed his exams. The following year he would attend the prestigious kindergarten she had chosen. Juri could now sleep soundly at night. Her son's future was secure.

This system of infant education is known in Japan as the "escalator system," and it determines a child's adult, professional future. Anyone who gets onto this track, which begins in preschool and continues through grade school and high school should end up eventually at the most prestigious university, which in turn paves the way to the most worthwhile career and the best matrimonial prospects. These private preschools belong to the universities and the finest educational institutions in Japan. In other words, academic careers can begin in preschool. It also depends, of course, on the parents' finances and on the infant passing the examinations.

Although the birthrate in Japan has dropped considerably, competition is rising for good preschools. Waiting lists are very long, and some parents even register their children when they are still in the womb. Tokyo's more prestigious maternity hospitals offer package deals including labor, birth, and automatic registration of the child at the best preschools.

Only one out of five or six infants passes the entrance exams to these preschools. They are asked to build a tower of blocks, exhibit powers of concentration and an ability to differentiate between colors. Being toilet-trained an unconditional prerequisite.

An infant fortunate enough to pass the exams and enroll will be taught the three major principles in life: polite behavior, social bonding, and rote learning. At the age of two and three, children undergo exercises in memorization. They are also conditioned to obey any order issued by an adult immediately and automatically.

The cost of these special preschools is high, sometimes as much as $500 or $700 a month and is often a financial burden for the family.

Education and achievement are deeply valued in Japanese tradition. In the year A.D. 700, schools were founded to ensure a suitable supply of future government officials. Teachers trained in Confucian philosophy were responsible for educating the sons of the aristocracy. As the social status of warriors rose in the twelfth century, sons of the samurai were also admitted to the schools supported by the feudal lords, which now offered training in martial arts. Later, male children of the lower social classes attended schools belonging to the religious temples, where Buddhist monks taught reading, writing, and mathematics.

With the opening of Japan during the Meiji period, Japanese leaders hoped that modernization and speedy industrialization would soon put Japan ahead of the rest of Asia. It no longer seemed practical to educate according to social status, and a general system of education was formed for all levels of society: aristocracy, samurai, merchants, and commoners. At the same time, education was made available to girls. Until then only upper-class girls received any kind of education, and this was only of arts practiced by ladies, such as music, flower-arranging, dancing, tea ceremony rituals, etc. Reading and writing had been exclusively masculine pursuits.

Several girls-only missionary schools were also founded during that period, teaching Japanese girls to read and write. By the year 1910, almost every child in Japan received an elementary education; but despite the existence of several high schools for girls, Japanese women were not admitted to universities, which were restricted to men only.

Only after the Second World War did equal education become available in Japan. The country adopted an education system based on an American model, consisting of six years in grade school, three years in junior high, and three years in high school. High-school education became compulsory after the war, and girls received the same schooling as boys. The postwar Japanese Constitution also declared that all people had the right to receive equal education according to their abilities. Thus, in 1947, the universities opened their gates to female students.

The Japanese education system soon turned into the driving force behind the successful Japanese economy, with Japanese women playing an important and responsible role.

Each Japanese mother begins her child's race to the top while it is still a fetus in her womb.

Her husband's frequent absence and his limited emotional ties with his children force the Japanese woman to focus all her energies on her children. It is no coincidence that she is known in the

West as the "best Jewish mother of all." Early childhood is usually a period of happiness for a Japanese child, where it is cosseted and protected by its mother and enjoys unlimited indulgence—until it is old enough to go to school. The Japanese child has warm emotional ties and a physical closeness to his mother not generally found in the West. Most Japanese mothers nurse their children for at least a year. The babies are carried on their mothers' backs (it is claimed that this is what enables a Japanese adult to fall asleep so easily on a moving train). Many mothers take daily baths with their children and share futons with them. No self-respecting Japanese mother would leave her child in day care, unless her husband is unable to support the family and she is obliged to go out to work. In that case, she will place the child in one of those institutions designated, by definition, for "infants whose mothers are unable to take care of them." Baby-sitters are unknown in Japan. No Japanese mother would relinquish her child to a strange woman. She takes her baby with her wherever she goes. This extremely close relationship also means that the child is allowed to get away with kicking and hitting its mother in frustration at not getting its own way.

The mother simply accepts her child's violent outbreak and waits for it to calm down, reasoning that children can't express their frustration in words, and have to work it out the best way they can. Japanese mothers also have different ways of expressing their love. Unlike her Western counterpart, a Japanese mother will not squeeze her child affectionately, nor cover its face and body with kisses or whisper loving words in its ear. The Japanese mother uses the *"obento"* to demonstrate her love for her child. The *obento* is a child's lunch box, which is usually a celebration in color and prepared with a great deal of care and deliberation. It might contain white rice wrapped in a green leaf, vegetables cut to look like flowers, a sausage carved in the shape of an octopus, and tiny slivers of meat or fish, all decorated with chrysanthemum flowers. The lunch box is placed on a napkin in a bag, handsewn by the mother herself. Textbooks and lectures teach mothers the art of preparing *obentos*. Japanese mothers strive to send in the most beautiful and nourishing one in the class. After all, a world-class *obento* lets a child know how much his mother loves him.

As soon as her child starts school, the Japanese mother, the *"Kyoiku-Mama"* (the parent responsible for the child's education),

A typical street scene in contemporary Japan where past meets future.
(*Alain Evrard/Liaison International*)

A homeless man sleeping on the sidewalk ouside a Tokyo bank.
(*Rory Lysaght/Liaison International*)

Homeless in a Tokyo subway.   (*Anthony Suau/Gamma Liaison*)

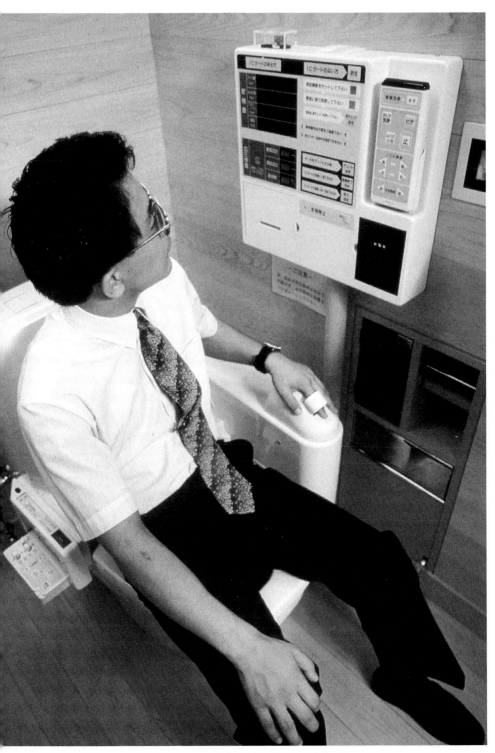

The "smart toilet" checks your health and can even advise if you are pregnant.
(*Kaku Kurita/Gamma*)

Drinking sake in a Rotenburo onsen or bath. (*Birmingham/Gamma*)

Zenshoji Zen Temple, 70 miles outside Tokyo, where Japanese pray to the goddess of gold, Golf Kannon. The 13 golf clubs behind her represent 13 Buddhist lessons.

(Kaku Kurita/Gamma)

Shrine to the giant daikon or "root of man," in Tagata. This is the center of a fertility festival that takes place in Nagoya every March. Pilgrims pray at this altar for a child, a spouse, or the return of a faithless lover.   (*Dieter Blum/Gamma*)

Cemetery of unborn babies.   (*Olivier Pighetti/Gamma*)

Firewalkers at Mount Takao.   (*Kaku Kurita/Gamma*)

With space at a premium, the Japanese have devised creative ways to put the dead to their final rest. These wall-graves are at Tame Cemetery in Tokyo.
(*Satoru Ohmori/Gamma*)

More creative solutions for final rest. These are gravestones at Shoho Temple in Tokyo. Shoho Temple is a modern 7-story building, completed in 1994. Each floor accommodates 200 gravestones.   (*Satoru Ohmori/Gamma*)

Members of a criminal gang or Yakuza. For them, tattooing is both a test of courage and a badge of identification. (*Dieter Blum/Gamma*)

Teenage fashions. (*Luxereau Christophe/Gamma*)

A Japanese bride and her family.   (*Satoru Ohmori/Gamma*)

Luxury treatment for pets.   (*Eric Pasquier/Gamma*)

Morning rush hour on the Ginza.   (*Anthony Suau/Gamma Liaison*)

Japanese men pour cold water on themselves during a purification bath to celebrate Coming-of-Age Day on January 15.   (*Itsuo Inouye/AP/Wide World*)

In another icy bath, Japanese men and boys pray for good health at a Tokyo shrine.
(*Atsushi Tsukada/AP/Wide World*)

Japanese salarymen exchange cards at a Tokyo exhibition. (*Itsuo Inouye/AP/Wide World*)

Another kind of card exchange: three youths present their cards to three prospective sweethearts, during a "proposal time" in Tokyo. Such meetings are part of the growing business of matchmaking, necessary in a nation where many complain they have trouble meeting members of the opposite sex. (*Atsushi Asukada/AP/Wide World*)

A barefoot boy walks over burning woodchips at Ichisan Jinja shrine north of Tokyo. Tradition says that those who take part in the annual firewalking event will be healthy throughout the next year. (*Ai Tsuyuki/AP/Wide World*)

A Japanese youth bows before the image of the King of Hill at Tokyo's Hoyoin Buddhist Temple. The red-faced king polices misbehavior and gives verbal advice to those who toss coins in the donation box. (*Koji Sasahara/AP/Wide World*)

will do everything in her power for the best education possible. In addition to her domestic chores, the Japanese mother will fight to get her child into the best schools, search libraries for useful books, spend hours helping her child with homework, prepare the child for exams, and promise the moon if the child succeeds. Many Japanese wives choose not to accompany their husbands on overseas transfers, preferring to remain at home so as not to disrupt the children's education, and protect the children from the emotional and intellectual upheavals involved in moving.

They take their children to music classes (and stay there with them); they go with their daughters to ballet lessons and spend hours with their offspring in public libraries. Every Japanese mother knows that only the best ones make it to the top, and the competition is fierce.

The *Kyoiku-Mama* has sole responsibility for their education. Their failure is her own, and their success will have a direct effect on her standing in the neighborhood and Japanese society in general.

Many Japanese families spend 20 percent or more of their income on their children's education. Enamored of statistics, they boast that the average cost of educating a child from the cradle through a good university is close to $200,000. Every Japanese home, no matter how cramped, has a quiet study corner with all the necessary equipment, including a desk and a small library. Because of the long school hours in the Japanese education system and the pressure to succeed, children are not required to help with housework. Only 28 percent of all Japanese children carry any kind of responsibility in their home, as compared with nine out of ten American children, who are called by the Japanese "bean-sprout kids," because they shoot up fast and tall, but lack content.

The Japanese media likes to compare the achievements of Japanese children with those of children in the West. The papers happily print stories of yet another Japanese child who outdid his Western counterpart in an international math contest, a Japanese girl who won first prize in an international English spelling bee, or another, who placed first in an international piano contest. Altogether, the Japanese believe their children are much more intelligent than those in the West. Thus, the Japanese educational system has a reputation as the best in the world. Japanese children do indeed win international competitions, because they are brought up and carefully educated to this end. The training Japanese children receive leads to success in examinations, and fills their heads with hundreds of thousands of facts and figures. But, if a Japanese child has to analyze a situation, draw conclusions, defend a viewpoint, or even ask questions, the inherent weakness of the Japanese educational system becomes apparent. Japanese schools repress original and creative thought. Spontaneity is a dirty word. Originality on a child's part will surely bring forth a letter of complaint to its parents, and a leading question will be met with a raised eyebrow. Japanese children do not know how to analyze facts, and criticism is not received favorably, because the teacher is the only one allowed to ask questions. Japanese schoolchildren are taught to accumulate information, formulae, dates, and facts.

The key principle in Japanese education is rote learning, sometimes until the early hours of the morning. The school year begins in April and lasts for 240 days. All schools have a dress code: the girls wear a blue, wide-collared sailor suit and the boys a black uniform with gold buttons. They carry the same school bags, the same lunch bags, and all wear the same hairstyles. Children whose hair is lighter-colored or wavy have to supply a note from their mothers confirming that this unusual physical appearance is hereditary.

Many Japanese schools require that their students wear uniforms in their free time as well. Some even demand detailed reports of their students' activities from the moment they walk out of the school gates. The school is entitled to invade the student's private life, with the teacher having the right to visit the child's home with no prior notice at any time of the evening to check if he's done his homework. Other schools insist that their students come to school by a specific route and forbid them to be in certain areas of the city. Schools determine how their students are to sit, how high they may raise their hands to answer a question and in what order foods should be eaten. There are also lists of permitted and forbidden books, and the school forbids the children (and their parents) to watch what they consider noneducational television.

This compulsory subservience leads many Japanese school children to acts of violence that the education authorities cannot ignore, much as they would like to. In 1985, violence in schools (*ijime*—a word which had turned into a nightmare) reached new peaks. Unpopular, or nonconformist, children were victimized by their schoolmates and teachers alike, since the Japanese believe that a protruding nail should be hammered in flat like the others. Tragic stories were published almost daily in the papers, of children beaten, ostracized, humiliated, and rejected. Thousands of children avoided going to school and many committed suicide. The case of thirteen-year-old Hirofumi Shikawaga, who hung himself in the men's room of a subway station in 1986, appalled the Japanese people. Hirofumi suffered from vicious abuse from his schoolmates, who finally organized a mock funeral for him. They decorated his desk with white funeral flowers, framed his photograph in black crepe, and lit fragrant incense for the purification of his soul. Although this took place in the classroom, the teacher did nothing to prevent it. In fact, he cooperated with the tormentors and even eulogized the victim, who sat all the while at his desk, with the white funeral flowers on it. Hirofumi hung himself immediately afterward, leaving behind a suicide note. He wrote: "I don't want to die, but this life is a living hell. Please stop such stupid things now. This is my last request." The boy's father exposed the story in the media and succeeded in extracting an apology from the teacher. As a result of public uproar, the Minister of Education announced that schoolteachers must not ignore violence in their schools, and that perpetrators would be punished. He declared the issue of supreme national importance.

Eight years after his suicide, in May 1994, Hirofumi's parents won their case against the boy's school in the Supreme Court of Justice and were awarded damages in the sum of $109,000.

The Ministry of Education published several papers regarding the parents' lawsuit, quoting statistics in its defense: Ten years ago, 155,066 schoolchildren were abused in school, but the number had fallen to 23,258 in 1992 and to 21,598 in 1993. Japanese experts in education admit, albeit grudgingly, that the numbers are probably higher. A great many child victims of abuse are reluctant to report the fact to the school authorities. Japan was once again shocked in 1994, when in November, thirteen-year-old Kyotoro Okuchi hung himself. He, too, left a suicide note, describing a long history of abuse and humiliation from his schoolmates. "They are hurting me so much and I can't take it any longer," he wrote in his farewell letter. Kyotoro's teachers had witnessed the boy's suffering. His face was often swollen from beating, but the school authorities did not investigate. There are many school principals and teachers who actually justify this system of abusing misfits in their schools. And once again, as in Hirofumi's case, the Prime Minister declared that Japan must find ways of ensuring that these tragedies are not repeated.

It is not only students who are violent toward each other. A recent report by the Ministry of Education revealed about four hundred cases over the last decade of serious injuries resulting from violence on the part of teachers. More than 2,500 schoolchildren were victims of physical violence, and the lightest form of punishment meted out by a schoolteacher is usually a slap on the face. Some children have suffered irreversible brain damage. Some have even died.

Winter is the hardest season of all for Japanese schoolchildren. The pressure grows almost unbearable between January and March, when they go through *"shiken jiguko"*—exam hell. Universities examine high-school graduates in five different subjects. It is for these exams, in fact, that a Japanese child has been preparing himself since kindergarten. If they pass the exams for Tokyo University or Waseda, the most prestigious universities, their professional future is secure. Each winter Tokyo's cheap hotels make a fortune selling package deals of room, full board, and transportation to and from the university, as well as counseling services. Traffic and weather conditions affecting examination days are reported by the media. Thousands of hopeful students crowd into temples to send up their requests on tiny slivers of wood which they hang on holy trees.

In March each year, the University of Tokyo publishes the names of all the students who will matriculate, and cameras focus on the happy, shining faces of those who have secured their future.

Then a Japanese mother can brag about her son, the student at Tokyo University, and rest on her laurels. He has succeeded in his mission. From now on her son will pay back her investment; she will get all the honor she deserves and the best daughter-in-law on the market.

Their school career is based on cramming for university entrance exams, but studying is not limited to the regular schools. Japanese children often need extracurricular help from special schools for exams, known as Juku schools. Students spend hours, often late into the night, memorizing and repeating their lessons. Sunday is their day off from school, so they study at the Juku from nine o'clock on Saturday evening until the early hours of Sunday morning. It makes no difference that they no longer absorb anything after one o'clock on Sunday morning. Their mere presence in the Juku in the middle of the night is ample proof to themselves and their parents that they take their studies very seriously indeed. Thus Japanese society conditions its future workers to be diligent, stubborn, resilient, and expert at rote learning.

Once accepted at a university, Japanese young people can rest. Japanese universities tend to give passing grades for presence rather than achievement. A degree at a Japanese university is virtually a foregone conclusion, and from the moment they are accepted at a university, students know the much-sought-after degrees will be awarded within three years, with little effort on their part. For them, the university is a place to have fun, relax, search for a suitable spouse, play sports, drink, and generally hang out, before entering the real world of work and social obligations.

A Garden for Unborn Children

*T*he wind blows through the garden for unborn children and thousands of multicolored pinwheels spin. When the wind stops, a dull silence falls. The statues of children stand side by side in double rows, as in the playground drill of Japanese schools.

The statues wear knitted caps, or hats with earflaps, in an array of fading colors. Their chubby bodies are covered with babies' bibs, sweaters, and warm winter coats. Some statues have been supplied with shoes for their long journey, bottles of milk, chocolates and other confections to sweeten their way. Others are decorated with umbrellas and heavy scarves to protect them from the cold Japanese winter. The statues carry soft furry toys, baby rattles, bells, pacifiers, Mickey Mouse buttons, and silk fringes, to keep them happy on their eternal journey.

The statues stare unseeingly out of blank eyes, and their faces wear expressions of infinite sadness. Even the gaily colored origami chains, cups of tea, bowls of rice, and crumbling incense sticks are unable to dispel the feeling of heaviness and discomfort hanging over the place.

These are the *Mizu-Ko*, or Water Babies, Japanese children who have never been born.

The Buddhist custom of *Mizu-Ko* dates from the seventh century. A poor woman in Japan, unable to feed another mouth, would end her pregnancy by standing in a freezing river for hours, until the contractions in her womb expelled the fetus.

After she aborted, she would sculpt a small clay doll, a symbol of the child that would never be born and was thus denied its present incarnation on earth. In secret, the woman held a ceremony, and dressed, fed, and pacified the doll. By giving it toys and gifts, the Japanese mother would placate the soul of her unborn child, so it would not disturb the peace of other members of her family. Her dearest wish would be for the embryo's soul to be reincarnated in a new child, to release her and her family from its vengeance.

The custom of *mizu-ko* was passed from mother to daughter. The father of the family and other male relatives played no part in the wife's decision, or her attempts to induce the abortion, or the ceremonies she subsequently held for the soul of the aborted child.

The first *mizu-ko* temple was built by a Buddhist priest some fifty years ago, and the ceremonies were held openly, no longer hidden as they had been for hundreds of years. After observing the unhappy lives of women who did not follow the ritual of *mizu-ko*, priests came to the conclusion that the women had not paid due homage to the souls of their unborn children. The first *mizu-ko* temple offered special services for the doll statues—from tending the garden, to dressing, washing, and feeding the doll statues, burning incense for them, lavishing them with gifts, and offering up regular prayers for their souls. A special goddess called Ji Zu was placed in the garden. It was her job to guide the lost souls on their way and protect them from danger until their next incarnation.

Sensing the financial potential in this ritual, other Buddhist priests built *mizu-ko* temples which specialized solely in day-to-day care of the Japanese water babies. Today competition is rife among the various temples—and the prices are exorbitant.

The most expensive of these temples is the Meika, where it costs about $700 to care for each doll statue, plus a mandatory hefty donation to the priests. About 300,000 *mizu-ko* dolls stand in the temple's garden, and they are joined daily by dozens more.

The issue of *mizu-ko* rituals has attracted considerable interest in recent years. People in Japan are demanding an investigation into the methods used to promote the sale of these dolls and the cynical exploitation of women's guilt over aborting unwanted pregnancies—and their fears of their unborn fetuses' revenge.

A state television network has investigated the so-called religious organizations which advertise and promote the sale of *mizu-ko*, a business which rakes in billions of yen every year.

"Is your husband impotent? Is he unfaithful to you? Are your children being beaten at school? Are they having trouble passing their university entrance exams? Are your parents sick? Do you suffer from premenstrual tension?" All these questions are flung at the already guilt-stricken woman, in free pamphlets distributed at newspaper stalls and post offices. The pamphlets include a telephone number which offers an instant remedy for all her trials.

Kuniko, a thirty-seven-year-old Tokyo woman, married with two children, was interviewed on TV—her voice and face blurred to preserve her anonymity. Kuniko had been invited to meet a woman who described herself as a "medium and marriage guidance counselor." The counselor questioned Kuniko at length on her problems and those of her family. Then the counselor suddenly dropped a bombshell. "Have you ever had an abortion?" Kuniko, who had kept this secret even from her husband, answered yes. It was then, as Kuniko later testified, that the counselor told her that she had noticed the spirit of the *mizu-ko* floating about her, making her fail in everything she undertook. The counselor then accused Kuniko of murdering her child, who had wanted to be born. Its soul had been selfishly condemned to wander the world for the rest of eternity. The counselor warned Kuniko that if she did not appease the fetus's soul, her children would be injured in an accident, her husband would divorce her, and she would end her life in terrible loneliness. The counselor did have a solution, however. All Kuniko needed was a *mizu-ko* doll for $1,200, to be paid in ten monthly installments to make it easier for her. She even offered to hire Kuniko as an agent for the company, to sell *mizu-ko* dolls to her friends. She could turn a profit, and cover the cost of her purchase.

Kuniko, who was terrified that her husband would find out about her abortion as well as the cost of buying the doll, told the TV interviewer that she had hidden the doll and was doing her best to appease it. Later, she took the doll to a *mizu-ko* temple, where she left it in the care of the priests, at a price, of course.

The company that sold Kuniko the doll called itself "The Buddhist Counseling Company." An investigation revealed that it was properly registered with the Japanese Ministry of the Interior and that, as a religious company, its profits were tax free.

A psychologist interviewed on the program tried to explain the mass hysteria surrounding the purchase of *mizu-ko* dolls. It was his claim that a Japanese woman feels terrible guilt if she has an abortion, and this becomes severe because of her inability to share her feelings with others. The abortion of her fetus and her failure to honor suitably its departing soul, envelops the woman in depression, so that every problem or hardship in her daily life is explained away as the unborn child's curse. The ghosts of these unborn, which haunt millions of Japanese women, can be appeased only with the help of a *mizu-ko* doll.

At the *Mizu-Ko* temple in the ancient city of Kamakura, the priest gave his blessing to boys and girls aged seven, five, and three years, dressed in gaily colored kimonos, as flamboyant as butterflies, on their special holy day, *Shichi-Go-San.*

Late in the evening, in the Garden of Children Who Were Never Born the pinwheels spun on as dozens of gaudily dressed children hopped and skipped down the stairs of the temple. The children ran across the garden with its thousands of silent statues and fell happily into the arms of their waiting parents.

The eyes of the unwanted Water Babies continued to stare unseeing in the silent garden as the cold Japanese night fell over the city.

A Different View of Abortion

"If the current birthrate continues in Japan, the population will decrease to around 40,000 people within seven hundred years," say Japanese statisticians. Exaggerated though this statement may be, it echoes a fear that Japan's industrial and economic power might decline because of a lack of human resources. Unlike most of Southeast Asia, Japan's population is dwindling.

A report published by the Japanese Ministry of Health at the beginning of this decade, caused demographic shock all over Japan. In 1989, only 1.24 million babies were born in Japan, the lowest annual birthrate in the last ninety years. In comparison, some 1.386 million babies were born in Japan in 1899, when birth registration began. However, the total population that year numbered 43 million, as compared with today's 124 million. Thus the average number of children in a Japanese family has declined from 5.1 in 1925, to 4.71 in 1930, 4.36 in 1937 and right down to 1.57 in 1990.

With statistics as grim as these, the Japanese rush to blame someone. Statisticians, politicians, and other public figures started in on the women of Japan, beginning with the yearly increase in the number of women who refuse to get married. And Japanese women marry at a relatively late age, around 25 years old, the oldest average marrying age in the world.

At the beginning of this decade, the Minister of Finance pointed out a reason for the low birthrate: Japanese women are too busy getting an education, and have no time to have children. His words caused an uproar among feminist groups and were retracted the following day by a spokesman. The low birthrate is, of course, directly related to the high rate of abortions in Japan.

An abortion is considered the most effective form of contraception, and the Pill is forbidden. As Dr. Koniao Kitamora, Chairman of the Japanese Family Planning Association said: "Abortion is a sure thing."

The Abortion Law was passed in Japan in 1948, and it permits abortion when the life of the mother or fetus are in danger, or because of the family's financial situation.

The Japanese are well aware of the high cost of raising a child and the astronomical cost of education and housing. Today, approval is granted for most abortions in Japan on the basis of financial problems alone. According to many of the Japanese women I spoke to, it is as easy to make an appointment for an abortion as it is for the dentist. For $500, and one hour in the hospital, the woman can go home minus her unwanted fetus.

The Japanese abortion market also flourishes because of the country's curious attitude toward contraceptives. Condoms are most popular and are sold in vending machines on almost every street corner. Intrauterine devices are rare and a woman who insists on one is usually required to have it put in under general anesthetia and spend a night in the hospital. Diaphragms are virtually unobtainable and the Pill, the most popular and effective form of birth control in the world, is banned in Japan. This ban is supported by the Japanese Association of Doctors and Gynecologists, who claim that the Pill constitutes a health hazard with undesirable side effects. Other supporters of this ban are Japanese conservatives, who claim the widespread use of the Pill will bring about a sexual revolution among the women of Japan and the sexual permissiveness common in the West. It is easy to detect fears that these Japanese men will lose control over the bodies of their women. This conservative viewpoint is staunchly supported by the gynecologists, who rake in fortunes from production-line abortions.

The invective against contraceptive pills is even repeated by some Japanese feminist organizations. "Remember the thalidomide babies," begins one anti-Pill argument. Indeed, 939 deformed babies were born in Japan to mothers who took this medication during their pregnancy.

Thus an absurd situation has evolved. In matters of contraception, Japan is a developing nation and birth-control policy is determined by men. The women prefer to leave these matters to them. The path to unwanted pregnancy, and thence to abortion, is very short.

Japan, with a population of 124 million, has an official rate of six hundred thousand abortions a year, although in practice, more than two million are performed. Many gynecologists prefer not to declare income from this lucrative business to avoid higher taxes, which explains the discrepancy.

Furthermore, the remains of about three hundred babies or fetuses are found each year. It is claimed that many thousands more of these tiny corpses are not found, nor will they ever be found.

And, of course, there is always the *mizu-ko* to soothe a guilty conscience.

Common or Garden Pornography

"**I** honestly can't understand the Japanese," said a senior Israeli journalist on an official visit as a guest of the Japanese government, "You should have seen the fuss they made at Narita Airport about a *Playboy* magazine I had. They confiscated it and gave me a lecture. But every newspaper stall in Tokyo is full of sex magazines—real hard-core stuff. How can they compare *Playboy* with the filth they sell here?"

Pornography is available in Japan everywhere you turn. Peep over the shoulder of a respectable Japanese businessman reading a newspaper, and you might see a picture of the Prime Minister next to a photograph of a naked girl masturbating with a vibrator. On your way out of the subway station, there are newsstands selling bizarre pornographic literature, fully illustrated. For example, pictures of a girl on a gynecologist's examining table, with a crazy doctor pushing eels and lizards up her vagina, or pictures of a girl defecating into a pot, the contents of which are used by her partner to paint his body in dark camouflage colors, or pictures of a girl having sex with a dog. Vending machines sell porn magazines on the street, and you can find the same magazines at your local grocer's or pharmacy. There are sex shops in the most decent and respectable of Tokyo's neighborhoods and hard-core porn movies are available at every video lending library. Many advertisements in

Japan include the sight of a naked woman; from milk, which is advertised by a blue-eyed, large-breasted foreign woman, down the line, to refrigerators. At home, too, you are not free of the plague of pornography, which is even advertised on children's TV programs. Foreigners living in Tokyo have to learn how to live with this phenomenon.

So why did Japanese airport officials confiscate my friend's *Playboy*?

Pornography is permitted in Japan on one condition only: that no pubic hair is exposed. Everything else is allowed, including pictures of a six-year-old girl being raped, sex with animals, descriptions of human feces coming out of the body, and other examples of a sick, warped imagination. Everything goes, so long as pubic hair is covered, censored, unseen. Underage Japanese girls appear, within the law, in the most disgusting pornography, including bestiality. There's no problem since they don't have pubic hair yet. Many Japanese porn "artists" draw their female models minus their pubic hair.

Since sex education is not part of the Japanese school curriculum, Japanese children receive this education from porn magazines. These, and the mass media, describe women as passive victims of rape, or screaming in ecstasy or pain. The pictures are humiliating, technical, cruel, and depict women merely as objects for men's entertainment.

I thought over the matter a long time, before daring to discuss it with a Japanese female friend. The conversation went something like this:

Me: Don't you think those illustrated magazines are appalling?

Friend: Yes, absolutely.

Me: And all those rape scenes on TV and sex descriptions at eleven o'clock at night?

Friend: Awful.

Me: So what's your opinion of pornography?

Friend: I don't look at it.

It's an honest answer. The Japanese have an amazing capacity for not seeing things they don't want to see. Embarrassing subjects, or sights that contradict their idea of esthetic harmony, simply don't exist.

A popular story in Tokyo tells of the foreigner and the Japanese man traveling in the same train. The Japanese, looking out of the train's window doesn't see the sad-looking houses, the heavy laundry lines, the smoke-spewing chimneys, the dirty factories, and the fields full of junk that the foreigner sees. The Japanese will see only the cherry tree, flowering amid the ugliness.

Pornography is a lucrative business in Japan. Hundreds of thousands of illustrated pornographic magazines are sold; sex shops do a roaring trade in porn movies; and popular porn queens make fortunes and get lots of public recognition.

Government officials refuse to release information on the exact sums of money spent each year on pornography in Japan. Foreign correspondents calculate that the money changing hands in this business is astronomical and virtually immeasurable. For example, Nikatosu, a producer of heavy porn movies, was in the top section of the Tokyo Stock Exchange for a long period, and business is booming!

Japanese sociologists, trying to explain the growing consumption of pornography, advise foreigners that the word "sex" in Japanese means "to play" and "in everything to do with games, there are no limits or inhibitions."

The relaxed Japanese attitude to sex and the body is found in their history, which describes a society with a totally nonjudgmental view of sexuality. There's a description from the Heian period (794–1185) of a nobleman, like the famous Prince Genji, who visits the rooms of every woman in the court every evening and not miss a single one. Mixed bathing has always been the rule in Japan, and men and women were not even embarrassed to defecate in public. The attitude to nakedness is generally accepting and extramarital relationships are routine.

There was no such thing as censorship in Japan until 1700, and the first censorship laws were legislated for reasons of economy. The law tried to limit the profits of merchants dealing in erotic art, like the *Shunga*—particularly graphic wood prints depicting exotic sexual poses. The *Shunga* pictures were named for the ancient profession of prostitution, which has been known forever as "Spring Sales." Prostitutes are still known as "Spring Saleswomen," a name which hints at the Japanese attitude to the profession and to the act. From this stems the name of these erotic illustrations, *Shunga*, "Spring Pictures." These pictorial guides contained explicit illustrations of sexual acts, in which the man is depicted with colossal genitals, together with useful hints on sexual hygiene. *Shunga* pictures often showed famous actors having sex with no less famous whores. The sex act was seen as artistic entertainment, to be performed with charm, expertise, and polish, accompanied by romantic courtship and dancelike love play. Most of the artists of the Edo period drew *Shunga* pictures, turning the act of sex into a celebration of the visually grotesque: gigantic genitalia, facial expressions full of sensuality, and impossible acrobatic poses.

During Emperor Meiji's reign (1867–1912), Japan encountered more sexually inhibited cultures. The Japanese adapted to the moves of the West. They began to believe that it was immoral for men and women to bathe together and installed narrow bamboo fences to separate male and female sections of the bathing houses. They also introduced tiny towels to cover up the most intimate parts of their anatomy. In their attempt to emulate Western culture, the Japanese developed an ambiguous attitude to sex. In the privacy of their own homes, they continued to be relaxed about the whole issue. Outwardly, they did their best to give the impression of a moralistic society.

Censorship in Japan causes confusion. Pubic hair is absolutely forbidden in pictures, and even pictures by famous artists such as Picasso or Goya undergo the scrutiny of the censor. Censorship is usually enforced by young girls with sharp scissors who carefully cut out pubic hair wherever it appears in illustrated magazines and books. On the other hand, pictures of rape and depravity are permitted.

The editors of *Ama* and *New Nudity* were tried in court for publishing pictures which showed a few stray pubic hairs, while the popular weekly *Focus* got away with authentic, special-lens photographs of Japanese public figures fornicating.

The attitude to what are known as "pink movies" is also confusing. These are cheap productions, which originated somewhere in the 1960s, in the wake of special legislation against prostitution. This limiting legislation coincided with the economic prosperity of the sixties, and only increased the demand for sexually explicit material. When movies of this sort reach the West, debates arise on the question of their pornographic or artistic merit. A Japanese pink movie includes, naturally, scenes of explicit sexual activity, with one limitation: no pubic hair may be shown. Some of these movies are rich not only in flesh and grunts, groans, and loudly expressed orgasms, but in brilliant cinematography and a fresh and provocative perspective on modern Japanese society.

In reply to criticism from educators and feminist groups, the authorities point out that the country has a very low rate of rape and sex-related crimes. The Japanese proudly quote statistics which show a rape ratio of only 4 per 100,000 people compared with a ratio of 50 per 100,000 in the United States.

Members of the Japanese Feminist Organization claim that Japanese women lag behind their American counterparts in their attitude to rape and sexual abuse by about twenty years. They reason that accurate statistics on rape are much higher than those published by the police, since many Japanese women are reluctant to report rape. Rape victims fear social ostracism. Normal family life—even finding a marital partner—will be very difficult if their rape is made public. Worse, they may be accused of seducing the man who raped them. Rapists in Japan rarely serve jail sentences. They are usually required to pay their victims financial reparations, using a scale which lowers in accordance with the victim's age, her social standing, and whether or not she was a virgin to begin with.

Because the Japanese are traditionally conservative and the issue is of low public interest, the current flood of pornography will continue to inundate the streets of Japan. Children will continue to learn about sex from obscene literature, Japanese men will continue to believe that women enjoy submitting to rape, and passive Japanese women will continue to star on the newsstands.

Japanese pornography is an ugly anachronism in a country which claims to be the most modern in the world.

Nights in Blue

*T*here was a reek of alcohol in the smoke-filled hall as a pale, skinny girl with a large red mouth that looked like an open wound, writhed awkwardly on the stage, her clumsy movements out of time with the earsplitting music. The spaced-out expression on her face was deadly serious and her eyes were fixed on an unseen point in the dark depths of the hall. The male audience, watching her openmouthed, grew impatient for the next phase of her act. The girl made one or two more snakelike movements before freeing herself of her clothes. A spontaneous grunt of satisfaction rippled through the audience as she stood stark naked on the stage. Robotlike, her face expressionless, the girl pulled out hermetically sealed and dated packages and handed out small pocket flashlights and rubber thimbles. Chattering nervously, the men covered their right forefingers and waited for action. The girl strode quickly across the stage, and passing from one man to the next, stood with her legs apart, as if waiting for a gynecological examination.

All pushed forward, even those in the second and third rows, to take their turn. They used their flashlights to light up the girl's crotch, and used their rubber-covered fingers to invade her vagina. The more inhibited were satisfied with a quick peep and a superficial dip, but the daredevils stuck their fingers in as far as they went, and thrust them in and out. With satisfied sighs, the men sat back in their seats and waited for the next act.

The girl, unmoved by all the invading fingers, kneeled on the stage waiting. The men below began playing the popular Japanese children's game of Janken-Fon (paper, scissors, stone). The winner, encouraged by the joyous cries of his friends, climbed on the stage. He was a salaryman, someone who worked for the Japanese government or a public concern, dressed in a conservative three-piece suit, smiling a wide, gold-toothed, smile. As the crowd howled, the man undressed, folding all his clothes neatly and arranging them in a pile alongside his shoes. He turned to the girl, wearing only a pair of brown socks to protect the innocence of his feet, and lay down on the stage. The girl, who looked as if she was in a deep meditative sleep, jumped up suddenly. From a small plastic bag, hidden behind the curtain, she pulled out a large bottle containing disinfectant, a towel, rubber gloves, and various other objects. With a practiced twist of the wrist, the girl shook the contents of the bottle, and poured them on the towel. She then used the towel to swab down the man's hands and genitals, as he sat loosely in front of her.

The highlight of the operation involved putting a condom on the man, and this she did with her mouth. After the lengthy and exhausting preparations, the girl lay down beside the man, waiting for something to happen. He mounted her, raising and lowering his flabby buttocks to the rhythmic clapping of the audience. The process, which clearly took too long for the young woman's liking, came to an abrupt end with a couple of sharp slaps on his behind. She shook his wrinkled body off her roughly and turned to the next in line. The man, in his socks, flaccid organ dangling, picked up his clothes and went down to join his cronies, who received him with loud cheers. The girls changed sometimes, but the activity went on for hours on end.

This club, which is advertised regularly in Tokyo tourist guidebooks, is not the only one offering sex shows with active audience participation. Many clubs of this kind can be found in Kabokicho, the prostitution quarter in the Shinjuko neighborhood. Current statistics reveal that the local population numbers some 3,500 inhabitants, who are joined by about half a million more every night. The largest concentration of sex businesses can be found in Sakura-

Dori—Cherry Street. It is the only place in Japan where you have to be careful walking the streets at night.

Activity begins in the early afternoon, which is when the quarter drops its respectable look and turns into the sin and pleasure center of Tokyo. That's when the shiny black Mercedeses slip down the alleyways. Their drivers, minus little fingers and dressed in loud flashy suits, wait for their bosses with commendable patience. At the same time, all the flimsily dressed, heavily madeup bar girls disappear into niches, lit up by red lights.

In Kabokicho, any sexual deviation can be satisfied, be it ever so perverted. When it comes to sex, Japan knows no limits and no prohibitions. The word "moral" is unheard of. When it comes to mankind's basic instinct, the Japanese fly on the wings of inspiration and show themselves at their very best.

Only in Japan can you find No Pan Kissa, coffeehouses where a waitress in a tiny miniskirt will serve you while the cafe's mirrored floor shows you that the young lady is not wearing any underwear. Other cafés supply their clients with a mirror attached to a long handle, with which to examine the private parts of every passing waitress.

Japan is also a place where you can eat a meal off a human table. The delicacies are served on the naked body of a young girl. Some Japanese men claim that the tastiest noodles come out of the vagina of this particular type of table.

The Japanese have also developed the massage holes. A penis, shoved through a hole in the wall, will receive a pleasant and satisfying massage from an anonymous entity in the next room. The price is very reasonable.

Another hole in the wall permits a man to look, secretly, at a girl getting dressed and doing all kinds of intimate things to herself. Perfect for Peeping Toms.

The visiting cards of call girls line every wall of every public telephone booth in Tokyo. The card bears a photograph of the semi-naked girl, personal details, and a number to call. Most of the cards insist that their owners are schoolgirls or students.

There are bathhouses everywhere. These used to be called "Turkish baths" *(Toruko)*, but their name was changed as a result of an official complaint lodged by the Turkish Ambassador to

Japan, who did not like the idea of places like this being named after his country. These places of entertainment, with the English-Japanese name of *"sopurando"*—land of soap—have become very popular. The door charge is twenty to forty dollars. Add another hundred to 350 dollars if you want "special pleasure."

To avoid immoral goings-on, Japanese law requires that a window be cut into each bathhouse door. Fortunately for the owners of these places, the law did not specify the window's placement. Thus, there are windows in all sorts of places on the door, except in the place which makes observation possible. Often, a towel is draped over the window to solve that problem.

There are several *sopurandos* which cater to the secret perversions of their clients. Here the girl might be asked to dress like a nun, a nurse, or a flight attendant. Clients who so wish, will be supplied with doctor outfits, and then can play doctor and delve deep into the girl's most private parts.

Sex entertainment in its most intense form is found on the island of Watakano in the Sea of Japan. This island has an official population of 500 inhabitants, but those in the know claim the real population, which has never been counted, is much larger.

This small island, about four miles in circumference, has about fifteen love hotels, thirty geisha palaces, and about forty bars.

A large number of women work on the island. Some are Japanese, and there are Filipinos, Taiwanese, and Thais, as well. The clients, mostly Japanese businessmen, think nothing of making a two-hour journey from Osaka to spend the night in the silken arms of a geisha or a hostess.

The love industry is the major source of income for the island's inhabitants. The income declared to the tax authorities is 500 million yen a year ($5 million), although the real sum is undoubtedly higher. Criticism is lobbed at the island's female workers for not declaring their fat earnings, but their employers, who take all payment in cash, cover them. Furthermore, because of its sparse population—the official headcount, of course—the island's inhabitants are not eligible for a regional policeman to uphold law and order. Depravity reigns, and no one even squeaks.

Nor was the Antiprostitution Law, passed in the fifties and responsible for the closing of many of the country's red-light areas, able to contain the love businesses on the tiny island. The island's tradition of prostitution dates from Tokugawa days, when it became a sexual haven for boatmen sailing on the Osaka-Edo (then Tokyo) route.

The only real problem arises when islanders are away from home and are asked where they come from. Their answer inevitably meets with howls of laughter.

Somewhere Between a Geisha and a Whore

I am sorry to say that during the five years I spent in Japan, I didn't interview a single geisha. The only one willing demanded a $1,000 fee for the interview.

"Try to understand her point of view," explained the go-between, one of my students, who had worked very hard to set up the interview and couldn't understand why I wasn't overjoyed by the terms. "As far as a geisha is concerned, time is money. When you interview her, you'll be taking up her time and you have to pay her."

I decided to forget it. Japanese geishas are not eager to be interviewed. Sometimes an interview with one is published in the papers, but she's usually elderly, or has left the profession. In fact, everything to do with geishas is kept secret, which only helps to fire the imagination.

I had always imagined a geisha to be a very young Japanese woman, breathtakingly beautiful, seductive, well versed in the art of lovemaking, a brilliant conversationalist, who had been carefully trained to keep a man happy. After an evening with a geisha, any man would find it hard to go back to a mere wife.

At least that's what I thought. I couldn't sleep the night my husband went to a geisha party with a group of Japanese businessmen. Passionate love scenes played themselves out in my mind as I

182 • *Shifra Horn*

waited impatiently for his return. The key turned in the lock to reveal my husband's tired face.

"How was it?" I asked him, before he'd even taken off his shoes at the threshold.

"Boring," he replied impatiently as he walked toward the bed.

"I don't believe you," I declared. "Is that all you have to say after spending an exciting evening with a geisha?"

"You wouldn't believe me, anyway, if I told you what happened there," he said, cutting off the rest of my unasked questions.

I felt very fortunate, therefore, when I was invited to my first—and last, as it turned out—geisha party. An evening with geishas costs a fortune, which only a few can afford.

Despite my high expectations and romantic notions about geishas, the evening was a great disappointment. The private dining room in the expensive restaurant, to which we had been invited by some Japanese businessmen, was invaded by three heavyset middle-aged women, dressed in expensive, elegant kimonos. Their faces were made up in a heavy layer of white-and-pink-tinted powder, and they wore large, stiff, elaborately constructed wigs. With wide, gold-toothed smiles, they sat down and began plucking at the *kotos*, Japanese string instruments, to please the guests during the meal. Later, they accompanied their music with high-pitched singing, which reverberated painfully in my ears and sounded more like caterwauling. Indeed, in Japan this kind of high-octave artificial voice is known as *neko-chan* or cat voice. It strains the woman's vocal cords as well as the listener's ears. As the atmosphere warmed up, after countless glasses of sake and cold beer, the geishas seemed in their element. They flirted with the men, tweaked the foreigners' chest hair, crying out in wonder (Japanese men usually have little or no body hair, compared with foreigners), fed the foreigners, who insisted on eating with chopsticks and, as the evening reached its climax, fashioned origami models. To me they looked more like good-hearted grannies, trying pathetically to keep their bored grandchildren entertained. Nonetheless, our Japanese hosts were enjoying themselves and participated enthusiastically.

We foreigners, who spoke no Japanese, and were unable to appreciate the geishas' charming and witty conversation, felt awkward, embarrassed, and helpless.

Only during my many trips to Kyoto, the ancient capital of Japan, did I meet the geishas from the storybooks. This was in Kyoto's famous geisha quarter, Gi-on. You can glimpse them in the narrow, twisting alleyways, between wooden houses, flitting from one restaurant to the next, holding in their hands parcels wrapped in *furoshiki*, a wide silk envelope traditionally used for tying up parcels. These geishas were younger and slimmer, but it was hard to make out their features under their heavy makeup.

The first geishas began appearing at parties around the year 1600, and strangely enough, were men dressed as women. Male geishas entertained the guests by beating on a drum and telling *Jo-Dan* stories—amusing anecdotes. Only in 1780, were these replaced in the entertainment world by female geishas, as poets, musicians, and artists of love.

In the reign of Shogun Tokugawa, the authorities had strict control over class distinction and separation. Only the upper classes were allowed to eat white rice, to wear certain clothes, and to live in large houses. Prostitution was also controlled. Thus special quarters were built in Kyoto and Edo (now Tokyo), in which geishas and prostitutes were separated into two categories, between which no mingling was permitted. Geishas, as women who had received the best possible artistic education, were considered respectable. Their talents included music, dance, and conversation and they preferred long-standing relationships with their clients, hoping for patrons who would set them up in their own geisha houses, thus releasing them from lives of hard work. Every geisha's greatest, and most secret, wish was to marry a rich client and to live free of financial worries.

Even today, despite the erotic image they have in the West, Japanese geishas are not considered whores. In many cases, a man will take a geisha as his mistress. Geishas will sometimes agree to have sex with a man, if he is willing to pay them a huge sum of money (several thousand dollars) for the pleasure. In any case, they do not see themselves as whores, nor does Japanese society. Whores in Japan are women at the very bottom of the social ladder.

Today, the status of geishas has declined. Young Japanese women are not interested in devoting their lives to old-fashioned arts or to the entertainment of male clients, if it means forgoing normal family life. There are now only 15,000 geishas all over Japan, and their number is declining. Moreover, modern-day professional hostesses are taking a share of the pie, by offering much less expensive entertainment and pleasure. In the past, most girls who became geishas were from poor families, who were unable to support them. If a daughter was blessed with a fair complexion and a certain grace, parents would sell her to a geisha house. At least she would be fed and educated.

A geisha's education begins at a very young age, on the sixth day, of the sixth month of her sixth year. This is the "three sixes" tradition, which will help her succeed in the lengthy education she is destined to undergo. The education is, in fact, never over, and the geisha continues to learn new songs, new dance steps, and hitherto unknown paper folds, for the rest of her life. The first two things a geisha learns are how to bow and how to open the shoji doors (sliding paper doors, typical of Japanese houses). Later, she is taught the tea ceremony, dance, song, the art of conversation, and how to play the koto and the banjolike shamisen.

At a certain stage in her studies, the girl has to take exams given to her by older, more experienced geishas. If she passes, she is given a new name and the life of geishas opens to her.

Her geisha graduation ceremony includes the giving of gifts. A new geisha has to visit every geisha house and restaurant which employs geishas, and give small gifts to the owners. With the gift, the young geisha is asking that the geisha house and restaurant owners remember her in the future. During her early months as a geisha, she is known as *shinbana*, or new flower. She continues to hold this title for a year after becoming a geisha.

The geisha's job is mainly to entertain her guests with various, traditional Japanese arts. This is the meaning of her name—"*gei*" is the word for art. Most geishas would like to have a rich patron, to supply all their needs, the most expensive of which are their kimonos. A hand-embroidered, silk Japanese kimono can cost tens of thousands of dollars, and these are the geisha's work clothes. The geisha is usually faithful to her patron and may even cherish the wish to marry him one day.

A real geisha will never open her door to foreigners, even very wealthy ones, who can shower her with diamonds and other precious stones. Anyone who wants to meet a geisha must be introduced to her by a mutual friend. Otherwise, he will never get anywhere near her. Geishas are never paid in cash. Their bill is sent to the client's place of work and the price depends on the kind of entertainment given, the meal, and the quality of the kimono worn by the geisha.

Between Hostess and Whore

*J*apanese geishas hate hostesses, who have been doing a brisk trade in recent years. The hostesses charge much less and compete with the refined, well-educated geishas. Foreigners and the uninitiated tend to identify hostesses as geishas, and geishas as hostesses, and all of them together as whores.

Some say there are half a million to one million hostesses in Japan today. Like her geisha counterpart, a hostess, too, is not considered a whore. Most are married, living with a partner, or divorced, and, having no profession, are obliged to support themselves as hostesses. Japanese hostesses are suffering serious competition from foreign women who flock in the thousands to the Land of the Rising Yen, in order to earn in one year what they could not earn in ten in their own countries.

Girls come from Southeast Asia: Koreans, Thais, Filipinos, and others. There are American girls, too, and European, not to mention several thousand Israeli girls, who have made their way to Japan to make good money in this business.

A hostess will have sex with a client if she wants to, if she likes him, or if the sum of money offered is attractive. A client who wants to spend more time with a hostess invites her to a restaurant, from whence intimate relations are only a step away. There are also whore-hostesses, known by the name of "one-night lovers." After a few drinks, the girl and her client agree to meet at a love hotel. If they get caught by the police, the man can always claim that the girl is his longtime lover.

It is the job of the hostess to show her client a good time. She welcomes him at the bar door with the traditional greeting, *"Irashaimaseh,* welcome," and leads him to his seat. She spends the evening pouring him the *mizu-wari,* whiskey and water, which Japanese men are so fond of. If the client takes out a cigarette, she must be quick and light it for him. She must also dance with him if he asks her, or sing with him to the musical accompaniment of the karaoke.

The hostess also has to laugh politely at her client's jokes and cooperate if he asks her particularly intimate questions. A hostess must do her utmost to make her client feel manly, desirable, sexy, and intelligent.

As I was told by No'a, a veteran hostess in Japanese bars: "The most important part of this job is to smile, smile until your mouth hurts and you want to cry. You have to look at them with admiration in your eyes and answer their moronic questions, which they ask you in pidgin English. When they get drunk they want to feel you up. They always ask to touch your hair or breasts. Even if you tell them firmly *'Dame*—No,' they'll try again at the first opportunity. Most of them are married, in their thirties or forties, white-collar workers with a respectable expense account from their employers."

An evening in the company of a smartly dressed hostess costs a paltry $100–1,000, which is usually covered by the man's expense account or his employer's entertainment and hospitality fund, which encourages workers to go out and enjoy themselves and get to know each other and their clients.

A hostess can earn between $200 to $1,000 or more a night. Her earnings depend on the number of men who demand to sit with her, the number of drinks she pours, and the kind of entertainment she provides. Sometimes she receives a very fat tip from a very drunk client.

Male Escorts

*G*eishas, hostesses, and bar girls entertain millions of Japanese men.

But what about the women?

Japanese women believe that what's good for men, is good for women. More and more clubs are catering to a female clientele in Tokyo—and the hosts, or escorts, are male.

"The New Queen" dance club is one of these. Male hosts take the night shift, thus releasing their female counterparts to catch the last train home. These young men, well dressed, wholesome, look like nice boys from good homes—the boy-next-door type who comes to cut his neighbor's lawn on a Saturday for a few yen.

Tokyo's more sordid nightclubs expect more of their male hosts. They are there to make the ladies happy. The women who frequent these places are married to industrialists, salarymen; they are the wives of doctors and engineers, and gangsters' women. Widows and divorcées are also welcome. In these clubs the common denominator among the clientele is money—lots of it.

Those requiring the able services of the male hosts are usually women in their forties and fifties, who are past the age of blushing and embarrassment. They are not inhibited about feeling up their hosts in public, because this is exactly what they came for. A client will kiss her host right on the lips, smearing a thick layer of lipstick around his mouth. She will not hesitate to pinch his hard little bum and exchange impressions openly with lady friends around the table.

The male host bar in Tokyo serves as a real haven for the city's women. Their host will play the role of magic prince with flair, fueled by expensive alcohol. A bottle of X01 whiskey, costing $1,500, or pricey French champagne can only add to the exhilarating experience.

When a woman visits a male host club, she can choose her own prince, but she must remain with her first choice.

The unwritten rules governing the behavior of Japanese women are upheld here. Even if a woman is surrounded by men, the only man who is allowed to pour her drink, light her cigarette, and rearrange a wayward curl in her perfectly coiffed hair, is the one she chose first.

Male escorts are not paid as well as their female counterparts. Income is usually supplemented by fat tips and gifts from a wealthy patroness, who takes her escort into her own private boudoir. However, she will not hesitate to throw him out when she tires of him. Veteran hosts are proud of the gold and diamond bracelets they receive from satisfied women. A story is told of one hefty tip of five million yen (about $50,000), received by an escort who worked wonders on the body of his benefactress. Japanese male escorts tell many stories of women who, after being widowed, fritter away all their late husband's insurance money. Another way to get revenge, even after death.

It's Done Differently in Japanese Hotels

*N*eed a room? Japanese hotels offer every kind imaginable. Some Japanese hotels are meant only for sleeping in and instead of a room, you'll have a narrow tube, which may remind you of a burial chamber from ancient Rome. Other hotels are not meant for sleeping in at all. Instead of a bed, there is a Jacuzzi or a swimming pool. Other establishments offer rooms reminiscent of hospital delivery suites, complete with gynecologists' examination chairs, with spotlights shining from every direction. These last are what the Japanese call "love hotels" and the one thing you don't do there is sleep.

It all started because the walls in Japanese houses are actually made of paper. The traditional Japanese home was usually inhabited by a young couple, their parents, and their children, and was not designed for privacy. You couldn't squeak, sigh, or groan without shattering the listening silence of the night.

A couple in search of privacy had to take off for the great outdoors. There, on the banks of a river, under the light of the silvery moon and to the sound of rolling water, they could bill and coo as noisily as they liked. But what to do in the cold Japanese winters, when the temperature plunged below zero? The Japanese invented the love hotel. No one really knows when this tradition began. However, in more moral days gone by, Japanese love hotels were meant for married couples only. While grandparents stayed behind to mind the children, the couple slipped out and spent a few enjoyable hours by themselves in an inn. Today, of course, modern love hotels also open their doors to couples who want to spend a night of pure sin.

You don't have to look far to find a love hotel in Japan. If, while strolling along the road, you spot the phantasmagoric palace of Ludwig, King of Bavaria, or a grounded spaceship, or an ocean liner anchored in the middle of the city, or a replica of the Statue of Liberty—you can be sure that you're come to a love hotel.

There are about 35,000 love hotels in Japan, of which 5,000 are right in the center of Tokyo. A two-hour stay costs around $30. If you want a special room, equipped with the latest technology in beds, you'll pay another $100, depending on the room, of course. Not expensive, really, for Tokyo.

When it come to the business of lovemaking, not a moment is wasted in Japan. You might have to cool your heels in a specially designed, intimate, waiting room, because the love hotel has a room-occupation rate of 150 percent.

The love hotels used to be called *tsurekimiyado,* meaning "drag her in," but now the woman chooses the hotel and the room. The man simply pays for the pleasure. The hotels decorate with women in mind.

The most famous love hotel in Japan is the "Caesar Meguro," situated in the heart of Tokyo. The hotel is built like a medieval fortress, complete with turrets, slits in the walls for shooting arrows, outer walls, a moat, and portcullises. The hotel has sixty-two rooms, whose names are enough to send a romantic shiver down any Japanese woman's spine. For example: Spanish Lust, Italian Swing, The Princess's Sigh, and The Royal Bedchamber.

As the gate opens, a thin, recorded voice welcomes the couple as they enter and wishes them a pleasant stay. If they came in a car, and parked in the hotel's parking lot, silent hands swiftly cover the license plates with a piece of wood or cloth, to make the job of sleuthing by cuckolded husbands or betrayed wives that much more difficult. There's not a soul to be seen in the hotel's reception area. Illuminated slides are projected onto a screen on the wall opposite the main door, depicting all the theme rooms in the hotel. If any show up dark, the room is in use. Now the lady chooses a room and presses a buzzer attached to its picture. A hand appears immediately from an opening in the wall. The hand, attached to an unseen body, passes over a key.

Payment must be made immediately and everything is done automatically. Even the mandatory "Thank you very much—*arigato gozaimasu*" is no more than a recorded message from the hotel's reception desk. From here, an elevator takes you up to the rooms.

The Royal Bedchamber boasts a circular, canopied bed, which can swivel. Above the bed is a ceiling mirror and a suit of medieval armor stands by the wall, watching the action in silent fury. The Time Capsule Room contains a vibrating bed, which can be raised or lowered like a dentist's chair. A picture of the Mona Lisa looks on, a mysterious secret smile playing on her lips.

For car-racing enthusiasts, there is The Last Race suite, which has a huge water bed in the shape of a Porsche, with an attached simulator to make the effect of auto racing more realistic. Another room looks like discotheque, with rock music and laser beams, crystal mirrors, and an ornate bar. Yet another has a transparent bath, shaped like a champagne glass, with warm, fizzy water pouring from the taps. All rooms are adorned with plastic flowers, red carpets, crystal chandeliers, and mirrors. The air reeks of stale cigarette smoke, cheap perfume, and alcohol.

Some love hotels have been designed especially for those who love water sports. Instead of beds, you'll find a giant Jacuzzi, a heart-shaped bath-for-two and even a small swimming pool, with a water slide leading you straight into the arms of your beloved. Those who enjoy dressing up and playing doctor can rent the necessary uniforms at the hotel and get straight to the serious business of mutual examination. You can also rent a full police uniform, including a wooden gun and handcuffs, and even a Rambo outfit.

The love hotels are incredibly clean. The rooms are made up quickly and efficiently between each couple; the maids are invisible, and the entire operation is run on a rotating bed system. The sheets are stiffly starched and sparkling white, pristine towels await the lovers, the toilets are spotless, and the bath clean and dry and shining. As in better Japanese hotels, there is a hair dryer, a new toothbrush, shampoo, body lotion and moisturizing cream, hair creams, perfumes, and a well-stocked bar. All the rooms also contain condoms and disposable vibrators, a TV with porn movies, and a video camera to capture the happy moments for future review.

A remote control for the camera ensures that the videotape

won't fall into the wrong hands. However, one popular bit of gossip involved a distinguished member of Parliament watching a porn movie with his friends. Suddenly, in living color, his wife appeared, having an enthusiastic sexual romp with a strange man. The story ended with a juicy divorce suit. Experts insist that the hottest, bluest, most professional porn movies pale beside those secret films of the genuine throes of romantic ecstasy in the love hotels of Japan.

For kinkier tastes, there is the Alpha Hotel, located between the Russian Embassy and the American Club in the heart of Tokyo. This one is for sadomasochists and its suites, or rather its cellars, resemble the dungeons of the Spanish Inquisition or the more up-to-date interrogation rooms of the KGB. Its twenty rooms offer ropes, shackles, whips, crosses, hooks for hanging, solitary confinement cells, and the inevitable gynecologists' chairs. Sinister names identify the rooms: the Marquis de Sade Salon, the Slave Market, the Mad Doctor's Room, or the Insane Asylum.

Just like Noah's ark, you can only get into a love hotel if you are part of a couple. If you arrive alone, the hotel manager might think that you have decided to commit suicide on, of all things, the palatial bed of King Ludwig of Bavaria. Japanese history is full of romantic suicides.

If you have no lover, and you're stuck in Tokyo late at night with nowhere to sleep, the capsule hotel is the thing for you.

This is a hotel for salarymen who have drunk too much and missed the last train home, or workaholics who stay in the office until the small hours and don't want to make the two-hour journey home, only to do it over again after a couple of hours' sleep. When there's a rail strike, or heavy snow has blocked traffic, the capsule hotels are an ideal solution. Half the price of the cheapest business-class hotel room, these capsules supply a small tubelike cubicle measuring three feet wide, three feet high, and six and a half feet long, which you have to crawl into. The cubicle is situated in a large room which looks like ancient Roman catacombs. The walls consist of four stories of these cubicles, one on top of the other.

Ladders are provided to climb up to the cubicles which contain everything needed for a good night's sleep: a mattress, pillow, blankets, an alarm clock, a radio, a small TV which also shows porn movies, a reading lamp, air-conditioning, an emergency button, a small shelf for your personal belongings, and a covering at the entrance to ensure your privacy.

Personal hygiene items are supplied by an automatic vendor at the hotel's entrance: a toothbrush with pre-applied toothpaste, a razor, a small towel, and a pair of disposable men's underpants. The hotels open at five o'clock in the afternoon and checkout time is by nine in the morning. These hotels admit men only. The house rules allow one person per cubicle. Guests are warned of surprise checks during the night.

These hotels, usually situated near railway stations for the convenience of people who missed their train, also supply *ofuro* and massage.

If you need to restore yourself in the middle of a work day, the Japanese have come up with a solution.

Shibata, a young entrepreneur, was well aware of his colleagues' suffering during the day from living it up the previous night, plus long commutes. In October 1994, he opened the first hotel for short naps only.

It is situated on one of the floors of an Osaka office block. Within walking distance of many offices, he set up ten small tents and five armchairs for aching limbs. The prices are low, in accordance with the limited amenities (there is no need to change sheets between guests): 300 yen (about $3.00) for a half hour catnap in a tent or 200 yen (about $2.00) for a half hour in an armchair. He figures most of his clients require a rest of at least one hour in an armchair, after which they can return refreshed and full of energy to their work and keep going for the rest of the day.

The Japanese prefer to spend their annual vacations in *ryokans*, more traditional Japanese hotels. *Ryokans* supply the same services as Western hotels, but with additional Japanese-style extras to make the guests' stay more enjoyable.

The *ryokan* staff offers a warm welcome at the entrance. Before you even notice, your baggage will be carried off on the arms, head, and strapped to the stomach of a small, ancient Japanese woman, with a wrinkled face and bent back. It won't do you any good to object, or to offer to help her. You, the guest, are forbidden to interfere, even if your heart is full of pity and you are concerned for the well-being of the poor old lady. If you succeed in freeing a suitcase from her determined grasp, you may well be endangering her livelihood.

You will be relieved of your shoes at the entrance and given a pair of soft Japanese slippers, which will be yours until the end of your stay, when your own shoes will be returned to you. If you want a walk outdoors, a pair of raised wooden clogs will be supplied.

Your walking baggage will lead you to the elevator, and from there to a typical Japanese room. There will be no furniture in the room, except a low table on the tatami and a *toko-no-ma*, a niche for ornaments, or pictures. The old lady, breathless from the exertion, will now offer a hundred apologies for her awkwardness and will rush to pour you out a cup of green tea, which smells of boiled seaweed, from a jug on the table. She will also peel the rice cakes for you.

The porteress, who in the meantime has been promoted to chambermaid, leads you to your private *ofuro*—Japanese bath. Shyly, she points out your toilet and the special slippers which you must wear when you use it. The toilet in Japan is considered a dirty place, so when you enter it your regular slippers must be changed. If you forget to change back after coming out of the toilet and walk about the hotel's corridors in your toilet slippers, you will be ridiculed by younger guests, who will point at you and gossip about the *baka gaijin*—the foolish foreigner. Toilet slippers are always dyed an eye-catching color, electric blue or bright red, and are usually embroidered with the letters WC, or, for those who are unable to read or to get the hint, a picture of a child peeing.

The chambermaid will persuade you to change into a *yukata*, a summer kimono, which also serves as a nightshirt. She will insist that you rush off to the *onsen*. She won't leave the room while you're changing your clothes—it's her job to help you put on your *yukata*. You might, heaven forbid, tie up the *yukata* on the wrong side and go out looking like a woman, since men and women have different ways of tying it up. You might even tie it sloppily and any negligence in your dress is a black mark against your chambermaid, who sees to your every need, like any conscientious Japanese mother. She doesn't even have to knock on the *shoji* doors before entering the room. Quite often, she'll pad in silently in her soft cotton glove socks and you won't even know she's there. She's always there, bringing you a bowl of fruit, clearing away dirty dishes, or simply making sure everything's all right.

On your return from the warm springs, scrubbed, steamy, and rosy red, you will be served your supper. A wooden tray, carved in the shape of a large ship, is borne into the room by a number of chambermaids, bent under an assortment of fish and other seafood, which flounder around in the pools of liquid between the leaves of lettuce and seaweed which line the inside of the ship's deck. The meal is washed down with beer and several glasses of sake, and courses of soup, salad, and rice. This sumptuous meal is included in the price of the hotel, and you will be charged for it even if you don't want it. The price of a similar meal in a Tokyo restaurant is higher than the cost of two days' full board in the *ryokan*.

Once the meal is over, you'll be urged once again to take a dip in the *onsen*. Yes, even on a full stomach. Japanese don't believe in our old wives' tales.

When you get back to your room you'll see why they were so eager for you to leave. The room has changed into something resembling an overnight camp for a Boy Scout troop. The floor is filled with futons from wall to wall. The table you ate on earlier is now leaning against the wall, its legs folded toward its base. Recreation time is over in the *ryokan*, now that the room is arranged for the night, even if it's quite early in the evening. With your stomach full, and your limbs relaxed from a hot mineral bath, you probably won't even feel like watching the closed circuit porn movies provided by the management. Anyway, Japanese porn movies always seem like a pale, puerile and censored version of their Western counterparts.

If, however, you have decided to make the most of your stay, you can take advantage of the night life the hotel offers. Most of the larger hotels have theaters, where Japanese plays are staged, as well as local entertainment shows. Other hotels present sex shows that rival the most outrageous strip bars in Hamburg or Thailand. You might feel like visiting a karaoke bar, where you can sing into a microphone with a sophisticated orchestral accompaniment, which makes you feel as if you're backed by a large orchestra. If you still can't sleep, you can hire the services of the *ryokan*'s geisha, who usually charges a fair rate. If you can't afford this, you can hire a bar hostess or even a call girl—the night doorman will be glad to help.

You will be awakened from your refreshing sleep at an unearthly hour. The shoji door will open a crack and a small plastic sign will be poked into your room bearing the following message in English and Japanese: "The morning paper will be here soon. Please welcome it with a happy face." And indeed, within a few minutes, the Japanese morning paper will roll into the room, and, again, the ancient chambermaid—who seems never to sleep but watches over you from the other side of the door, counting every breath you take—will urge you to go to the *onsen*. When you return you will find that all the futons have disappeared into the depths of the large wall closets, and on the table, your breakfast awaits you: green tea, hot sticky rice, fish soup, Japanese pickles, and dried fish. If you insist, they will prepare some coffee and an omelette especially for you. And again, after your meal, the *onsen* awaits you.

The cheapest *ryokan* costs about $150 per person per night including breakfast and an evening meal. A particularly luxurious *ryokan* can cost as much as $2,000 per person per night.

Because of the high cost of real estate and its distance from any hot springs, it is hard to find really good *ryokans* in Tokyo. Most are located in volcanic areas, where there are plenty of hot springs and boiling mineral water.

There are many Western-style hotels, since every profit-minded international chain is eager to open several branches in Japan. A room in one of these hotels looks just like one anywhere else in the world, except for one difference: here you will receive Japanese-style pampering. In addition to the soap, shampoo, and bath foam, you will also find body lotions, aftershave, hair cream, perfumes, combs, hairbrushes, razors, ready-to-use toothbrushes, shower caps, fluffy bathrobes, and, of course, the traditional yukata. You will also be supplied with an electric kettle, which heats up the water automatically, and cups and bags of green tea. Guests at the Hotel Seiyo Ginza are in for the biggest surprise of all, but they must first prove that they have a hefty bank account and plenty of friends and supporters among the international aristocracy.

The telephone number of Hotel Seiyo Ginza does not appear in the Tokyo telephone directory, nor in the yellow pages, nor can it be reached through the city's telephone exchange. Anyone who wants to stay at that hotel can't just walk in off the street. He'll be turned away politely but firmly at the entrance. Even if the reservation is made over the phone, he will undergo a brief interrogation to determine his background. Not just anybody gets into Hotel Seiyo Ginza.

It all began when Sieji Tsutsumi, one of the richest people in Japan and the brother of the richest man in the world, was unable to find a hotel in Tokyo which met his high standards. He wanted an intimate, elegant hotel, like the best European ones, without forsaking the benefits of traditional Japanese hospitality. Tsutsumi's idea was simple: a special hotel, offering the personal service of a traditional Japanese *ryokan* and the conveniences of a posh European hotel.

And most important, his hotel would be situated in Tokyo's most prestigious quarter, the Ginza, the heart of the city.

Thus, for an investment of $70 million, Tsutsumi built his hotel and named it Seiyo—the Japanese equivalent of "more Western." The hotel is the most expensive in the world with a clientele of billionaires, millionaires, kings, and princes, as well as the run-of-the-mill rich and famous. One might find Elizabeth Taylor reclining on a white silk chaise longue in the coffee lounge and meet Dustin Hoffman in the gilded elevator, or see the Sultan of Oman eating sushi. A hotel of this sort needs no advertising; news of its existence spreads among those circles who make sure the news go no further. There are no giant signs shouting out the hotel's name, or a lobby the size of a railway waiting room, and no shops. Instead, there is a discreet entrance off a side street and pleasant doormen who welcome every guest warmly and refer to him by name, as they help him climb out of the hotel's limousine—a Jaguar or a Rolls-Royce, no less. The hotel has no reception desk and guests register in an elegant lounge, at a gilt-and-leather-covered wooden desk, surrounded by wonderful flower arrangements which are changed daily. In the reception room, the guest is received as if he were an old friend and then led to his room.

The twelve-story Hotel Seiyo has eighty suites. Each is unique.

No two rooms are alike in size, color, or interior decor. The emphasis is on restraint and a simple sophistication which offers the guest maximum comfort. The temperature in each room is controlled by an individual air-conditioning system, which also ensures optimal humidity. Here no guest need ever wake up in the middle of the night with a parched throat because of the air-conditioning. If the guest suffers from insomnia, he can always watch the TV, kept discreetly in a handsome wood cabinet, or listen to stereophonic music, or watch one of more than two hundred latest releases available from the hotel's video library.

Business calls can be made on one of two telephone lines and there is a fax machine, fitting perfectly into the handsome cabinet. If he wants peace and quiet, the guest has only to press a button which sends a message to the computer room—"Please Don't Disturb." A team of 250 highly trained workers stands at the guests' disposal. Each guest is assigned a personal secretary, who takes care of all his needs, large or small, including translation and interpretation, typing, sending out mail and fax messages, buying tickets for the kabuki theater or a movie, ordering a limousine or a private helicopter, and even seeing to gifts for members of his family.

A special feature of the room is its bath. Baths in Japan are for relaxation, meditation, or intimate social encounters. The Seiyo's huge bathrooms have been designed with this in mind, with Italian marble tiles, gold taps, and picture windows overlooking the Ginza quarter of Tokyo. The guests are supplied with three kinds of soap, their favorite shampoo, toothpaste and a host of other luxurious necessities. The bath is wide and deep, and you can take a shower in the adjoining stall, where you can also enjoy a massage and a sauna.

Thus pampered and wrapped in the expensive soft robe supplied by the hotel, the guest is ready for bed. If he can afford it, the guest may prefer a bed designed by Hermés. This giant bed is covered with silver fox furs and offers seven kinds of pillow, from the simplest goosedown, to a special wrinkle-preventing pillow filled with small pearls, which massages the neck during sleep and invigorates the blood circulation. A synthetic pillow is also supplied, for those who suffer from allergies.

Should a guest wake up in the middle of the night and need anything, the hotel's staff is at his service around the clock.

In the morning guests wake up to the pleasant voice of the telephone operator, who greets them with a "Good Morning." Ten minutes later, a silver coffee pitcher arrives with an English newspaper. The liquor in the minibar, hidden in a smart mahogany cabinet, is the best and most expensive available and is included in the bill.

And as for the price: the least expensive room in the hotel, usually used by the guest's valet or secretary, costs $500 a night. A suite costs between $1,200 and $2,000 a night. Add to this 10 percent tax and a further 10 percent service charge. In Japan you don't leave a tip.

The hotel's restaurants offer exceptional cuisine. Kit-Chu is the most expensive Japanese restaurant in Japan, with waitresses dressed in exquisite kimonos. A meal for two can cost upward of $1,500. If you crave French food, you'll find the best here. The chef studied under the legendary French chef Roger Verager. The restaurant has a wine cellar which would not embarrass a Rothschild; some fifteen thousand bottles containing three hundred different kinds of wine. A modest five-course meal for two, with a moderately priced wine, costs around $600. Food is served on Japanese Noritake plates—a different color for each season of the year. You can order baby squash stuffed with goose liver or green mushroom mousse or lobster cooked in citrus, caviar-stuffed pheasant and clear consommé, with twenty-four-karat gold leaf floating on it. Each diner is attended by four waiters, for the best and most efficient service.

I could go on: the hotel's doors and windows are designed to keep out any hint of noise from outside; the fresh flower arrangements arrive at the rooms daily; or the complimentary chocolates and the brandy laid on the pillow when the bed is prepared for the night; and the thousands of other little details that make one's stay at the Seiyo Ginza an unforgettable experience.

After a vacation in a hotel like this, who wants to go home?

The Japanese Brain

Japanese Intestines are Longer By a Yard

"*W*e Japanese are built differently." I heard this statement over and over again from my first day in Japan.

"Japanese women take sick leave every month at the onset of their periods. Western women don't need this, because you are stronger and more resilient. Japanese women are fragile. Any kind of strain during their period can be detrimental to their health." So I was told by the chairwoman of the Japanese Feminist Organization, when she explained the Japanese "Menstrual Law," which requires employers to release female workers from work for three days during menstruation. A similar rationale keeps birth control pills unavailable. "Japanese women who take the Pill may suffer undesirable side effects and cancer." This is the general medical opinion in Japan. The fact that millions of women all over the world use contraceptive pills, proves nothing to Japanese doctors.

International pharmaceutical companies trying to introduce new medicines to Japan often encounter decades of foot-dragging. "Japanese physiology is different from that of Westerners. Any new medication must be thoroughly analyzed and tested before it can be used on members of the Japanese race," is the usual rationale for endless delays.

A Japanese diamond dealer's wife, an intelligent woman who had spent several years in Israel with her family, once told me that she had never taken any medicine prescribed for her by an Israeli doctor without first phoning her private physician in Japan. "You Israelis are made differently," she explained. "Medicines prescribed for you are not necessarily good for us."

"Japanese intestines are a yard longer than the intestines of foreigners. Therefore, beef imported from the USA does not suit the Japanese digestive system," said the chairman of the Japanese Agricultural Cooperatives, to the Tokyo Foreign Correspondents' Cell, at a news conference.

The Japanese are exposed to constant brainwashing; which tells them they are like no other nation on the face of the earth, different in culture, traditions, and beliefs. The Japanese are told over and over that they belong to a special and extraordinary race, unlike any other, and this is the secret of their success.

This theory of racial superiority was amplified by Dr. Tsunoda Tadanobu, of the Tokyo Medical School. In his pseudo-scientific best-selling book, *The Japanese Brain*, he explains, among other things, why a Japanese audience is quiet during a concert, while a Western audience fidgets and coughs. The reason, he states, is the different shape of the Japanese brain.

Dr. Tadanobu claims that Western brains separate rational thought in the left lobes and emotions in the right lobes. But Japanese brains mingle rational and emotional thought in their left lobes. The Japanese people respond to the sound of the wind, the ringing of bells, sounds of laughter and tears, the song of a cricket, and the notes of Japanese musical instruments with their left lobes. The Japanese are particularly sensitive to the sound of coughs and snorts during a concert, since the music and the coughing are both picked up in the left lobe of their brains.

According to this scientist, fundamental differences between Japanese and Westerners can be explained by this theory. In the West, people tend to be rational and logical in their dealings with the natural world, while the Japanese are more emotional and prefer to seek harmony with nature.

Dr. Tadanobu's theory has become popular among scientists, politicians, and Japanese people in general, who use it to point out the vast differences between them and the people of the West.

This theoretical difference in brain structure also creates unique differences in the Japanese language. In Japanese, for example, vowels serve as whole words: *"i,"* stomach, or *"e,"* picture. Since in many other languages, most vowels are meaningless, they are taken up by the brain's right lobe. In Japanese, the vowels, used also as whole words, are taken up by the brain's left lobe—which is exactly what happens when a Japanese listens to the sounds of nature. Japanese brains develop differently owing to the character of the Japanese language. Dr. Tadanobu also claims that a Japanese person educated in the West will become like a Westerner, because his brain functions will alter.

Moreover, he and other Japanese researchers claim that their language is blessed with *kotadema*, a particular spirit which inhabits only Japanese. They assert that the Japanese language has pure words, words which express deep emotional significances, beyond their semantic meaning. Japanese words are finer, and have richer and more varied meanings than those of Western languages, which are crude, direct, and unemotional.

These theories of the psychological complexities of the Japanese people and the innate superiority of their language, bolster the idea that, the Japanese people are unique and better. These theories are encouraged and supported by the Japanese government, which publishes countless papers and articles on the subject. A particular kind of literature known as *Nihon-Jin-Ron*—Theories on the Japanese—emphasizes that their racial uniqueness makes the Japanese nation culturally, racially, and economically superior, and will eventually turn Japan into the greatest power on earth.

Body Language

The Japanese waiter met us at the entrance to the restaurant; his arms were folded across his chest and he was mumbling something unintelligible.

We were starving as we took our seats at a table in the dreary country restaurant, which was decorated with small statues of the gods of fortune. It was the only restaurant we found open after grueling hours of driving on the jammed freeway out of Tokyo.

The waiter returned to our table, and repeated his mumbling. He made the same gesture with his arms, only now he seemed more determined and less inviting.

"I've got a feeling we're not wanted here," I whispered to my husband, beneath the waiter's stony glare.

"I've heard that country restaurants usually don't speak English and prefer not to serve foreigners. He obviously can't translate the menu for us. We may as well leave," my husband said.

The waiter, who had gone into the kitchens, was peeping at us suspiciously from behind the pots and pans, one hand waving in front of his face as if swatting an invisible fly.

We left the restaurant with empty stomachs and drove on for miles to the next restaurant.

I encountered that arms-crossed-over-the-chest gesture hundreds of times during my stay in Japan. It is commonly used to express: "No entry," and sometimes "Forbidden and out of the question." I eventually interpreted the swatting-flies gesture as an expression of negative sentiments.

Foreigners to Japan consider these gestures the epitome of bad manners. For the Japanese, they are an unspoken component of the Japanese language. With the Japanese, every movement, nod of the head, facial expression, vocal sound, blink, murmur, smile, and even silence, express messages that baffle Westerners. Many foreigners learn Japanese, but no teacher explained to us the meaning of the mysterious smile hidden behind an upheld hand, the sharp intakes of breath, or the thunderous silences. These had to be learned from experience.

Sometimes, in a conversation with a Japanese person, you will find that the most important part of the sentence is unsaid and it is up to you to fill in the blanks.

This nonverbal communication is typically Japanese and may be a result of Japan's homogenity: a single language, a common religion, and similar social ethics. The Japanese are often able to complete in their minds a friend's unfinished thought, to understand every tiny stir in the person with them and almost to read their minds. They value harmony above all, and deliberately and consciously avoid direct conflict. It is difficult to create discord in a nonverbal conversation. They may also sidestep embarrassing situations this way.

The simple act of being quiet is of considerable importance in Japan. From his companion's silence, a Japanese can sense and understand what is not being said. A great many poems have been written and proverbs handed down over the years in praise of quiet. "Those who know, say nothing; those who speak, know nothing," is an elegant summary of the Japanese respect for silence.

A foreigner in Japan on business, facing a lull in the middle of negotiations, might fill the void with small talk. This is the worst thing he could do. A Japanese silence can be interpreted in several ways. Besides offering a pause for thought, silence can hold a wide variety of conflicting emotions, contentment or discontent, disagreement or even complete agreement, which is unnecessary to express in words. A foreigner to Japan will react correctly only if he is aware of this and is able to respond with a silence of his own.

The Japanese will never say the word *"iie*—no" outright, even when they disagree, or are not interested in proposals they have been offered. The word exists, of course, but during all my years in Japan, I heard it only once, from the mouth of a three-year-old tyke who refused to eat his porridge.

An adult Japanese wishing to express displeasure, or trying to explain that something is hard or impossible, will draw air through his teeth making a sound like a hissing snake. If you hear this, you'd do well to rescind your request or proposal.

The Japanese are also famous for their frozen, inscrutable expression, similar to a Western poker face. This classic facial expression, handed down over the centuries from the samurai, is favored by Japanese men. In samurai days, expressing emotion was considered weak and undignified. Nowadays, the frozen face is used as emotional armor, especially when a Japanese man must mix with a crowd, or feels his privacy is threatened. Often the poker face conceals a multitude of negative emotions and a strong desire to be somewhere else.

Of course, Japanese are only human, and they smile and laugh and know how to show that they are happy. Strangers, seeing Japanese people smiling, or laughing their heads off, won't always understand the reason for this joviality.

Sometimes, in fact, there really is no apparent cause for laughter. A Japanese may have experienced a tragedy, yet he laughs. But this laughter is full of deep sorrow, nervous, inhibited, and not from the heart. It serves as a mask for deep emotional discomfort.

In Western culture, we look people straight in the eye. A shifty look is considered dishonest or unreliable. In Japan, a direct look, especially at someone who is your senior, is perceived as invasive and vulgar. Japanese children are brought up to look at people at an invisible point somewhere in the middle of their necks. If a Japanese person doesn't meet your eyes, take it as a sign of respect.

It is very important in Japan to keep your distance. You must be careful not to invade someone else's space. Don't pull up a chair in too friendly a way, to get closer to someone, nor may you pat someone on the shoulder. If you do, a Japanese will feel threatened. Keep at least twice the amount of distance between yourself and a Japanese person as you would with a Westerner. If your Japanese acquaintance moves his chair away from you, don't be offended and don't be tempted to move closer to him.

These norms are especially difficult to follow for those people who make a habit of kissing everyone they meet. A Japanese will consider even the most innocent kiss on the cheek from a woman involved with him solely in business negotiations as a grave affront to his manhood.

The Japanese have a complicated repertoire of body language. Every movement expresses a feeling, an emotion, a response, or signals a situation. For example, agreement is expressed in a vigorous nodding of the head. If a Japanese wants to refer to himself, *Watashi*—I, he will point with his finger to the end of his nose. The word "man" is expressed with a raised thumb and "woman" with a raised little finger. The raised little finger also often refers to a second wife or mistress.

The sign for eating is more theatrical. One pretends to hold a bowl under one's chin and puts imaginary rice into one's mouth with chopsticks.

Shitsurei shimasu, excuse me, especially if one is obliged to get through a crowd, is expressed with the right hand, spread open in front of the face, making small cutting motions in the air. The Japanese all around you will disperse.

Japanese girls express their embarrassment with a nervous and irritating giggle, holding their right hands over their mouths.

And then there's bowing. If a Japanese wants to attract someone's attention, he will make a point of bowing before this person and, of course, the higher the status, the deeper will be the bow of the person wishing to curry favor.

Anything to do with voice is taken very seriously in Japan. Westerners, who are known for being loud, must learn to control their voices in Japan, and use a lower vocal range. A loud voice is considered vulgar as well as threatening. Many Japanese women adopt a high-pitched squeak known fondly as *neko-chan*, a kitten. With this voice, they are trying to adopt a childish helplessness and cuteness, and appear nonthreatening. You often hear this voice from the mouth of a hotel receptionist or a telephone operator. Foreigners in Japan find it hilarious.

The Japanese are highly clothes-conscious. An adult Japanese would never dress in bright colors or flashy styles. They rarely use scents or aftershaves.

The Japanese don't display affection in public. It is extremely rare to see a Japanese couple kissing under a streetlamp or even holding hands. They would be mortified at the sight of a foreigner kissing his wife in public.

It is important to learn some Japanese—without it, a stranger in Japan is at a complete loss, but without an understanding of body language and what is unspoken, the words alone are of little use. A Japanese person's unspoken words may well be critical in business negotiations. What is unsaid must be understood.

A Journey of Survival

*A*lmost everyone who negotiates with the Japanese accuses them of having no nerves, being irrational, inconsistent, putting their opponent down, falling asleep in the middle of a difficult discussion, and generally behaving badly. However, foreign businessmen should make a point of learning the Japanese rules of the game.

The first and most important rule: be prepared. If you've come on a commercial mission, make sure that information or anything else you need is readily available. You will find the Japanese are better prepared than you are. Take care of the smallest details, don't dismiss anything as unimportant, and make yourself thoroughly familiar with your material—or success is impossible.

Read everything you can on Japan, speak to people who have been there and are experienced in negotiating with the Japanese. Heed their advice.

It's a good idea to rest well before beginning business negotiations, especially after a long trans-Pacific flight. The Japanese relish marathon discussions, which can last for days on end without a break. Shake off jet lag, and acclimatize yourself to the weather and Tokyo's fast pace.

Carefully go over every issue raised during the negotiations. You will make a good impression. The Japanese like their adversaries to be serious and conscientious.

Make sure you understand the nuances of the word *"hai"*—"yes"—since it is not always possible to know exactly what a Japanese means when he says it. Sometimes the word "yes" means "I understand," or "I agree with you," or "I am listening and am concentrating," or "I am keeping up with what you are saying," and so on. Thus, when a Japanese says "yes," he is not necessarily about to sign a contract with you. Don't forget that it is impolite to use the word "no" or answer in the negative. A foreigner who begins a sentence with "I don't agree with you," will probably shock his Japanese counterpart.

It is crucial to sum up in writing everything said at a meeting. Even if the Japanese side doesn't like the idea—a summary of the proceedings may prevent future misunderstanding.

It is a good idea to prepare a draft of a contract or an agenda of points to be raised at the meeting before it begins. Such a document can be very useful during the various stages of negotiation.

Make sure a business meeting with Japanese people does not end on time. Many foreigners tend to press their Japanese counterparts into setting dates—this is not done in Japan. Try to act like your hosts—patient and accommodating.

Expect lack of order and inconsistency when dealing with the Japanese. An observer from the outside might feel that the Japanese change their minds because they are confused and have no clearly defined policies. Foreigners may come away from negotiations frustrated and assume that the Japanese were deliberately trying to unbalance them. But the Japanese are not always perfectly organized and sometimes disagree among themselves.

Try to pay close attention to the stand taken by the Japanese negotiating team during a discussion. They usually don't like to make statements or requests outright and are apt to hide behind statements in officialese.

Don't get nervous during periods of silence. Foreigners aren't used to these and might resort to unnecessary chatting in an effort to fill the gap. Play the Japanese game and stay silent too.

Japanese are very fond of ceremony. Have business cards printed in both English and Japanese—the larger hotels will do this. Without these, the Japanese will not know how to address you during your discussions. A businessman without a visiting card has no identity. When you are given a card from a Japanese colleague, thank him, address him by name and place the card carefully in a small wallet designed to hold them. If you treat someone's card with contempt, leave it behind on the negotiating table, or clean your nails with it, you'll lose the deal.

You must never press the Japanese, even when what they are saying is unclear. They don't mean to confuse—this is simply their way of expressing themselves. They would be very surprised if a foreigner offered them his exact meaning and expectations. As far as they are concerned, it is always better to prevaricate and act with caution.

Don't jump to conclusions. If, in the midst of the foreigner's presentation, the Japanese start talking among themselves in Japanese, don't take this as bad manners or an interruption. One of the participants probably didn't understand something of what was being said in the foreign language and is asking for clarification.

Make a point of bringing an official gift to the participants in the negotiations. They, no doubt, have prepared one of their own, and it is traditional to exchange gifts. Take great care over the wrapping of the gift. A carelessly wrapped gift will give a bad impression of its giver. If the original gift wrapping has wrinkled during your long flight to Japan, you can always ask the hotel chambermaid to help you rewrap it. Every Japanese woman is an expert at gift wrapping.

Never refuse a dinner invitation. Social occasions, such as dinner at a restaurant, give your Japanese hosts the chance to get to know you in an informal atmosphere, away from the negotiating table. With a little wine or whiskey in your belly, a pretty hostess or two and pleasant music, most of the barriers will drop. During the meal, forget all your Western squeamishness and eat everything you are served. If you leave anything on your plate, your hosts, who chose the most expensive restaurant they could afford, will be sure you didn't like the food and they will take offense.

If your Japanese hosts suggest a weekend away at a hot springs spa outside Tokyo, say yes. Even if this entails scalding your completely naked self in near-boiling water, it's worth the suffering. A great many barriers (and not only clothes) can be removed with the Japanese at these communal baths. What's more, this is a sure sign that your negotiations were successful and the contract is as good as signed.

What Makes Them Laugh?

The Japanese sense of humor is difficult to fathom. The Japanese themselves treat the issue as if it were a grave national secret. If you ask what makes the Japanese laugh, don't expect much of an answer. They don't tell jokes in Japan.

Japanese humor is certainly evident in their TV programs. TV studio audiences almost die laughing at every twitch of the host's eyebrow. Nearly every program on Japanese TV has hysterical canned laughter, or even the real thing, if it's recorded live. If you turn your TV on for only a few minutes you won't be able to help getting the impression that Japanese TV is hilariously funny.

TV jokes can be divided into three categories, starting with sports jokes. Imagine watching baseball players getting balls thrown straight in their faces again and again. The Japanese host supplies an ecstatic voice-over, while shrieks of uncontrolled laughter come from an invisible audience in the background. The camera focuses on the players' faces as the balls smash into them.

There are the morning jokes, in which an entire TV crew creeps into a Japanese home (it's quite easy to get into a Japanese home through the shoji doors). As lights flash in their eyes, the family wakes up suddenly. The audience is beside itself with laughter, especially at the sight of a couple jumping up stark naked, startled by the sudden bright light, or a little boy waking up, confused by the commotion. The TV crew usually gets fed a full breakfast, prepared by the housewife, who can't stop laughing at having been the victim of a practical joke.

In the "hotel fun" category, a television crew enters a room in a love hotel during the early hours of the morning. The camera zooms in on the disarray: the articles of clothing haphazardly thrown, the used condom discarded in an ashtray beside the bed, and finally, on the couple itself, fast asleep in the middle of the giant heart-shaped bed. The couple awaken and cooperate willingly, the woman modestly shielding her breasts with the sheet. The invisible audience screams with laughter.

Similar practical jokes are filmed in ordinary hotels as well, perhaps showing a girl fast asleep. The audience dies laughing as the host peels her embroidered bra off the back of a chair. The host, who is whispering into his microphone so as not to wake the girl up, is shaking with laughter, and so is the cameraman—the picture is rather wobbly. The scene ends when the girl is awakened, sometimes by having the bedclothes pulled off her, or by the host getting into the bed with her and pretending to be asleep.

As she awakes, the girl first blanches, and then turns a bright red—not least for being caught with disheveled hair and no makeup.

Tak-eshi-Jo is Japan's most popular TV show and belongs in the category of sport humor. Groups of young people, costumed as sushi, horned beetles, barrels, and so on, are made to ford a difficult object such as a hanging rope bridge or floating barrels. At the same time, footballs are shot at them from an enormous cannon by another group of people dressed as crazy kings. The clumsy players in their funny clothes fall into the mud, into the water, or onto a pile of fresh cow dung—and the audience roars. The host laughs as well, and so do the people who are smeared all over with mud.

The funniest programs on Japanese TV are the sex shows. Dressed like a doctor, the host examines a female patient, who wears only a pair of flimsy panties, lying on an operating table. The "doctor" listens to her heartbeat with the aid of a huge stethoscope, pinches her nipples, and murmurs a bogus medical diagnosis.

Home video clips showing various mishaps involving children or animals are also quite popular.

Japanese TV likes to showcase freaks. The fattest woman on earth, for the kind of money only the Japanese would pay, agreed to appear on TV with her breasts exposed and to place her over-flowing flesh under the kneading and pinching fingers of the pro-gram's openmouthed host. I have never seen such a motley collection of hideous, disfigured, and pathetic creatures as I did on Japanese TV comedy shows. They came from all over the world, quite willing to display every detail of their genetic misfortunes to the entire Japanese nation—for a price, of course.

But merely exhibiting these people was not always enough for Japanese TV. NHK, a reputable TV channel, managed to hire the woman with the largest breasts in the world. Stark naked, she was taken to a male-only bathhouse, where she crept behind the men soaping each other and helped one of them to scrub his back. This grateful fellow, eyes stinging with soapsuds, returned the favor and tried to soap his helper, until the moment his hands encountered the biggest breasts in the world. The Japanese audience in the studio was choking with laughter and almost needed mouth-to-mouth resuscitation.

I'm sure you've got the idea by now that the Japanese do have a sense of humor. Their jokes might be less sophisticated and rather childish, even sadistic sometimes, but they find them funny. And how.

Japanese intellectuals are quick to explain that the Japanese don't like sophisticated humor, the kind that needs thought and analysis before you start laughing. When a man spends long hours in an office and gets home only after a lengthy and arduous jour-ney in a crowded train, all he wants is to unwind. He doesn't want to think the joke out or have it explained. What a weary, hard-working Japanese needs is immediate satisfaction.

Japanese TV humor accurately reflects modern Japanese cul-ture: prohibitions, social restraints, strict formalities, social hierar-chies and class distinctions, constant efforts to behave correctly and follow the rules to avoid embarrassment to others or shame to oneself, and, of course, a great deal of suppressed anger and almost superhuman emotional control.

Humor offers escape from reality. It enables you to channel stress into other, more acceptable outlets; to unburden your anger and unload constant, painfully achieved self-control—all you need is an outburst of purifying laughter. Almost everybody who ap-pears on a Japanese comedy show finds himself in an embarrass-ing situation, and the more embarrassing and ridiculous it is, the more he laughs. The unmentionable subjects of daily Japanese life, can be held up in front of the camera and ridiculed uninhibitedly. The viewer experiences a catharsis which helps preserve his sanity.

A Japanese TV comedy show which would make a Japanese viewer go berserk with laughter would, at best, leave a Western viewer indifferent. Many newly arrived foreigners spurn this kind of humor as infantile and idiotic, although their children probably love it. The longer these same foreigners spend in Japan, however, the more desperate they become for just this kind of slapstick humor. It's the only way to relieve some of the pressures created by the culture and its people.

So if you ever find yourself watching a Japanese TV comedy show, try to remember that the Japanese find it very funny. And be glad you're not a guest on one.

The Butcher's Son

*I*met Hideo Yamamoto at the Tokyo Press Club. Hideo handled public relations for an American airline company. In his spare time he was an amateur opera singer. He was devoted to his family and very proud of his beautiful daughter, a gifted pianist. His family lived in a modern and comfortable home on the outskirts of Tokyo, and Hideo himself was a member of the local golf club, which indicated a large income, since in Japan, golf club membership fees can cost hundreds of thousands of dollars. Everything about Hideo spelled success and self-confidence, and he always made sure this was the impression we, the foreigners, had of him.

After Hideo had left our table one day, Edward, an English journalist in charge of the club's gossip, bent over to me and whispered: "Poor Hideo."

"What happened?" I was worried.

"Didn't you know?" he asked.

"No, really, is he sick? Has his wife left him?" I asked. "He doesn't look as if anything's the matter."

"What do you expect?" Edward asked. "Should he go around the streets announcing that his father's a butcher?"

"A butcher?" I didn't understand. "What's that got to do with it?"

"You really don't understand, do you?" said Edward. "The fact that his father's a butcher makes him a member of the untouchables, the lowest of the low."

I couldn't believe my ears. This is the kind of thing you hear about only in India, I thought. "But why is Hideo a poor thing? He's got a family, a talented daughter, money, and lots of friends here in the club."

"That's just it," said Edward. "Because of his background, no Japanese company would employ him, and only a Western company is willing to hire him. Haven't you noticed that only foreigners are willing to get close to him? He's got no friends among his own people, but it goes deeper than that. His daughter, Akiki, can't marry anyone from a class higher than her own, and will have to make do with a butcher's son, or the son of a leather tanner, or a street cleaner."

"I thought," I said to him, appalled, "that there is no longer any class distinction in modern postwar Japan. I thought all that was stopped by General MacArthur."

"Aren't you the naive one," said Edward, pleased at shocking me. "You don't know anything yet." His voice had an ominous note.

I thought no more about what Edward had told me, but then I heard about a young university graduate who married a fellow student. According to Japanese tradition, marriages are arranged by the young couple's parents, after thoroughly researching each other's backgrounds. This particular girl married for love, without asking too many questions about her young husband's family. By the time she found out that her new husband came from the wrong side of Osaka and was a member of the caste of the untouchables, she had already given birth to a beautiful, healthy baby son. She left her home, her husband, and her infant and sent her divorce petition afterward by mail. By Japanese standards, she had excellent grounds for divorce: her husband belonged to the *burakumin*, which means "sons of the small villages."

The cleaning lady at the Tokyo Jewish Center also received "special attention" from the Japanese secretaries. I never saw them so rude and unpleasant as when they were ordering her to clean. "She's one of the lower classes," I was told by my gentle Filipino secretary. "You'll never get them to treat her with any respect. This is something too deeply rooted in their tradition."

The Japanese are reticent about the subject of the untouchables. They are especially reluctant to discuss the matter with foreigners. Ostensibly, the problem does not exist. No sociological research is done on it, it is not mentioned in guidebooks, and rarely in the papers, and the TV stations completely ignore it. Government officials simply shrug their shoulders when confronted with the issue, and say that it no longer exists. You can find passing references to the subject in Japanese history books. But does it happen today? "Modern Japan has no racial problems. Japan is an egalitarian society. All citizens are equal." And this is the message that the Japanese are constantly trying to get across in their conversations with foreigners. "The *burakumin* class? Yes, I believe it once existed, but not anymore, of course," the Japanese say, doing their best to camouflage reality. They prefer to sweep their *burakumins* under their tatami, in a closed room, so the neighbors outside won't see or hear anything.

You won't even find the word *"burakumin"* in a Japanese/English dictionary. The word *"buraku,"* which means ghetto, or the place where the untouchables live, is translated simply as "village."

Japanese word processors don't include the words *buraku* or *burakumin*—as if these words don't exist. Japanese publishers will admit reluctantly that they are obliged to use a special computer function to print it.

But about three million Japanese know full well what it means to be a descendant of the *burakumin*. Even if they graduate from a university and marry the right person (if that person doesn't have an inkling of their background), they and their children will bear the stigma of their lowly status. The fear of discovery will haunt them all their lives, and the chances of creating a new identity for themselves are practically nil. Their higher-caste countrymen will always be able to ferret them out, and when they do, the results are extremely unpleasant.

Every year, several hundred members of this caste commit suicide. They have little chance of finding a partner outside their social class, and promotion at work is impossible. They can be geniuses at school, but they will always bear the mark of the untouchable.

The Japanese admit that the *burakumin* are no different from anyone else in their physical appearance, their speech, their religion, and their morals. But these people still constitute the largest, best-hidden minority group in Japan.

The origins of the caste of the untouchables is unclear. The first *burakumin* ghetto was probably built during the ninth century A.D. The people known as *burakumin* were banished there, probably because they made their living doing jobs that contradicted the laws of Shinto and Buddhism. These religions believe in reincarnation, preach purity, and forbid the harming or killing of animals. The *burakumin* were known at that time as *"eta"*—contaminated—and did work which was unacceptable to the Shinto and Buddhist religions: butchery, tanning, dung collecting, and burial. To this day, the descendants of the *eta* work at these professions, which no other Japanese, however hard up, would do. These people are paid the lowest wages in Japan, and if they lose their jobs, they often become homeless.

In the past, the Japanese government left them out of its national census. They were considered subhuman and therefore not worth counting. Their villages were never even marked on maps of Japan. It was during the reign of the Shogun Tokugawa that the first laws were passed which discriminated against the *eta*, restricting these miserable people to certain jobs, forbidding them to marry outside their caste, to visit the home of people in higher castes, or to own land. They were also forced to pin a strip of leather to their clothing to identify them wherever they went.

New laws passed by the Japanese government during the 1970s, which declared that all citizens of Japan are equal and outlawing the term *"eta,"* were unable to dispel this deeply ingrained racist tradition.

About four thousand *burakumin* ghettos exist in modern-day Japan, most of them around Osaka, in the area between Kyoto and Nara and in the old part of Tokyo. A total of some two million untouchables live in these ghettos, half of whom have broken away from their childhood homes in an attempt to find a better future, although this, too, is uncertain. Statistics published by the *"Burakumin* Liberation League," which has its headquarters in Osaka, show that about 70 percent of the *eta* would leave the ghettos, if they were able to do so. Around 7 percent of them are on welfare (as compared with a 3 percent national statistic), and less than 70 percent of them graduate from high school (compared with 98 percent of the remaining population of Japan). Only five percent of them go on to higher education.

The total average income for an *eta* family (if the wife is also employed) is between one-half and one-third of the national average. Today they live in small, overcrowded, smelly, crumbling houses, with no sidewalks, insufficient street lighting, and no modern sewage systems. Their neighborhoods suffer from general neglect, and if you take a walk along one of their streets, you'll feel you've gone back in time.

Japan's private detective agencies make good money from investigating the background and ancestry of potential brides and bridegrooms. A good detective can uncover a tainted ancestry as far back as six or seven generations ago. This immediately brings about the cancellation of any engagement or wedding arrangements. No one would knowingly marry someone from this low caste and risk tainting his children for generations to come. Employers, too, would fire a worker on the spot, if there was suspicion that he was an *eta*. Until quite recently, government-run registries supplied private detective agencies with information on the *eta*. Today, these registries are classified and data is released only with a special government authorization.

In 1979 a series of books, titled *Burakumin Chimei Shukan,* was published, which included the names and addresses of all the *burakumin* in Japan. Many Japanese companies made use of these lists to weed out undesirable elements from among their workforce.

The issue is of no concern to those Japanese people who are poor, but not members of the race of untouchables. On the contrary, "It's always good to know that there's someone worse off than we are," say Japan's manual laborers.

Recent criticism from intellectuals has prompted the Japanese government to improve the lot of these untouchables by pouring money and other resources into the ghettos. The *Burakumin* Liberation League is demanding penalties for racial discrimination against the *eta*. For the first time, the High Court of Justice forced a man to pay damages for refusing to marry his fiancée, after an investigation uncovered her lowly origins.

The League now meets with people, companies, and organizations accused of discrimination. Although these are quick to beg forgiveness of the *burakumin* and offer large sums of money in compensation, they do not stop discriminating.

It seems unlikely that this racism will ever be completely eradicated, mainly because of Japan's overwhelming conservatism, which is stronger than any legislation. Anyway, abolishing the caste system would seriously diminish Japan's blue-collar workforce.

A Homogenous Society

"*J*apan is a homogenous society," proudly declared former Japanese Prime Minister Nakasone while traveling in the U.S. in October, 1986. "As a single-race country with a single culture, we have been able to achieve so much," he stated. Furthermore, he claimed that Hispanic, African-American, and other minorities had negatively affected the level of intelligence and intellectual achievement in the United States.

This was not the first time that Nakasone had expressed these sentiments. True, he made his speech in Japanese before a Japanese audience, with the aim of encouraging a feeling of national pride. However, unfortunately for him, there were several journalists in that audience, who were all too willing to run off and report his opinions to the international media.

It is not surprising that Nakasone's words created an outcry in the United States. They also received sharp criticism back home in Japan. But Nakasone was only expressing an opinion widely held in Japan: there are no minority groups in the country. This homogeny, which government officials describe with so much pride, is, in their opinion, the secret of Japan's economic successes.

In 1985, Japan's Foreign Ministry published a diplomatic report congratulating the nation on its economic success, and attributing this success to Japan's racial homogeny. Many politicians in Japan admit openly that their nation is fortunate for not having had to integrate foreigners into their society.

In 1980, Japan presented a report to the United Nations which categorically denied the existence of ethnic minorities in Japan.

This is not true.

Japan has, for one, an ethnic native minority: the Ainu. This Japanese minority is subject to racial discrimination; their lands have been appropriated and they are forced to live on reservations. These people are known in Japan as the "Ino," which is a derogatory term for "dog."

Archaeologists believe that many tribes of people traveled from Siberia across Asia to North America thousands of years ago, and that those tribes settled in North America before the arrival of the white man. According to this theory, more tribes of the same race arrived in Japan from neighboring Korea. The North American Indians and the Japanese Ainu may be distant cousins.

The histories of the two peoples show similar discrimination and similar problems. Late-nineteenth-century American Indians were banished to reservations to make room for white settlement. At around the same time the Ainu tribes were uprooted by the Meiji government and sent from the north of Japan's main island to the freezing wild island of Hokkaido. Like that of the North American Indians, the history of the Ainu tribes is a tragic one of exploitation and discrimination.

Some twenty-five thousand Ainu now live on Hokkaido, and it is the policy of the government of Japan not to recognize the Ainu as an ethnic minority.

Unlike the rest of the Japanese, the Ainu are broadly built, light-skinned, and tawny-eyed. The language they speak is quite different from Japanese. Ainu men, unlike Japanese men, have dense body hair. They are known derisively in Japan as "hairy barbarians."

Surveys show that many Ainu have experienced racial discrimination. About 7 percent are on welfare, and only about 80 percent of their children finish high school (compared with the 98 percent national average).

The Hokkaido Oteri Organization claims that at least sixty thousand Ainu live today in Japan under false names and borrowed identities.

Ainu culture is similar to that of Alaskan Eskimos—essentially a fishing and hunting culture. Like Eskimos, the Ainu like to offer a visiting stranger the entire contents of their home. They wear colorful, decorated robes, meant to guard them against evil spirits, and use poison-tipped arrows for hunting. The composition of their poison is a closely guarded tribal secret.

The Ainu believe in totems: the owl and the bear and other animals are considered gods. The tribes are not nomadic and prefer to settle in one place, in straw and wood huts. They believe in an afterlife, and traditionally burn the house of a dead woman, so that she may use it in the next world.

The Ainu have recently organized themselves as a political force and have applied to the United Nations for official recognition and for the financial aid granted to minorities by international organizations. The Ainu have also spoken out against the policies of the Japanese government, who persistently claim that Japan is a homogenous state.

The issue is largely ignored in Japan. Distinguished researchers point out that the Ainu are Japanese in every way, and that their language and beliefs are deeply rooted in prehistoric Japanese culture.

Whether the Ainu tribe will achieve official recognition depends on their tenacity and ability to demand their rights and to gain support. Otherwise they will become no more than a faded memory in history books and anthropological studies.

There are other ethnic minorities whose existence the Japanese authorities completely ignore. These are the inhabitants of Japan's southernmost island of Okinawa, as well as the Japanese-born ethnic Koreans.

Okinawa is the largest of the Ryukyu chain of islands, which are closer to Taiwan than to Tokyo. These islands were controlled in the past by both Japan and China, and benefited from the cultural influence of China.

In the 1895 Sino-Japanese War, the Japanese invaded and controlled these islands. At the beginning of the present century, Okinawa was the poorest of Japan's territories. When asked where he came from, an Okinawan would probably say Kyushu, a southern island, closer to Japan. Until quite recently the phrase: "Okinawans and Koreans need not apply," in help-wanted ads, was commonplace.

During World War II, every Japanese soldier was under orders to willingly give up his life for the Emperor. In response, as a result of misinformation, several hundred people committed suicide in Okinawa, one of the war's major battlegrounds. Whole villages chose to die rather than be taken prisoner by the American army. Of the 240,000 of Okinawa's war victims, 150,000 were noncombatant civilians.

A 1984 survey by the Japanese Ministry of Education showed that only 7 percent of the schools on Okinawa fly the Japanese flag. Nor is the national anthem heard in Okinawan schools in the morning, as it is in the rest of the country.

Today, the local population of Okinawa seeks to preserve the island's unique culture and traditions. Under American occupation, the Okinawans were allowed to study and learn about their origins. Once the island was returned to Japan, in 1972, however, whole chapters of Okinawan history were deleted from national history books.

The people of Okinawa are determined to continue their struggle for official recognition by the Japanese government; like the Ainu, they must arouse public sympathy for their plight.

Japanese-born descendants of Koreans suffer a different and more severe form of discrimination.

According to Takao Goto, an expert on the Korean minority community in Japan, 60 percent of the Korean minority have lived in Japan for three generations. Numbering 2.5 million, most are still obliged to register with the Ministry of the Interior and to carry the identity card of a foreign citizen. Like all foreigners in Japan, the Koreans are required to record their fingerprints at the Ministry of the Interior, as if they were criminals. Korean political activists are thrown into jail or forced into hiding if they refuse to be fingerprinted. Toward the end of the eighties, the authorities made great efforts to hunt down these fingerprint refuseniks. Entire families of Koreans were taken down to the registry offices and forcibly fingerprinted.

Those Koreans who try to integrate into Japanese society by changing their names and identities are openly rejected and scorned. A Korean employee will not be promoted at work, his salary will be lower than that of his Japanese colleague, and his children are treated as outcasts and often forbidden to marry Japanese.

The Japanese treat the Koreans with contempt, giving them derogatory names such as "garlic eaters" and "dogs,"and find it rather hard to reconcile themselves to facts now being uncovered by historians. In the ninth century A.D., most of Japan's aristocratic families, and probably the Imperial ancestors as well, came to Japan from Korea.

The present-day Japanese Koreans came (or, more accurately, were brought) to Japan during the present century. Entire Korean villages surrendered to occupying Japanese forces during Japan's rule of Korea between 1910 and 1945, and were shipped in overcrowded boats to Japan, where they were forced to labor in the coal mines and at building military fortifications.

Only recently have horrific stories been published of Korean women, forced to become prostitutes for the Emperor's soldiers during the Second World War. Korean historians claim that between 100,000 and 200,000 women and girls were kidnapped and used as "comfort women" for the Japanese army controlling the front lines between China and Southeast Asia. Initially, Japanese officers allotted one girl to three soldiers, but toward the end of the war, the ratio became one girl to one hundred soldiers according to eyewitnesses and survivors. Japan successfully ignored this appalling chapter of her history for many years, but the issue surfaced in 1991, when Japanese Prime Minister Kiaichi Maizawa paid an official visit to South Korea. The first Japanese prime minister willing to make amends for past atrocities was welcomed in Korea with widespread demonstrations.

Korean historians assert that Japan's World War II treatment of Koreans resembled the long-ago slave trade between Africa and the United States. Only recently have hitherto secret documents revealed the maltreatment of Koreans in Japanese forced-labor camps. Japanese newspapers are now willing to publish stories like these, triggering an unprecedented examination of national responsibility for war crimes.

Japan, under the influence of the West, is becoming gradually aware of the civil and social rights of its ethnic minority communities. The *burakumins*, the Ainu, the Koreans, and the Chinese, as well as members of other ethnic communities, born and raised in Japan, have the potential to unbalance Japan's harmony and social order. And Japan is neither racially pure nor homogenous.

Hinoa·Uma: Fire Horse Women

"**Y**ou'll never believe what I've just found out," our American friend said at a Friday evening party. He was one of the foreign headhunters who came to Tokyo to find workers for his overseas clients. "We've been looking for female workers and I've interviewed several hundred so far. Not one of the applicants is exactly twenty years old. Some are twenty-one, some nineteen, but not a single one is twenty. When I checked their birth dates, I discovered that not one was born in the year 41."

According to Japanese tradition, a new era begins with the crowning of each Emperor. Thus, the year 41 means the forty-first year of the reign of Emperor Hirohito. In other words, 1966.

It wasn't until January that we discovered the answer to this mystery. Each year, on January 15, Japanese youth celebrate the end of the second decade of their lives, and their entry into adulthood. Dressed in their best kimonos, the young men and women go to the nearest temple and receive the priest's blessing.

That same year, headlines announced that only 1.3 million young people reached adulthood, and stressed that this number was half a million less twenty-year-olds than the previous year, which was the lowest number of twenty-year-olds since 1899, when Japan began calculating its yearly birthrate.

Of the 1.3 million celebrating the passage to adulthood that year, around 700,000 were young men and 650,000 were young women. These twenty-year-olds made up only 1.1 percent of the entire population of Japan, the lowest number ever registered. The following year, 2.4 million young people reached the age of twenty, almost double the number of the previous year.

What happened in 1966?

It was a Fire Horse year, according to the Chinese astrological calendar which the Japanese use. According to ancient Japanese belief, a Fire Horse woman is destined to murder her husband. Obviously no bridegroom can be found for her. She can never become a wife and mother and is fated to live in loneliness and poverty.

This is not the only superstition related to the Chinese zodiac. To be born in the year of the tiger also has unpleasant consequences. A baby girl born under this sign is destined to grow up into a rebellious, shrewish girl, adventurous and unruly. No Japanese boy will marry a woman like this. As for a boy born in the year of the Monkey—he may end up a thief.

Newspaper clippings from the year 1965 showed that Japanese belief in the grim prospects of Fire Horse women was deeply rooted. The country's gynecologists held open discussions on the disturbing increase in abortions that year. "Superstitious parents," said an article in *Asahi Shimbun*, "cannot bear the thought that about half of all babies born are female. So a woman gets an abortion in order to avoid a tragic fate for a potential daughter. Other parents of daughters born during that accursed year changed the date on their birth certificates, hoping this would save them from their terrible destiny. Fear of creating Fire Horse daughters also caused a steep drop in marriages that year.

In the end, however, Japanese boys and girls born in 1966 benefited, despite the superstitions. The low birthrate in the year of the Fire Horse meant far fewer children enrolled in school. Fire Horse children did not have to compete for places in the more prestigious schools. Job promotions and a swift rise to the top were made easier because of the relatively few candidates for each position.

The next Fire Horse year is 2026. Who knows what it holds in store?

The Jewish Connection

Star of David

*T*he Japanese and the Jews is the name of a book by an anonymous author, who wrote under the pen name of Isaiah Ben Dasan. The book was published in 1970 by Yamamoto Shoten and was very soon turned into a best-seller in Japan, where nothing at all had previously been known about the Jews. The author chose anonymity, although informed sources are willing to swear that he is none other than Mr. Yamamoto himself, a well-known Japanese intellectual and publisher, and a fervent supporter of Israel. Mr. Yamamoto and his wife have visited Israel on many occasions at the head of Japanese delegations wishing to learn more about the Chosen People, the subject of the book.

Isaiah Ben Dasan, or, if you prefer, Mr. Yamamoto himself (who is now dead), tried in his book to find similarities between two nations, so different and far apart from each other geographically— the Jews and the Japanese.

The book's first page is decorated with a Star of David, surrounded by the Japanese circular rising sun. The Jewish Star of David, explains the author, is known in Japan as *kagome*, the basket weaver, and is the familiar family crest of one of Japan's leading aristocratic families.

Japanese researchers have been using this symbol and others like it to support the theory that some of the Lost Tribes eventually found their way to, and settled in, Japan. The late Professor Ikuro Teshima was a fervent believer in this theory and founded the Makuya cult, which is well-known for its unreserved admiration and support of the modern State of Israel.

In his book, *The Ancient Jewish Diaspora in Japan or the Tribe of Hada*, which was published in 1971, Professor Teshima suggests that in ancient times some Jewish tribes may have settled in Japan. The first researcher to suggest this was Dr. Yoshiro Saeki (1872–1965), a world-renowned expert on the subject of cults and offshoots of ancient Christianity in the East. Dr. Saeki studied Persian and Hebrew at Oxford, knew several other languages, and was a follower of the Scottish missionary McLloyd, who hypothesized that the Japanese are descendants of the Ten Tribes. On his return to Japan in 1907, Saeki visited the small island of Ikushima, where he discovered something which changed the whole course of his studies: the tomb of an ancient tribe called Hada and a temple called "Osake Jinja," "The Shrine of King David." A phonetic reading of the temple's Chinese name creates the word "David."

After forty years' research, Dr. Saeki concluded that the Hada tribe are part of the Jewish diaspora, which adopted the Christian religion at some later stage. This theory was supported by several Japanese experts in ancient Christian religion. According to Dr. Saeki, the tribe of Hada arrived in Japan during the first century A.D. or even earlier, long before the arrival of Buddhism, which came in the year A.D. 552.

During his years at the university, Professor Teshima served as Dr. Saeki's personal assistant and when Dr. Saeki died at the age of ninety-four, he took upon himself to continue with the research.

Further support for the theory of the ancient Hebrew tribe was afforded to Professor Teshima during a visit at the Temple of King David on the island of Ikushima, where he discovered the mask of the King Ko, on which was carved an ancient Chinese symbol meaning The Western territories of Syria and Persia. The high priest at the temple told him this was an ancient mask belonging to the tribe of Hada. When Teshima showed a photograph of the mask to his mentor, Dr. Saeki, the latter jumped for joy, saying that the mask looked exactly like the face of a Jew, with its hooked nose, round eyes, and beard—and nothing at all like a Japanese face.

On one of his visits to Israel, Professor Teshima, who believed that the Hada are descendants of the tribe Zebulun, even met with the late President Zalman Shazar and explained his theory. In his book, *The Jewish Diaspora in Japan,* Professor Teshima offers a long list of evidence identifying the Japanese Hada tribe with a nomadic Jewish tribe which made its way across the Silk Road to Japan.

It was in 1948, the year of the founding of the State of Israel, that Professor Teshima saw the Divine Presence over the volcano Asso. It was then, too, that he founded the Makuya cult, and swept with him thousands of Japanese believers in the Bible, personal closeness to God, and the divine mission of the Jewish people. His first visit to Israel in 1964 was followed over the years by dozens of groups of Makuya, who have become well-known for their excited dancing in the streets of Jerusalem and their outspoken support for the State of Israel. Cult members have also staged several demonstrations and rallies all over the world and have become a strong pro-Israel lobby in Japan.

During the 1973 Yom Kippur War, at a time when the whole world was suffering a huge energy crisis due to the Arab oil boycott—and Japan was especially hard hit—the Makuya took to the streets of Tokyo, in a giant demonstration in support of the State of Israel. As the demonstration ended, Professor Teshima collapsed and three weeks later, on Christmas Eve, he died at the age of sixty-three. Thousands of his disciples now follow in his footsteps, convinced of the holy alliance between the Japanese and Jewish nations and the sacred mission of the Jews on earth.

Another very popular cult in Japan, especially among Israel's young "backpackers," is known as "Bet Shalom" (house of peace), which was founded in 1938 by the Protestant priest, Takashi Otsugi, after having a vision of God. The priest was told during this vision that the Holy Land would be given to the Jews, and he was asked to pray every day for the peace of Jerusalem and the coming of the Messiah. When the priest tried to preach his doctrines, he was persecuted by groups of Japanese militants. After Japan suffered defeat in World War II, and as a result of the new democratic government which allowed freedom of religion, he was able to preach and teach with no fear of reprisal. The numbers of his followers grew quickly, and there are now about one hundred churches all over Japan belonging to this cult.

In 1971, a small hostel was built in the churchyard at Kyoto, whose sole purpose was to supply free hospitality to visiting Israelis. Similar hostels were founded in Tokyo and Hiroshima, and they offer Israelis hearty hospitality, a good breakfast, and much warmth and support. Groups of Israeli tourists often arrive to the sound of Hebrew songs, sung in the angelic voices of the church's Dawn Choir. In an atmosphere of support, surrounded by Hebrew books and after eating an excellent Israeli-style breakfast, what Israeli tourist wouldn't feel absolutely at home?

There are, however, other groups in Japan who insist that Jewish history in that country is very brief and insignificant—that unlike in Europe and America the Jews left no mark on Japanese society. Even the small number of Jews living in Japan in the middle of this century were swallowed up and integrated into the country's 124 million strong population. As the historian Takashi Morematso (who was a great supporter of the Jewish people) said: "Most of the Japanese don't even know what a Jew is. They wouldn't recognize one if they saw one, and they know absolutely nothing about the Jewish problem."

Nevertheless, one or two Jews did succeed in leaving their mark on Japanese history. One of these is the businessman Jacob Shiff, who helped the Japanese government to raise large financial loans in the U.S. and England during Japan's war with Russia. Although this was Shiff's personal revenge for the 1903 Kishniev riots (in which dozens of Jews were slaughtered), he was decorated by the Japanese government and dined at the table of the Emperor of Japan.

Japanese soldiers were first exposed to anti-Semitic propaganda, during the Russian Revolution, when fighting on the side of the anti-Bolsheviks in east Siberia. The Jews were blamed for the revolution. By 1919 the first anti-Semitic literature had appeared in the Japanese language and included sections from the *Protocols of the Elders of Zion*. This was soon the basis for all anti-Semitic literature in Japan.

Hitler's rise to power and the German alliance with Japan produced a new wave of anti-Semitism, which drew its inspiration from Nazi propaganda. Hitler's claims that behind the amassed force of the Allied war machine stood an avaricious little Jew fell on ready ears. Although the Japanese authorities never actually adopted an official anti-Semitic propaganda, certain public bodies undertook research into the "secret of the Jews," special institutions were formed to study the effect of Jews in the world, and papers were published on the subject. Dozens of books about the secret of Jewish power and the potential danger the Jews held for Japan were published in Japan during the war. The Japanese believed that German anti-Semitism was actually based on a fear of Jewish genius and alleged supernatural powers.

The Jewish question was raised frequently in the Japanese Parliament and press during the Second World War. The public was made aware of the issue by way of large exhibitions in the country's department stores. Although the Japanese government never adopted an official anti-Jewish policy, anti-Semitism was rife among intellectual circles in Japan and was widely accepted in the universities.

Tokyo's small Jewish community has been increasingly concerned in recent years by increasing evidence that anti-Semitism might be growing in Japan.

In fact, anti-Semitism has existed in Japan since the dawn of time. Thus, for example, one venerable Japanese dictionary defined a Jew "as avaricious, stingy," another called a Jew "a money lender," while a more modern one defines a Jew as "a person who is not to be trusted and whose main activity involves money."

Japanese businessmen often use the term "Jew" in the course of negotiations, meaning "with a character like this, you'd better beware and take care." Of course, they are very sophisticated about it and merely hint that "he must be a *kyu* and an *ichi*," *kyu*, meaning the number nine and *ichi*, one. Together they add up to ten, which in Japanese is *ju*, or Jew.

Japanese book shops are well stocked with books on Jews and Judaica. "The Jews are responsible for the fall of the dollar and the rise of the yen. All of Japan's economic problems are caused by the Jewish connection with the international money market. The Jews are working behind the scenes and controlling the leading American companies such as IBM, General Motors, Chrysler, Standard Oil, and others. The United States is in fact a Jewish superpower, the Jews control the media." This is only a partial list of so-called facts presented by the Japanese writer, Uno, in his books. Uno, who heads the Institute for the Study of the Middle East, defines himself as a "Christian fundamentalist." Over the past few years, his books about the Jewish issue have headed the Japanese best-seller lists for months on end. In his first book, *If You Know the Jews,*

You Know the World," Uno claims that it was the Jews who were responsible for the 1929 fall in the New York Stock Exchange, and that they are planning something similar for Japan. This book was especially popular among businessmen. Japan's large banks bought thousands of copies for their workers, as compulsory reading on the "state of international economics." His second book *If You Know the Jews, You Know Japan,* Uno declared confidently that the Jews' claims regarding the Holocaust are highly exaggerated.

Uno's books are not unique. Books about Jews by other Japanese "experts" feature photographs of Orthodox Jews on their jackets, or green banknotes, or a collage comprising portraits of Lenin, Kissinger, and Charlie Chaplin. The titles promise revelations on *The Jewish Program to Conquer the World, How to Read the Protocols of the Elders of Zion,* and *How to Succeed on the Stock Exchange Like the Jews.* Other books offer detailed descriptions of "Jewish genius" and contain informative suggestions on *How to Bring Up Your Child to be as Smart as a Jew.* Comic books show the Jew as a greasy old reprobate, with a thick cigar stuck between his fat fingers.

The Jews have been blamed, among other things, for the comics themselves. Serious articles in the newspapers complain that it is the Jews who are responsible for the flourishing comics industry in Japan, which causes so much distress to conscientious Japanese parents.

There is no shortage of anti-Semitism in magazines and newspapers, as well. An entire issue of a historical magazine was devoted to the subject, "The Jewishness of Mystery," in which it was claimed that the Jews were responsible for the Watergate scandal, and the corruption at Lockheed, in which a former Japanese prime minister was involved.

How can there be anti-Semitism in a country which has no Jews? And how can the Jews be a symbol of avarice and greed in a country which has such a short Jewish history? Dr. Teshima, a lecturer in Hebrew literature at a United States theological seminary, tried to answer precisely this question in a paper entitled "What Is Anti-Semitism Doing in Japan?"

Teshima, who describes Uno and his ilk as "ignorant vulgarians," explains that the recent bloom in anti-Semitic literature in Japan is symptomatic of the fear the Japanese have of the yen's increasing strength on the international money market, thus causing an economic crisis and bringing about the need to fire workers in

Japan's export industries. Uno's books provide superficial explanations and shallow solutions. Teshima sums up his paper by saying that, although there is no real danger of active anti-Semitism taking hold in Japan, this cancer must be cut out before it has the chance to spread.

Anti-Semitism appears in Japan because the nation feels threatened by the strange and unfamiliar world outside. The mere act of having *The Protocols of the Elders of Zion* translated into Japanese served to express confusion and the thin line between respect for the intelligence and wisdom of the Jews, and inherent fear of them. Since the reign of the Emperor Taisho (1912–1925), whenever the Japanese people have been overcome by a collective xenophobia, they have used the image of the Jew as scapegoat, although most Japanese have never even seen a Jew in their lives.

Professor Ben Ami Shiloni believes that although anti-Semitism in Japan drew its ideas and symbols from the anti-Semitism in Europe, the Japanese saw in the Jews the ultimate personification of the European culture which threatens their country. The stereotype of the successful, covetous Jew is none other than a caricature of Western Man, to whom these characteristics are attached all the time. Thus the double standard in relation to the Jew, who symbolizes everything that the Japanese both admire and hate in the West.

The Jew, therefore, is always a distant, dull threat, who symbolizes the evil beyond. Sometimes, when necessary, he is brought forward—as happened during the eighties, when the rising wave of anti-Semitism that washed over Japan expressed the fear of Western response to Japan's thriving economy and the threat Japan might pose to the world economy.

As the storm raged around his anti-Semitic books and made him into a wealthy man, Uno professed not to understand what all the fuss was about. He gave countless interviews, in which he claimed repeatedly that he was not anti-Semitic, and that he had written his books only as a sort of entertainment. The main objective of his books, he said, was to inform his readers about the Jewish religion and the biblical prophesies. He felt that "the books were very useful to the Japanese people, who are interested in getting to know themselves and their lives."

Uno himself headed Japanese missionary groups on several visits to Israel and even visited some of the government offices. One of the dignitaries honored by a visit was the late Prime Minister

Menahem Begin, who was warned of the dangers involved in a complete retreat from the Sinai Peninsula. He claimed also to have visited Yitzhak Navon, Shimon Peres, Yitzhak Shamir, and Geula Cohen.

Most of Uno's writings, however, have never reached the Japanese man-in-the-street. He may have heard some mention of Jews when he studied *The Merchant of Venice* in school. He knows nothing of the Holocaust, and as far as he is concerned, Israel is just another far-off country, which is sometimes involved in trouble.

Every day, at one of Tokyo's more crowded centers, the Shibuya railway station, you can see hoards of black-leather-clad Japanese youths dancing in front of the Yoyogi Park. Their stiff multicolored hair and metal decorations make them look for all the world like any other other group of punk rockers all over the western world. There they are, raising their arms in a stiff, Nazi salute to the joyful cries of their friends. Their swastikas and other Nazi decorations are bought in a popular Tokyo store with the revolting name of World's End, which sells all the Nazi kitsch you can imagine, from swastika pins to Third Reich flags and SS badges and framed pictures of Hitler. If you're interested, you can also get a good whip there as well. The shop itself is decorated with horrific drawings of skeletons dressed in striped concentration camp pajamas and photographs of crematoria.

A giant beer house that opened in 1990 in Tokyo's fashion center, the Omote-Sando, takes you straight into the atmosphere of Nazi Germany. The decor is an exact replica of the 1936 Berlin Olympics. Nazi flags, swastikas, and video clips of Hitler offer a spine-chilling backdrop for thirsty beer drinkers.

These people haven't read Uno's books, and they haven't exactly made a study of the Holocaust or of the Jews. All they're doing is having fun.

The Righteous Gentile

*I*t all began one morning when Yukiko Sugihara, wife of the Japanese Consul General in Kovna, Lithuania, looked out of her bedroom window to find the source of the strange noises coming up from the yard.

An odd-looking group of strangely dressed people, the men sporting long beards, stood huddled behind the locked back gate of the Consulate building. They sounded desperate, obviously crying for help. It was six o'clock in the morning, and as she stood there looking on in astonishment, the group grew larger by the moment.

Her life and that of her family changed beyond all recognition that late-August morning in 1940. Even had she had any suspicion of what awaited her, she most probably would never have considered acting any differently or making an effort to change the course of events.

In the drawing room of her small house in the coastal town of Ofuna, near Tokyo, beneath an oil picture of a sunset over Jerusalem, painted by her middle son, Yukiko is unable to stem her memories. The story pours from her lips for at least the thousandth time.

"My late husband ordered me to take the three children and hide in the bedroom closet until we were sure that the crowd outside was not hostile. At my husband's request, the housekeeper, Boris, went out to find out what was the meaning of their presence there. Boris reported that he had counted about two hundred people, who said that they would soon be joined by several thousand more. They were all Jewish refugees, who had made their way to Kovna from Eastern Poland, in an effort to escape the Nazis. They were so desperate that several of them even tried to climb over the fence into the Consulate area."

From that morning on, things would never be the same in the home of the thirty-nine-year-old Consul General Senpo Sugihara and his family. Sugihara had been posted to Lithuania in order to follow the movements of the Russian and German armies and to report his findings to the Japanese Foreign Ministry. He had been chosen for the job because he was fluent in Russian and six other European languages. Sugihara was, in fact, a spy who enjoyed diplomatic immunity.

"That morning," related Yukiko, whose lovely face seemed unaffected by the passing years, "we were exposed suddenly to all the horrors of the war. It was impossible to ignore the people at our gate. I was obliged to peep out at them from behind a curtain because every time they caught a glimpse of me, they would begin weeping and begging for help.

"At my husband's request, a five-man delegation was allowed into the house, and it was then that we learned for the first time what it was they wanted. All they asked for was to be supplied with transit visas so they could travel accross Japan to the Dutch island of Curaçao.

"It was the only way they could escape the Nazis, who were getting closer and closer to our region. That was also when we started hearing the horrible stories of the concentration camps and the annihilation of the Jews. We felt terribly responsible for them. Unfortunately, the week before, we had received an official order from the Soviet government to close down the Consulate. They had given us only two weeks to pack and organize our move. We realized that if we were to help the Jews, we had no time to lose, since every hour was fateful.

"My husband quickly sent a telegram to the foreign ministry in Tokyo, describing the situation and asking for urgent permission to issue the Jews visas. The reply was negative, and the crowd outside was getting larger with every passing day. We knew that if we didn't help them, they would die. My husband sent a second telegram, but it, too, was rebuked."

After two negative replies, Sugihara decided to bypass bureaucracy and the Japanese Foreign Office clerks. He sent an urgent telegram to Matsuoka the minister himself, in which he described the sorry plight of the refugees and reported that all they were so terribly in need of were twenty-one-day transition visas. Sugihara demanded a swift reply, since he had been ordered to leave Kovna. This telegram, too, was refused by the Japanese Foreign Office.

"For three days we were under siege," remembered Yukiko. "Our cook informed us that she had no intention of going out to shop, so that we were literally without food. Our three sons were still little, Hiroshi was four, Tsiaku two, and I was still breastfeeding a four-month-old baby. The fears and worry made my milk dry up, and the poor baby screamed all night. We were trapped in the house, and we couldn't stop talking to each other. My husband was the only Japanese representative at the Consulate, so I was the only one he could discuss things with. And throughout those confusing hours, we knew that my husband's diplomatic career was in the balance against the lives of all those people out there. After weighing up all our options, we decided to disobey the orders from the Japanese Foreign Office. This initiative on the part of my husband was considered extremely grave: a blatant disregard for official orders, especially during a time of war. But we were unable to put a career against the lives of hundreds of people. What would happen to us as a result of not following orders was absolutely incomparable with the bitter fate awaiting those Jews if we did nothing to help them."

All that time, while Sugihara and his wife were debating what to do, they had no way of knowing that, back in the Japanese Foreign Office, clerks were playing with the idea of settling the Jewish refugees from Europe in Manchuria, at that time a Japanese-occupied Chinese colony.

The book *The Fugo Plan,* written by the former chief rabbi of Japan, Marvin Tokayer, and published in 1982, revealed for the first time documents that prove Japan's colonial strategy and vision with regard to the Jews. The mastermind behind the program was Colonel Yasue Norihiro, who had translated the *Protocols of the Elders of Zion* into Japanese. After a tour of Israel in 1927 as a guest of the Zionist Leadership, Colonel Norihiro published his book, *The Jews*, in which he described the Jews as a powerful force whose aim it was to take over the world. Now Japan was making plans to use this power to her own ends. Japan was in need of clever, wily, experienced business people; wealthy and well-educated people, who would develop that primitive and obscure piece of land known as Manchuria. Here was a rare opportunity for Japan to open her gates to thousands of Jews. Nonetheless, none of the telegrams sent by Consul Sugihara received a positive reply, for the simple reason that this so-revolutionary plan had not yet received official approval.

Sugihara, who knew nothing of what was going on in the Japanese Foreign Office with regard to Manchuria, set the wheels in motion to save the Jews in Lithuania. Like any other well-organized clerk, he sent a telegram to Tokyo informing his employers that, in spite of everything, he was about to issue the visas. Then he went and told his news to the thousands waiting outside.

"When my husband told them of his decision, they became very agitated. Some of them tried to climb over the fence and get into the Consulate," Yokiko remembered. "My husband tried to calm them and explained that they would all receive a visa and that they would each have to wait patiently for their turn to come. Later we started handing them out numbers and the queue became more orderly."

From the early morning until late at night, Sugihara wrote out the visas himself, in his neat handwriting. Yukiko helped him. "Most of the applicants had no passports, so that the visas we issued had to be handwritten by my husband. Surprisingly, however, the more visas my husband managed to write—and there were hundreds of them, the queue got no shorter, in fact, it just kept growing."

Altogether, Sugihara issued some five thousand visas. He kept waiting for a response of some kind from Tokyo. But he heard nothing.

"They obviously couldn't imagine how many visas I was actually issuing every day," wrote Sugihara in his memoirs. In order to save the lives of as many Jews as possible, the family delayed by a week their departure from Kovna. "Even as we were leaving the house in Kovna on our way to our next posting in Prague, there were still people crowding around our gate, waiting for a visa. On the way to the railway and even through the train window, my husband was still writing out the permits, because all the rubber stamps were already packed away and he passed them over to the upheld hands on the platform."

Thanks to Sugihara, about five thousand Jews, most of them Yeshiva students and their families, were saved.

Sugihara and his courageous deed had very nearly fallen into oblivion. Very little of what happened to him and his family during and after the war was known to the Jews whose lives he helped to save. The Japanese Foreign Office, however, waited for Sugihara patiently for years, in order to settle up their score with him. Toward the end of the war, Sugihara and his family were captured by the Russian Army in Romania, his final posting, and thrown in a Siberian concentration camp together with German prisoners of war.

"We were the only Japanese family to be captured in Europe during the war," said Yukiko. "Life in the camp was hard. We suffered from the cold, hunger, and no medical supplies, but worst thing of all was the fear—we didn't know if we would be held in the concentration camp forever, and never be allowed to return to Japan. But after fifteen months, we were told that we could go back. We knew that the journey home would be a hard one, but we had no idea just how long and how hard."

Since the Russian railway had been damaged during the war, the family was told that they would have to make their way northward overland across Siberia to Japan. The Russians preferred to keep the fact secret that there was a Japanese family being held among the German prisoners of war, so they were forbidden to leave the train carriages throughout the entire six-month journey. Yukiko Sugihara's greatest fear the whole time was that her husband would not be permitted to return to Japan.

"We kept hearing rumors, that my husband, who spoke Russian as if it was his mother tongue, would be very valuable to the Russians, who wouldn't let him leave Russia that easily. All through the journey until we finally arrived at a small port inside Japan, I never stopped worrying."

In April 1947, the family arrived at a defeated, battle-torn Japan. In June, Sugihara was called to the Japanese Foreign Office. He was prepared for the fact that he would be made to resign, like all the other diplomats who had been in Japan's Foreign Service during the war.

The procedure involved the presentation of a letter of resignation. He could then expect to receive an alternative position, or a recommendation for a senior position in civilian life. But the clerks who accepted Sugihara's letter of resignation informed him that he was not entitled to a recommendation, and in Japan, anyone who doesn't have a recommendation may as well be dead because he'll never be able to find a job.

In his memoirs, Sugihara was bitter about having been dishonorably dismissed from the Foreign Service for disobeying orders during his term of office in Kovna.

"I don't quite understand what happened," he writes in his memoirs. "After Kovna, I was Consul General in Prague, in Germany and then in Romania. Why did the Japanese Foreign Office wait so long to punish me?"

Sugihara, who was unable to find any other kind of work, began selling lightbulbs so that his family wouldn't starve. But Yukiko admits that her husband was never a great success as a door-to-door salesman.

Fortunately, and thanks to his perfect English, he was able to find work as a translator with the American occupying forces. This gave him a regular income and meant that his family could survive the difficult years after the Second World War.

Later, Sugihara moved from one job to another until he finally found a good position with a Japanese commercial company, in whose service he was even sent to Moscow, where he remained for sixteen years.

All those years, the Jews whose lives he had saved had been trying to track him down. Some of these Holocaust survivors had settled in Israel and risen to senior government positions, like the former Minister of Religious Affairs Zerah Warhaftig, and the former Knesset Speaker, Menahem Savidor—but Sugihara seemed to have disappeared off the face of the earth.

Still, there was one of the survivors who never gave up. Mr. Yehushua Nishri, who by a strange coincidence, returned to Japan, not as a refugee this time, but as economic attaché at the Israeli Embassy in Tokyo, spent every spare moment tenaciously trying to find the man who had saved his life. In 1968, he finally succeeded in finding Sugihara, who was back in Tokyo on a holiday from Moscow.

Sugihara was immediately invited to visit Israel, where, in a special ceremony, he was given the title "Righteous Gentile." The prime minister of Israel asked him what the State could do for him, and his request was granted forthwith. Sugihara's youngest son, Noviko, who was born after the war, was accepted to study at the Hebrew University of Jerusalem. Today, Noviko speaks Hebrew like a native, works in the diamond industry, and spends most of his time traveling between Israel and Japan. Sugihara's oldest son, Hiroshi, serves as a commercial intermediary between Japan and Israel. The middle son, who is an artist and lives in the family home in Tokyo, paints the landscapes of Jerusalem and the desert from pictures his father sent him during his visit to Israel.

All three brothers and Sugihara's widow, Yukiko, who despite her advanced age has lost none of her vitality and beauty, work hard at restoring their father's lost honor. In Israel Sugihara is a hero and a savior, and has even had a forest planted in his name; but people in Japan are not honored for disobeying orders, even if this meant saving lives—and the Japanese Foreign Office has a long memory.

Sugihara the elder died in 1986. Shortly before his death he was asked if he had any regrets at having sacrificed a promising diplomatic career for the sake of saving the lives of Jewish refugees, and all the pain and suffering this caused his family. "As a human being," replied Sugihara, "it was the only thing I could do."

It was only fifty years after Sugihara had saved the lives of those Jewish refugees in Kovna that his name was finally absolved. With the fall of communism in the Soviet Union and the liberation of Lithuania, Sugihara's name was cleared there, too, and a street was named in his honor. It was only then that the Japanese Foreign Office sent a representative to visit the widow. Thus, at last, she received a hint that her husband's humanitarian act was recognized formally by the Japanese government. In a brief item in the *Jerusalem Post* dated October 22, 1991, readers in Israel were informed that the Japanese government had decided to exonerate the name of the Righteous Gentile, Consul General Sugihara.

With her husband's name finally exonerated, Yukiko Sugihara now involves herself in giving lectures both in Japan and all over the world in favor of peace and against militarism and racism. Sometimes she quotes a poem she wrote in the train, when the dozens of outstretched hands begged for their passport to life:

> The window of the train rushes by
> as hands reach out
> begging
> for a passport to life

And Yukiko ends her story with these words: "I am sure that my husband is watching over us from up there, and that he is very satisfied."

Transient Community

*T*he last time anyone saw the elderly Jewish gentleman whom we shall call Mr. Landsman, at Tokyo's Jewish center was when he was about to move into a retirement home. That was the day he brought with him a long metal crate full of books, clothes, and household utensils, which he wanted stored in the center's basement. That's what he told anyone who asked about the contents of the crate. People said that the crate also contained a jar of ashes, the remains of his dead Japanese wife, with whom he had lived for forty years in Japan, and were willing to swear that they had heard him asking the center's rabbi if the jar of ashes could be buried with him in a Jewish grave, when his time came. Boaz, the building's deputy concierge, swears that since the crate was left in his safekeeping, he was disturbed each night at the same hour, by eerie sounds and whisperings. Even the ear-piercing rock music constantly blaring through the sophisticated sound system he is so proud of did nothing to silence the strange voices from below.

But, apart from the regular appearances of Landsman's wife in the darkened basement of the elegant Hiru-O Jewish Community Center in the richest of Tokyo's residential quarters, it seems that Mr. Landsman himself has been forgotten by everyone.

Although he had lived in Japan for over forty years, he never became fluent in the Japanese language, and since his friends at the old people's home never learned Yiddish or English, he was destined to live out the remainder of his life in total silence and loneliness. The heads of the Jewish community who had donated the money necessary to keep him in the Catholic charity institution could not understand why he chose to live out the last days of his life in that place, rather than returning to his homeland and moving into a respectable home in Miami, with other people of his own age and background.

Every few months the community's rabbi would remember Mr. Landsman and take the trouble of visiting him at the retirement home, where he lived with a few dozen other Japanese, ancient and wrinkled, and dry like parchment. The rabbi came back from one of these visits one day, with a strange look on his face.

"It's a miracle," he told anyone who was willing to listen to him. "You wouldn't believe it, but Mr. Landsman asked to read the Sidur with me, and he read it wonderfully, truly wonderfully."

And here I would point out that Mr. Landsman, who was nearing the very distinguished age of one hundred years, was completely and incurably senile and very often did not remember to whom he was talking. The day after the sudden and unexpected reading in the Sidur, Mr. Landsman died. He was buried according to tradition in the Jewish cemetery in the port town of Yokohama. It so happened that the jar containing his wife's ashes completely slipped everyone's mind, and, to Boaz's great consternation, the Japanese lady never found eternal peace and continued her rather noisy search for her dead husband's remains.

A typhoon was blowing the day he was buried, and the only people at the graveside was the rabbi and a *minyan* of picture-selling Israelis, who decided to forgo a day of business for the sake of a greater good. The small gathering was joined by two short, elderly, lilac-haired American ladies from the Bronx who had come to accompany their older brother on his final journey. The sisters' story dispelled at last the mystery which had always surrounded Mr. Landsman.

During the Second World War, Mr. Landsman had been a well-known and highly respected physicist, one of the team of scientists who planned and produced the first atom bomb.

"He couldn't handle it," said one of the sisters. "When he saw the pain and tragedy he had helped create with his own hands, he swore an oath to atone for what he had done. He joined the International Peace Movement and came to Japan in order to teach and preach peace. He refused to leave Japan, wanting to live out his life in the country which he had helped cause such unforgivable sorrow."

Mr. Landsman was only one of 350 Jews who constituted what was known by the distinguished, and somewhat demanding, term "Japan's Jewish Community."

Their redbrick headquarters was funded by the wealthier members of the community. Its street wall proudly bears a large Star of David and a menorah. The center offers very expensive religious services. It has a Conservative synagogue, with no separate section for female worshipers, and a collection of ancient holy books from Russia, a ritual bath, with black acid rainwater (from Tokyo's polluted air), a Judaica library, and a Hebrew school.

The center also supplies community and sport facilities, rather like the British Colony clubs in the exotic East: a swimming pool, a restaurant, library, a shop selling Jewish souvenirs, and a great many parties and elegant dinners, on all the High Holy Days or whenever a distinguished guest arrives from Israel.

"Ours is a transient community," the veteran chairman, Mr. Citrin, liked to say of his flock. "They come here for a year or two, or three, and then they go back to where they came from." Unlike them, Mr. Citrin, who was born in China, was in Japan for good. Apart from him, the Jewish community includes a few old Russian, Yiddish, or heavily accented English-speaking widowers, married to nubile young Japanese maidens, and a handful of very wealthy elderly widows, some of them distinguished Japanese matrons, who have kept up their connection with Judaism for the sake of the children. Another group consists of the Holocaust survivors, several Jews of Polish origin, whose lives were saved by Consul General Sugihara in Kovna. And a few Jews of Iraqi, Persian, or Indian origin, who hold a commercial monopoly over sales of pearls and precious stones in the Far East. All these live in pleasant harmony and with few disagreements, alongside some American families with small, noisy children who attend Sunday school every week—and the families of Israeli diplomats and Israeli commercial representatives in Japan. The only real disagreements, and these did tend to arise at regular intervals, concerned the restaurant's menu, which at the time was nonkosher. As doyens of the community, the Russians demanded that the menu include borscht, chicken Kiev, piroshki, and stroganoff (which they wanted made out of Kobe beef, for which beer-fed calves are massaged daily until they are slaughtered, a process which produces a particularly tender texture to the meat). The dishes of Mother Russia were prepared for them by Chef Otto, who was especially sensitive to their gastronomical whims.

The Americans, who made up the community's noisy majority, were serious devotees of health food and demanded that all the cholesterol-heavy, saturated fatty, putrefying dead meat be replaced on the menu by a salad bar, like the one they were used to at the American Club. And we Israelis, we were pining for good old falafel, tahini, and moussaka, the kind we used to get at home.

No compromise, however, could solve the serious disagreements around the gefilte fish issue. This dish had to be prepared each year for the Jewish holidays at Passover and New Year and the kind that dominated this particular kitchen belonged to the Russian school of thought—heavy, solid, and dark brown in color, from being cooked in caramel. An unusual temporary coalition was formed between the Israeli and American contingents, who demanded that their fish cakes be lighter-colored and finer-textured. Soup knaidelach presented another problem each springtime, and special meetings were held to discuss the various schools of thought, those championing the hard kind and those the soft variety. A different recipe was tried each year, but it was never possible to please all of the people all of the time. The Russians liked theirs airy and light, while the Israelis were firm in their demand for the more solid kind of knaidelach.

Old Rachmanian, the Persian jewel dealer, never took part in the noisy culinary arguments—he had found himself the ideal solution. Nor did he ever eat at the community table. "Too expensive and tasteless," he used to tell me when he came for morning prayers on Saturdays, holidays, and at the beginning of each month. His own personal valet-cook-waiter–private secretary, whom he had brought with him from India, was adept at preparing a wide variety of the Persian Jewish dishes he loved. He kept a huge freezer at his home, in which he stored large quantities of carefully packaged cuts of kosher meat, imported from Denver, Colorado, and Australia. On his eighty-fifth birthday, the merchant's seven sons and their wives came from all the corners of the United States to collect their old father and take him back with them. The huge freezer remained in the apartment. It was impossible to get it out through the door, and no one understood how it had been carried up the five stories and pushed through the narrow opening in the first place. Rachmanian couldn't remember either. "It was so long ago," he said, "who could remember something like that after so many years?"

It was easy enough to satisfy the gastronomic passions of ninety-five-year-old Mr. Brown. He never made any complaints about the quality of the food on his regular Sunday visits to the center's buffet lunch. He used to tell me such obscene jokes about strudel and borscht that even people at the other end of the long room could see me blushing to the roots of my hair. Mr. Brown used to like to talk about everyone with everyone, but he never volunteered any information about himself or the reason for his long sojourn in Japan. Stubborn rumors had it that he had lived in Tokyo since the end of the Second World War. They would whisper that he had actually been a CIA agent, "planted" in Japan undercover posing as a toy salesman. He had liked the place and was more successful in business than he had been as a secret agent, so he decided to stay, even after the death of his Japanese wife. Every winter he would fly to Hawaii, together with other elderly members of the community, who found the harsh Japanese winters too cold for their old bones to bear. One frozen December Sunday, he turned up as usual at the restaurant and told me that he was leaving for Hawaii the following day, to warm himself up. As usual, he tried to attract my attention with some of the most obscene jokes I had ever heard in my life. When he realized he was getting nowhere with me, he made off in the direction of another old man, and tried his dirty joke on him. The old man blushed deeply and looked down at his fingernails in embarrassment. Mr. Brown went on his way and the next day, as he landed in Hawaii, he collapsed and died.

At a management meeting later that week, the Israeli mainte-
nance worker told Mr. Brown's last joke, the one I was unwilling
to listen to, and it was the foulest one of all.

Narkiss was another member of the community. She was a
Belgian-born artist, married to a Japanese man, who was also the
only one in the center to read the Israeli daily, *Ha'aretz*. Wherever
he went he would leave behind him flimsy pages of the newspaper's airmail, overseas version—floating in the swimming pool, in
the dining room, and on the library floor. The Hebrew he spoke,
which he had picked up during his few years in Israel, was better
than that of his wife and their daughter, who looked for all the
world like a Japanese doll and chattered freely in French, Japanese, and Hebrew.

I could go on to describe Ruthi, the widow, a Japanese convert
to Judaism, who had married a Chinese-born Jew, and who, after
his death, had become a pillar of the community and a devout
Jewess—so much so that Israelis meeting her for the first time
were sure she had been born and raised a Jew. And the Jewish
lawyer who owned a collection of old and rare Japanese artifacts,
and was also, of course, married to a Japanese lady; or the Jewish
editor of a popular best-selling Japanese daily pornography magazine, or the Jewish shipping magnate, and others, too many to
mention.

How, in fact, did the Jews find their way to Tokyo?

After the 1905 Russian Revolution and the 1917 Bolshevik Revolution, many Jews escaped from Russia and made their way to
Manchuria and China. Some went on to Japan. With the Japanese
invasion of Manchuria in 1931 and the atrocities perpetrated
against the Chinese population, the Jews picked up their chattels
and moved to Shanghai, Hong Kong, and Japan. They were later
joined by the Holocaust survivors from Kovna. At the end of the
Second World War, the Tokyo Jewish community flourished. A
large number of American servicemen were stationed in Japan
with the Occupation Forces in 1945 and joined the community of
Jews who had come from China. Later, when Japan had recovered
from the trauma of war and began redeveloping her economic
power, Jews started flowing in from all corners of the earth and settling in Tokyo. Jews are the most insignificant of Japan's minori-

ties and are totally swallowed up in Tokyo, that gigantic city which houses some twenty-four million people during daytime hours. Despite its size, the Tokyo Jewish community holds a place of honor in all the city's foreigners' clubs. Members of the Tribe of Moses have made their presence felt all over the place. At the Foreign Press Club, in the computer companies, as members of the PTAs in the International schools, at sports tournaments, at the American Club, and especially at the Sunday morning antiques fair at the Togo Shrine and in the Yoyogi Park, where the opening ceremonies took place for the last Tokyo Olympics.

Members of the Jewish community could be seen every Sunday morning, touring the fairs and markets of Japan, in a never-ending search for Japanese antiques. Lectures, family outings, and any other events were pushed aside to make time for the obsessive collection of made-in-Japan bric-a-brac. The families would get together in the evenings and compare notes with each other on the bargains they had managed to pick up during the day. What, in fact, were they looking for? Painted silks, kimonos, antique pictures, Japanese wood carvings, colorful Imari pottery, wooden Japanese sideboards, Japanese dolls in kimonos, fine glassware, exquisitely beautiful bamboo carvings, and, of course, all sorts of objects and things which would just lie uselessly around their homes. I don't know who it was who infected all the others with the collecting bug. Most people would probably point an accusing finger at Shmuel, the center's president, a gentleman from the West Coast of the USA, who had come to Japan on a four-year mission for a computer firm. His home got gradually more and more stuffed with objets d'art, which were hung on the walls, placed on the floors, and filled every available space in the closets, sideboards, or shelves. If you opened a closet door in his home, you were seriously risking having an ancient, precious, and very fragile Japanese vase fall on your head.

Nothwithstanding the nastiness with which the community referred to its president's mania for collecting, one particular find of his succeeded in disturbing everyone's peace of mind. It was on the eve of Yom Kippur in 1989, which fell on a Sunday—market day—and the president arrived back at the center in a state of extreme agitation, holding a parcel under his arm, wrapped in a Japanese kimono. The center was buzzing with activity at the time, with last-minute preparations for the final meal before the fast, and the synagogue was undergoing a thorough cleaning and scrubbing. Nevertheless, it was impossible to ignore the look of excitement and joy on our president's face, as he burst through the open Chinese-carved library doors.

"You must have a look at what I found today in the market," he said to no one in particular.

We dragged ourselves slowly toward him, as Boaz whispered to me angrily, "I wonder what he's found this time. A stuffed cat from the days of the pharaoh, no doubt, or broken bits from the tablets of the decalogue."

Irritatingly slow and with hands shaking, Shmuel pulled the painted kimono off the article he was holding reverently in his hands. When he had finished, we stood there openmouthed.

"You found that in a street market?" we asked in disbelief.

Even the most cynical among us could not remain indifferent to his find. What we saw was a Torah scroll, dressed in an exquisite red velvet covering and decorated with silver pomegranates and bells, which we later discovered turned out to have been cast in the style of the Far East, as if commissioned by a Tibetan or an Indian craftsman. The covering was removed carefully to reveal the scrolled parchment, which had been written with incredible clarity by a scribe.

"I couldn't believe my eyes, either," he said. "I saw the silver pomegranate poking out from between all the other junk and Imari plates. When I asked to have a look at the book, the Japanese vendor admitted that he didn't really know what it was, but that he thought it might have been written by some mysterious sect, somewhere in the East. I couldn't get any more out of him than that."

"And what about the price? How much did you pay him?" we asked impatiently, well aware of the outlandish prices usually paid for Torah scrolls.

"The vendor reckoned that he'd paid a high price for it and asked me to give him two hundred dollars."

The rabbi, who had been informed of the Day of Atonement miracle, came running up. "It's truly a genuine king's ransom," he whispered in awe, as he examined the scroll, "and on Yom Kippur, of all nights."

The same Torah scroll was used that year in the Simchat Torah festivities. No explanation has yet been found as to how such a valuable piece of Judaica found its way to a Japanese antique fair in the yard of a Buddhist temple in Tokyo.

The End of the World

*W*hen the end of the world comes, some Japanese will flock in by the thousands to Takayama City. They alone will be saved from the catastrophe which will destroy the world. The survivors will re-populate the world with a new race, pure, strong, and free of thousands of years of warped history.

Takayama City in the middle of the Japanese Alps, on the island of Honshu, is prepared for the end of the world. Everywhere you look in the tourist town of Takayama reveals ample evidence of the approaching Apocalypse.

But try to find the temple of the Mahikari sect in books or maps and you won't be able to. It doesn't appear on municipal maps of Takayama. If you ask a municipal clerk about the temple, he will shrug his shoulders and pretend he didn't understand the question, as if there was something to be ashamed of, hidden away. But try as they might, the town's inhabitants cannot ignore the existence of the strange entity of Sukyo Mahikari, the Temple at the Center of the Earth, towers over the entire town, far above the straw roofs of the traditional wooden buildings. For believers, it is the holiest place on earth. About ten miles out of town, on the very top of Mount Kurai, stands the gigantic temple with a sparkling, solid gold roof which dazzles everyone for miles around. A huge Star of David adorns the roof's golden edge.

In 1959, Okada, the sect's founder, fell off his horse and broke his back. He then had a spiritual revelation: the God Su appeared before him and asked him to found a pure and chaste community, free of all the evils and materialistic poisons which contaminate the human race and threaten to bring humanity to the very brink of extinction.

The God Su revealed himself again in 1984, as Okada lay unconscious on his deathbed, and described to him the holy Temple of Solomon in Jerusalem, which he wanted recreated in his honor. The plans for the temple were transferred spiritually to Okada's sixty-year-old daughter, Keyshu Okada, who built an accurate replica of Jerusalem's First Temple atop Mount Kurai. Okada died in 1984 and never saw the new temple. The sect is now led by his daughter.

According to the temple's publicity department, "none of the laborers fell sick, nor were there any accidents or injuries while the temple was built, and the town of Takayama enjoyed wonderful weather during the construction." The brochure goes on: "Many have joined the sect as a result of the wonders bestowed upon the laborers by the God Su."

The temple is the size of a sports stadium and topped with a golden dome, which cost some forty-five billion yen (about 450 million dollars). It is generously decorated with Stars of David around its perimeter, on its windows, and inside the hall itself. For the sake of symmetry, no doubt, there are gigantic swastikas on the pillars flanking the temple's entrance.

Members of the sect explain that the top point of the Star of David symbolizes God, and the lower point, man. The two points on either side symbolize the harmony and reciprocal relationship between God and his creations. Aware of our sensitivity, as Israelis, to the huge swastikas, the temple's PR man explains that this is actually a prehistoric symbol belonging to ancient religions, which signifies four different powers opening and closing clockwise and counterclockwise.

The sect considers itself an essential part of the salvation of the world. Its members are responsible for creating a heaven on earth. The human race, brainwashed by the evils of materialism, has forgotten God and the real purpose for its earthly existence. It has created spiritual pollution and fouled the environment. The solution lies in the purification of souls and a return to spirituality. One of the sect's objectives is to practice purification, which they achieve by reflecting an ethereal light from the palms of their hands. This technique is so simple that even a child can learn it in a three-day course. The light cures the ills of the soul and the body, purifies one of all depravity and contamination, and points the way to the path of righteousness. The light must also be shone over fields, over a good meal, and over passersby, since the more people exposed to the light, the quicker the world can be cleansed of its troubles. It is not necessary to go as far as Takayama in order to benefit from the ethereal light. People passing by the busy Tokyo railway station, Shibuya, may be asked politely by sect members to soak in the light shining from the palms of their hands. In Takuyuma, on a gray building with a large Star of David on its front, it is possible to transcend reality, spread out on tatami mats, and enjoy the ethereal light shining from the hands of a sect follower. Through the teachings of the God Su, the sect has recruited about half a million believers in Japan, South America, Australia, and Europe.

Once a month, thousands of believers meet to synchronize their positive energy. However, unlike their god, whose philosophy is one of humility and modesty, the High Priestess Keyshu, her father's successor, is extremely conspicuous in her ostentatious kimonos, each of which is valued at several thousand dollars. Only she is admitted to the the inner sanctum at the Mahikari Temple, which no one else has ever seen.

Devotees of the sect believe that their temple is the source of ethereal light on earth and it is open to believers in all religions: Christians, Moslems, Hindus, Buddhists, and even Jews. The God Su is common to all of them.

According to Professor Sosumo Mazuno of the theological department of the University of Tokyo, some 20 percent of Japan's population are involved in one way or another in the new religions. New religions were already emerging in Japan about 150 years ago, but only after World War II, when restrictions on religion were abolished, did new religions flourish. Some sprang up immediately after the end of the war, like *Denshinkio,* the religion of electricity, which worships Thomas Edison. Some 720 new religions were registered in Japan in 1951, and were it not for laws preventing tax fraud by religious organizations, their numbers would have increased at a terrifying rate. Japan's rapid economic growth during the early 1970s coincided with a parallel surge of new religions. All large bookstores have entire departments set aside for books on spiritualism, meditation, telekinesis, UFOs, and supernatural phenomena.

The devotees of some new religions deify the sect's leader, and treat him or her as a god. Many other religions do not demand that their worshipers follow religious ritual—their only objective is curing physical or mental ailments. The Japanese on the whole have tolerant attitudes to the issue of religion and leave it mostly up to the individual. A Japanese will suffer no inner conflict if, during a single day, he lights incense to the gods in a Shinto temple, attends a Buddhist funeral—and gets married in a Protestant church in the evening. The Japanese are pragmatic about religion. A new religion might prove helpful now and again.

Today's new religions are partly the result of the urbanization of Japan after the Second World War, when millions of people migrated to the industrial cities, desperately seeking work. They abandoned traditional mores along with their villages, where religion held an important position in everyday life. These new city dwellers flocked to new religions, in response to the overwhelming pressures of life in industrialized, postwar Japan. New religions pop up in Japan at a rate of more than one hundred a year, offering everything: exorcism, prayers for the salvation of intelligent extraterrestials, and utopian pipe dreams.

How these new religions survive financially is a mystery. Claims that many of these religions take unfair advantage of their tax-exempt status are probably true.

I exited the railway station near my home. A man wearing a pink elephant mask, stepped up, offering bags of oranges and white balloons with pictures of happy elephants to the passersby. The passengers walked past him quickly, ignoring him. I stopped, curious. Pleased, he pushed a bag full of fragrant oranges tied with ribbons at me and handed a balloon to my son, who stood there staring, wide-eyed.

Holding my loot, I made my way to the platform and joined the silent passengers, waiting for their train. Suddenly I noticed that I was alone with my son. The long line of Japanese people I had just joined had vanished. I held the bag of oranges in one hand, while my other hand held on to my son, proudly flying his helium balloon. Suspicious glances slanted in my direction. I looked down at my clothes. There seemed nothing wrong with them. My son, too, looked no different than he always did. Suddenly an old Japanese woman, bent-backed and dressed in a gray kimono, made her way toward me. Watched by the admiring eyes of her countrymen, who kept a safe distance from me and my son, she pulled the bag of oranges out of my hand and grabbed at the balloon. *"Dame,"* she said. (Forbidden, taboo.) She repeated it several times.

I was astonished at the abrupt way she had broken one of the strongest taboos of Japanese etiquette—one must not interfere with or disturb the peace of a stranger. I assumed that she had a good reason for her actions, and that my son and I were in danger of some sort. I threw the bag of oranges in the nearest garbage can and, despite my son's loud protests, released the balloon, which flew up to the blackened ceiling of the subway. Only then did people return to stand next to me, with the same poker-faced intensity which gave away nothing of the minidrama which they had just seen. This was my first experience of that detested sect, the *Om-Shinari-Kiu,* or the Supreme Truth.

This sect practices celibacy, self-mortification—holding yoga poses for hours on end, lengthy fasts, and long periods of solitary confinement. When the Tokyo police raided the sect's stronghold and found starving human skeletons, their leader, Shoko Asahara, was living in luxury. His bulging stomach and fat, rosy cheeks bore witness that he did not deny himself the pleasures of the flesh.

The more widespread of these religions have become wealthy and powerful. The best known, *Soka Gakai,* boasts over six million followers, schools, a university, control of the Komaito political party—part of the governing coalition—and a publishing empire.

Another group, with more than five million followers, is the *Risho Kosei Kai,* which owns a huge pink temple, built in the shape of a wedding cake, a hospital, and the largest concert hall in Japan. One of the sect's leaders goes on peace-preaching missions around the country. His eventual aim: receiving the Nobel Peace Prize.

Biako Shinkokai, the White Light Organization, is the religious group that prays for peace for a "superior existence." Its believers pray for all 168 countries with which Japan has diplomatic relations. Israel is one. The Israeli Embassy in Japan receives a large bouquet of plastic flowers from the group on Israel's Day of Independence. A note saying, "Pray for World Peace" is attached to a broad white ribbon around the everlasting flowers.

Many sects use aggressive marketing methods, such as the

Kofuko-No-Kagaku, Human Science and Happiness, which has already recruited some forty thousand devotees. The sect's leader is Riohu Okawa, who claims that he alone has access to a spiritual level defined as "the ninth dimension." He channels Christ, Buddha, Confucius, Mohammed, Elijah, Nostradamus, and many others, including Beethoven, Picasso, and Van Gogh. Of all these, the *Om-Shinari-Kiu* cult represents the most serious threat to the serene population of Japan. Its members are the ones behind the friendly elephant masks.

On March 20, 1995, Japan and the world were appalled when several containers of Sarin (a poisonous nerve gas) exploded in Tokyo subway stations, painfully killing twelve and injuring more than five thousand people. Seventy-five of them critically. Police raided sect headquarters but failed to find its leader, Shoko Asahara. Dozens more nerve gas canisters were found. Members of the sect were preparing for the end of the world in the year 2000, anticipating a world war which would eradicate all evil. Only the righteous members of their sect would survive.

Despite the far-reaching manhunt for sect members, poisonous gas exploded again in the subway station at Yokohama. Not content with killing their own countrymen, the sect also prepared a "gift of love" for the American people. Another gas attack a month after the one in Tokyo, this time in Disneyland. The *Baltimore Sun* reported that two Japanese males were apprehended at Los Angeles International Airport two days before the planned attack. The two had with them written instructions for preparing the lethal gas and a videocassette giving full details of the target area.

Apart from the great wealth and valuable property their leaders have accumulated, the only thing these religious sects have in common is total superficiality. Not one offers any discernible wisdom or philosophy. Most offer escapism and a sense of social belonging, to their believers.

Japan's economic conglomerates are suspicious of workers who follow the new religions. This is an issue that potential workers must resolve before being hired. Japanese conglomerates hold that membership in a religious sect constitutes a conflict of interest and detracts from the employee's absolute loyalty to his employer.

Japanese sociologists claim that people who seek out new religions are actually attempting to escape the boredom of their lives.

They believe that Japanese society is materially wealthy but spiritually poor. Many people in Japan suffer from anxiety and permanent stress and from other psychological disorders as well. Other sociologists reason that the Japanese, unable to keep up emotionally with their country's accelerating modernization, tend to feel that the end of the world is near. New religions offer salvation for troubled souls, cures for psychosomatic illnesses, calming meditation for anxiety, and a feeling of belonging. Thus, the new religions have become a form of psychological therapy for the masses.

Take, for example, the aged teacher Sengo-Ku, for whom Japanese women abandon their husbands, children, parents, and lifelong ambitions. Dozens of girls and young women, some of whom have been recorded as missing by the Japanese police, have turned up in a quasi-Christian commune in the southern island of Kyushu.

The media have been hurling insults at the sect's leader for years, calling him a pimp and an old adulterer, and accusing him of keeping a harem. Because of media persecution, Sengo-Ku and his flock moved out of Tokyo and settled in Kyushu. There, they continue to hold their services and rituals, far from the public eye and away from the prying, sensation-seeking media.

The media has rarely let up hounding and harassing him, and because of this Sengo-Ku has always refused to be interviewed. When I decided to arrange a meeting with him, my Japanese colleagues teased me, saying that I would have as much chance of talking to him as I would Emperor Hirohito. My Japanese friends did not take into account that Sengo-Ku believed the Jewish nation would be ultimately responsible for peace on earth. I asked him for an interview and did not forget to mention that I was an Israeli. He and several followers traveled seven hundred miles to Tokyo by Shinkansen—the Japanese fast train.

Sengo-Ku arrived at our meeting accompanied by six well-dressed, beautifully madeup, lovely, young women. These women, whom he referred to as "Daughters of Zion," were all dressed in smart black-and-white suits, for reasons of modesty and so that they would not be distracted from their scriptural study by wearing bright colors. Each one wore a gold Star of David with a crucifix at its center—the sect's sign.

With care and the soft, feminine concern that daughters might extend to an ailing father, they surrounded their leader, who turned to them with unspoken understanding.

Sengo-Ku (the women called him *"ochan"*—uncle) was dressed in an expensively cut suit, and did not fit the poisonous image the Japanese media presented of him. He had been born and raised in a devout Buddhist family, and founded the sect in 1960, after he experienced a religious vision during which he had seen the first Hebrew, Abraham. He realized that he had been chosen for a mission, and began spreading the word, and pamphlets, which he handed out to passersby at bus stops and railway stations in his hometown of Osaka. After dozens of women and girls left home to join him, Sengo-Ku became a controversial figure, so much so that the issue was raised in the Japanese Diet Parliament.

He spoke in his defense. "It is hard for outsiders to understand us. Japanese society is based on clan and family life, and our kind of extended family does not fit this mold. The young women with me did not leave a family; they returned to one. They did not desert a husband, they have found him. God is our Father, we are a family, and everyone is equal before God." He added that the underage girls in his sect ran away from home because of trouble with their parents. Their parents, instead of being pleased that the girls return to school and live within a warm, supportive, religious family headed by Sengo-Ku, are actually suing him for seducing juveniles.

The sect's women are known as "Daughters of Zion," because of "Jerusalem, Zion, which has played, and is yet to play, an important role in the history of the world." Together with their leader, they live in a large seven-room house, with a big prayer hall. Housework and cooking is shared equally among all the women.

The sect runs on a regular daily schedule. Mornings are devoted to Bible study both New and Old Testatments, in Japanese and in translations into various other languages, with the aim of finding the version closest to the original Hebrew. In the evening the women undergo a metamorphosis. From serious, modest, studious, and bashful young ladies, they turn into a different species: heavily madeup and dressed in seductive clothes. They then go down to the sect's nightclub, which is also known as Daughters of Zion. There they work as hostesses.

My questions regarding their occupation brought on a wave of giggles, well hidden, according to Japanese tradition, behind dainty, upraised hands. No, they do not have intimate relations with their gentlemen guests. Their job is to pour wine and engage in religious discussion. The atmosphere in the nightclub is oddly religious. Two Bibles are placed at the entrance and the coasters on the tables bear biblical quotations. The clients keep these coasters as good-luck charms. And the clients are not barflies, but men with religious tendencies. Later, the women admit to me that many of the men who come to the club do so out of curiosity.

Why do they work at this profession?

"We have to make a living at something, don't we?" say the women, their eyes wide and innocent. No, they don't want to marry, or go back to their husbands. Their religious studies give them total satisfaction. In Japan, they believe, the family is the most important thing in a woman's life. But they have a family, and what's more, they also have God.

Sengo-Ku, who came all the way from the southern island of Kyushu in order to meet me, the first Israeli woman he had ever laid eyes on, never stopped talking about the creation of the Jewish State, its importance to world unity, and of the stupidity of the Western Christian world, which is unable to understand the importance of Israel's mission on earth. "The Jewish nation has special qualities, and ultimately will be responsible for peace on earth. We are nurtured by the love of the God of Israel, the Jewish nation, and its teachings, and if other countries felt as we do, then peace will come to the world."

"Sengo-Ku, what is it you want most?"

"To bring all the women of my sect to Israel, and see with my own eyes the land of Abraham and the birthplace of Jesus Christ."

A Question of Hebrew

"Why Do You Want to Learn Hebrew?"

"*W*hy do you want to learn Hebrew?" I asked my Japanese students in my beginners' class at the Hebrew school.

It wasn't until I had established a much deeper relationship with my pupils that I dared ask such a question—usually toward the end of the third semester.

Their replies were as varied as those answering them.

The Hondas were studying Hebrew because they wanted to read the Bible in its original language. There were many others like them: old Cheneo, Kim, who was a member of the Korean minority, and a few Japanese monks and nuns, as well.

Mari wanted to study Hebrew because it was her dream to teach Japanese to Israelis at the Hebrew University of Jerusalem, and she needed to be fluent in Hebrew to do this.

Imaii was considering converting to Judaism, had been to Israel many times and visited its schools to learn the methods of the Israeli education system.

Noriko, who called herself Na'ama and wore her hair braided around her head, wanted to study Hebrew at a kibbutz *ulpan,* or intensive language program. She had to learn the basics first at the Yotsuya *ulpan.*

Yoko Orata, an internationally famous flutist had appeared several times in Israel with the Israel Philharmonic Orchestra. Yoko was friendly with Israeli players and wanted to talk freely with them in their own language.

Hideo, a journalist, was to be sent to Israel together with his family, by the Japanese News Agency, Kyodo.

Uno, the priest, on the other hand, believed that the Japanese are descendants of the Ten Lost Tribes of Israel, some of which settled in Japan. As the descendant of such an ancient and distinguished tribe, he wished to learn the language of his ancestors.

Unlike these pupils, who talked openly about their reasons for studying Hebrew, others preferred to keep their motives secret. I usually managed to find out why later on, when I was asked to help them somehow, or when I heard gossip about them, or as I got to know them better. More than once, some of these secrets left me amazed and shocked.

At the Hebrew School at Yotsuya-San-Chome, I first came across the word *sensei*. "What do you mean by *sensei?*" I asked my pupils, when they began calling me that during the first month of school.

"Translated freely, it means someone who was born before. In other words, someone who is a lot older than I am," said Uno, the old priest.

I looked over my Japanese students. Most, if not all of them, were near, or above, sixty. If the word corresponded to chronological age, why were they making me so old, I wondered.

They saw my confusion. "When we call someone '*sensei*,' it's to show respect," they explained quickly.

"I see," I said. "*Sensei* is the same as 'old man' in the Bible."

"Yes, but not quite," they added. "*Sensei* can also mean someone very young." At the end of the lesson I asked them to define every type of person they would call "*sensei*" and this was their list: *Sensei* is someone who is your senior worker, big-built, older, wise, strong, authoritative, someone with a degree, a politician, a rich man, a doctor, a lawyer, someone who has traveled widely, a policeman, a chef, a doorman, an expert at acupuncture, a sportsman, a TV anchorperson, a top fashion designer, a society hairdresser, and of course, a teacher; a teacher of Ikebana, of embroidery, a teacher of martial arts, a university professor, an elementary school teacher, a kindergarten teacher, and a teacher of Hebrew.

Japanese society can be divided into those who are called *sensei* and those who call others *sensei*. The Japanese believe in class distinction, starting with the Emperor, whose ancestors were born to the Sun Goddess, and moving down the hierarchy of the country's aristocracy, the samurai, the middle classes, the lower classes, children, women, and the untouchables. A part of all these castes, but in a special and separate social category all their own, are the "*sensei.*"

Unfortunately, teachers in Israel are not held in such high esteem. I was lucky to teach in Japan. In fact, as far as a teacher in Japan is concerned, the sky's not the limit. *Sensei* status confers great respect and a salary to match. In the Japan of the Shogun Tokugawa, schoolchildren were taught to believe that "the teacher is like the sun and the moon." The word *sensei* is used to honor a variety of occupations, at almost every level of the Japanese social hierarchy.

The respect afforded to the people worthy of the honorific *sensei* is virtually limitless. Self-abnegation, flattery, giving up one's plate of food or the best seat at a sumo wrestling match, are all proper ways to show one's respect.

When a person is introduced as a *sensei* to a group of people, everyone in the room becomes eager to please the honorable one. If you are a *sensei*, you are certainly better than I.

A *sensei* has complete authority over those who refer to him as such. They depend on him and honor his decision. He often serves as confidant and advisor coping with other peoples' troubles, solving problems, and offering counsel. You must never keep a secret from a *sensei*. It is his job to help, and he should be familiar with the most intimate details of your life. As a teacher, he must be involved in his student's life and help in whatever way he can. There is no way to evade this, even if the problems he is expected to solve are much too big for him.

Which is what happened to me. As soon as my students started calling me *sensei*, my fate was sealed. So far, in Japan, no one has ever been able to escape the karma of a *sensei*.

My satisfaction at my distinguished status as a Hebrew *sensei* in the big city of Tokyo was short-lived. A letter arrived in the mail addressed (in Hebrew) to the "Low-down teacher" ("Hamora Shfela").

So much for my new status, I thought.

I felt downright humiliated. Someone obviously wished me ill. Hard as I tried, I was unable to imagine anyone who would want to call me such a horrible name. My relations with my students were good; I had no enemies in the class. I tried to remember if I had inadvertently hurt anyone's feelings, or paid too little attention to any one of them.

Feeling utterly dejected, I reread the letter. What a relief! The writer had made free use of the letters L and R, using them interchangeably, as is customary among the Japanese. I could relax. My student, Imaii, who wanted to send me a letter in Hebrew, had simply decided to "Japanese" my name.

As I held the letter in my hands, I remembered the day I introduced myself to my new students, who whispered among themselves that it sounded *"muzukashi"*—difficult to pronounce. This Japanese word connotes a particularly difficult problem or something that has the power to unbalance mental equilibrium. The "R" in my name gave me unnecessary grief in Japan. The average Japanese is unable to pronounce this unfriendly letter, which undergoes a process of metamorphosis in his mouth, to emerge finally as an "L." Thus my name in Japanese became Shfela, which means "lowdown" in Hebrew.

I decided to use our next session together for teaching the shortened form of my name, "Shipi." I wrote it on the blackboard, in large white Hebrew letters and transcribed it into Romanji, which is the phonetic way of writing Japanese words in the Western alphabet.

I saved myself further heartache and my devoted students no longer unwittingly insulted me.

"Teacher, What Is a Joke"

*T*he word "joke" does not exist in the Japanese language. In fact, when they want to describe a short, amusing story with a punch line at the end, the Japanese use the English word "joke."

As I was told by frustrated, *gaijins* (foreigners) in Japan, I would be better off not telling jokes to the Japanese. They don't understand it anyway, and they'll roll about laughing when the joke is explained, because this is what they think is expected. But if you must tell a joke, don't forget to use the word "joke" before you start. They'll laugh at the end, without your explaining the joke, because everyone knows the word "joke," means you laugh at the end.

All told, their sense of humor is different from ours. Moreover, the Japanese have their own traditional farce, the *Jo-Dan* that they find hysterical and we don't find remotely amusing.

I used an exercise book called *One Thousand Words* to teach them Hebrew, which included a simple, well-worn little joke, the kind we used to tell each other in third grade and laugh our heads off.

I had to use this book for this class, and I could not skip chapters—my students would miss out on some basic words. Anyway, my diligent students had already covered this chapter a week in advance (without even being asked to).

I decided to jump in at the deep end.

"Today, we're going to learn a joke," I said in Hebrew, and immediately translated the sentence into English, using the familiar word, "joke."

Suspicious whisperings filled the classroom.

"What do people do when they hear a joke?" I asked.

"They laugh," they replied solemnly.

I read them the joke, pointing out and explaining the words which were new and unfamiliar to them. An ominous silence fell on the class.

They obviously don't understand, I thought, and translated the joke into English.

I expect they don't know where to laugh, I thought. I translated the punch line, and asked the right questions, explained the ridiculous aspects of the story, drew the story on the blackboard, and even added a little skit I made up on the spot. When I'd finished my act, I looked at the class. They were stunned, their frozen faces looking at me in total misapprehension.

To my great consternation, unlike other Japanese I knew—businessmen, journalists, and actors, who would die laughing at the sound of a joke—my class seemed to have chosen intellectual integrity. The students didn't get the joke, so they didn't laugh. I had always told them not to pretend to understand if they didn't comprehend a lesson.

My students, hardworking, honest, and decent, sat there silently listening to my desperate attempts to explain my joke to them. To ease my distress, I wrote their homework assignment on the board: "Write a joke for the next lesson."

I could sense rising panic. After a few moments of hurried whispering, Kim raised his hand: "Please, teacher, we don't know any jokes."

I sat there miserably and stared at my students, and tried to explain.

"You can find a joke in a street situation, in joke books, and by talking to people," I said.

The following week, most of my students were absent. Their absence told me that they were unable to find jokes and thus were unable to do their homework. Turning up in class without having done your homework was almost worse than death.

The homework handed in that week was meager and the "jokes" strange and complicated. The Japanese *jo-dan* had been pathetically translated into Hebrew, and brought tears of despair to my eyes.

I did find some solace in Janette's joke, which ran like this:

"A little girl saw a pregnant woman in the park, looked at her huge stomach and said:
What's that?
That's my baby, was the reply
Do you love it?
Yes, I love it very much, she said happily
Then why have you eaten it?"

A normal kind of joke, funny even. But this did not surprise me. Janette wasn't Japanese. She had been born and raised in the United States, in an American family. Her Hebrew was accurate and fluent, much better than that of the rest of the class. The other attempts made me feel like a complete failure. My introduction to pleasures of Western humor had fallen flat, and I made up my mind never to include any more jokes in my teaching syllabus.

Only hardworking old Kim, who used to travel for miles from his home on the army base at Yokota to his weekly Hebrew lesson, did not hand in any homework. For a whole month afterward I sensed that something was bothering him. Kim, who had never missed a lesson and always handed in his homework assignment on time, had been forced to break tradition.

A month after the lesson on jokes, we were learning about shopping in a store. Their homework assignment was to describe how they do their shopping. This was Kim's chance to let me know of the agonies he had suffered in his attempt to find a joke. It went something like this (as translated from Hebrew):

The Bookshop

Kim went into bookshop and walked between the bookshelves to find a joke book and didn't find. He asked the shopkeeper:

Kim: I want to buy one joke book. I need to write one joke. Do you have a joke book?

Shopkeeper: Sir, you don't need joke book to write joke, because many jokes in street.

Kim: I tried to find it and I couldn't find one. Because I grew up in first Korea under influence of Confucius culture. People don't tell light stories and many think and tell only serious and heavy things. So I have and have not sense of humor. But I need to write joke for homework assignment.

Shopkeeper: I know your trouble. And your pains. I understand that the former Prime Minister, Nakasone talked lightly, made many promises and did not keep them. And the short Prime Minister Takashita talks heavily and seriously.
The shopkeeper go between bookshelves and takes small book.

Shopkeeper: Here this book will ease your troubles.

Kim: Thank you very much. How much does it cost?

Shopkeeper: One thousand two hundred yen. Thank you very much.

This reminded me of the joke about the man who came home and found his wife naked in bed. In the bedroom closet, he found three Indians and one Englishman. "What are you doing here?" he asked. The three answered together: "We're from the previous joke."

Who Are You, Kiyako-San?

*T*he first time Kiyako came teetering on her high-heeled boots into the Hebrew class at Yotsuya-San-Chome, we all caught our breath for a moment.

I don't know if it was because of her ostentatious clothes, heavy makeup, or perhaps her incredible beauty. To call her appearance provocative would be an understatement. She stood out among other students, all modestly dressed women or stern-faced priests, and was quite different from the average Japanese woman, who keeps her dress modest but elegant.

Seemingly oblivious of the frigid Japanese winter, Kiyako was wearing a very short skirt and a tight, low-cut blouse, which showed off her ample breasts. A tight elastic belt cinched her narrow waist. She had heavy theatrical makeup on her eyes and the small, cherry red lips so admired by the Japanese.

Kiyako turned up suddenly in my beginners' class, about ten lessons into the semester. I asked her if she had ever learned any Hebrew before, or even seen Hebrew writing; she said she hadn't.

I suggested that she sign up for the new course, which would begin in two months. She refused and insisted that it was urgent. She had to learn Hebrew quickly and now. I couldn't ask her at this early stage why she wanted to learn the language, but judging from the way she looked, I didn't suppose she was interested in reading the holy scriptures in the original. I placed her at a desk.

During the first lesson, she sat ramrod-straight in her chair, trying hard to absorb and internalize the tone of the language, which was so foreign to her. At the end of the lesson I sat with her for about half an hour to read out the Hebrew letters and explain their significance. She picked it up immediately. By the end of the lesson she was able to read four words and the first two pages in the book *One Thousand Words*. I wasn't too surprised. I had already come across similar cases of Japanese people determined to learn Hebrew.

She had her homework assignment prepared for the next lesson. Her handwriting was wonderfully artistic and looked as if it had been done by a calligrapher. She refused to intrude on the lesson itself, but by her upright stance, it was obvious she was not missing a word.

The third lesson was similar. Her progress was so swift that I was unable to find a logical explanation for it. In the fourth lesson, she raised her hand for the first time to answer a question. Her Hebrew was amazing: fluent, accent-free, and her answer was correct and accurate.

"I've been studying five hours every day at home," she replied to the question I couldn't help asking. "I get home from work in the evening, take care of my daughter, and then sit down to study."

Kiyako soon made up for lost time and became the best student in the class. She was able to answer complicated questions and knew words that the others had never heard of. I was amazed by her fluency and the fact that her Hebrew had no hint of a Japanese accent.

One day she came to class with her four-year-old daughter, Uni—the name came from the word Universe, explained her mother—a perfect copy in miniature of Kiyako herself.

"I've nowhere to leave her," she explained apologetically, and promised that the child would not cause a disturbance. In Japan, a mother must spend all her time with her children. If she is obliged to leave them for any reason, she would prefer to do so with her mother, or another close female relative. Almost everywhere in Tokyo you can see women with small children in tow.

Uni sat still and straight, just like her mother, and kept herself occupied throughout the two-hour lesson. She never once opened her mouth to ask a question or even to ask to go to the bathroom.

I went to her at the end of the lesson, to see what she had been so busy scribbling. I was astonished. For two hours, this child, who was not yet four years old, had been accurately copying all the Hebrew letters and words off the blackboard.

As suddenly as she had appeared and with no advance notice, Kiyako ceased coming to Hebrew class. Janet, who had befriended her, told me that Kiyako had divorced her husband—a rather daring step for a young Japanese woman to take—and that she was now living in the picturesque town of Fuji, in the foothills of Mount Fuji.

"She's living with her mother, who is helping her bring up Uni," Janet told me, and added that because of the distance from Tokyo, she thought that Kiyako would not be able to resume her Hebrew lessons.

A letter I received later confirmed Janet's story.

I heard of her, from time to time, from friends at the Israeli Embassy in Tokyo. She spent a lot of time in the Embassy, I was told. Kiyako had begun appearing at Embassy receptions and the Israeli national holidays celebrated at the Jewish center. There she would be, in a very short skirt, dipping a piece of apple in honey at Rosh Hashanah, or nibbling a matzoh at Passover.

Rumor had it that she was having an affair with one of the Embassy's security officers. "But it isn't serious," the gossips added. "He's got a girlfriend in Israel, and she's about to join him in Japan."

Every time she saw me at a community function, she would apologize and say that she was no longer able to study Hebrew, because she lived so far away and was busy looking after Uni. She did not elaborate on her reasons for wanting to participate in the events at the Jewish center and the Israeli Embassy.

One day, Boaz came up to speak to me. He was an Israeli who had made his home in Japan and was my deputy at the Jewish center. He knew everything that went on in the lives of everyone around him.

"Did you know why Kiyako wanted to learn Hebrew?" he whispered mysteriously. "She has offered her services to the Mossad. She wants to spy for Israel."

Exactly one year after I had left Tokyo, I received an emotional letter from my former student, Satoko Honda. After learning that I was planning to write a book about my Hebrew class in Tokyo, she wrote to remind me of all the sad and happy times we had shared together. At the end of her letter, she mentioned Kiyako: "Did you know that Kiyako wanted to be in the Mossad?" From the rest of the letter, it was obvious that Kiyako had not succeeded in fulfilling her dream.

Or perhaps she did, but I'll never know.

My contact with her ended when I returned to Israel. I never found out the truth behind Kiyako's burning desire to learn Hebrew.

All I Wanted Was Someone to Speak Hebrew To

"*M*y name is Harada." She introduced herself in fluent English. "I believe you give lessons in the Bible, and I'd like to study with you."

We arranged over the phone to meet at the Yoyogi-Koen railway station near my home.

Harada was waiting for me at the station, which was full of smartly suited people rushing to and from work. She was an ageless Japanese woman, full-figured and dressed in a gray, nunlike suit.

"Which book were you interested in studying?" I asked her after the mandatory preliminary niceties.

"I think I would prefer Genesis," she replied in Hebrew, without a trace of a Japanese accent.

"You speak Hebrew?"

"A little and not very well," she replied, with typical Japanese modesty.

I read her the first chapter of Genesis. When I had finished, she asked hesitantly, to read it out herself. Her reading was faultless. I would have recommended her as a reader for the daily radio Bible program. Harada took particular care with all the vowels, dots, and enunciation. She pronounced the guttural "R" in a way that would not have put a Yemenite rabbi to shame. From the way she read, it was evident that she understood every word.

I began to analyze. Here again, she was obviously well versed in Hebrew. She was able to read Rashi, understood the commentaries of the medieval sages, and added aspects from Legends. Harada also offered a learned argument over this or that translation into ancient Greek, as well as into Latin.

Her knowledge of the material which I had recently taught my class at the Bible House in the Ginza neighborhood, was definitely deeper than my own. Harada distinguished between the different sources from which the piece was composed, and exhibited the kind of accuracy that only a practiced researcher into the Bible could equal or understand.

"Harada-San, where do you know all this from?" I couldn't resist asking her.

"From an important Israeli personage," she replied.

She began hesitatingly to tell me the story of her life. During the sixties, Harada, a devout Protestant, was a student at a theological seminary in Tokyo. Her dearest wish was to study the Bible in its original language in the holy city of Jerusalem—and this was made possible by the same important Israeli personage who paid a visit to Tokyo and met her at a reception at the Jewish center. When she heard of Harada's wish, she promised her that the day would come and she would be a student in Jerusalem. Within a month, she already had her tickets and study grant. Harada learned Hebrew at a language school, and then she went on to get her BA and an MA. Meanwhile she also met and married a Japanese man who was studying the history of Israel. "We soon became quite an attraction there in Jerusalem," Harada told me, with a nostalgic smile. I have heard that this important Israeli personage was no less than Golda Meir herself, although there is no official evidence to support this.

From Jerusalem, Harada went on to the Vatican, where she completed her Ph.D. Fired with missionary spirit, Harada found herself one day in a convent in the French Alps. "I was a Catholic nun," she said dryly, with no attempt at any kind of explanation or further details.

At the same time she also divorced her husband, who is now a professor of Hebrew and history of Israel in the science and technology town of Tsukuba. She herself teaches Hebrew and Bible stories at the Theological Study Institute in Tokyo.

She also informed me that she was one of the team of experts who produced the new translation of the Bible into Japanese. She did this over a period of two years in total isolation in a wooden hut, in the cold, far-off northern island of Japan, Hokkaido.

"I almost went out of my mind with loneliness."

The job of translating, which had been completed at the time we met, is considered the most advanced Japanese version of the Bible. I myself used this version in teaching my Bible class in the Ginza quarter.

Before we parted, she asked shyly how much she must pay me. I refused payment, and insisted that in this case I should pay her for what she had taught me. Harada was insistent, and so was I.

"All I wanted was someone to speak Hebrew to," she said shyly as we parted. "I am surrounded only by Japanese people, and I miss the sound of the living language. I like to hear the changes and innovations in the language, to hear slang and to talk."

I told her she would always be a welcome guest at our home. I would be pleased to meet her, to talk, to exchange opinions on various chapters in the Bible, but at no charge, of course.

Harada called me a week later, in order to postpone our next meeting, claiming that she was busy. The next meeting didn't take place because of a prior commitment on my part and thus our meeting, which I looked forward to, was postponed from week to week.

In fact, I never met Harada again until my return to Israel.

We spoke at length on the phone, exchanged ideas, consulted on teaching material, and planned a date for our next meeting, which never took place.

I told the story of Harada to my friend Kozo, with whom I was particularly close.

She soon gave me a mouthful. Kozo usually pleasant and understanding, had a sharp side.

"When will you ever learn?" she said, hissing as the Japanese do when someone manages to upset their equilibrium, or acts in a typically stupid *gaijin* way. "I'm surprised at your lack of sensitivity," she continued, rubbing salt in my wounds. "Of course she didn't come back to you, nor will she ever. You were supposed to accept payment. She wanted to meet you and you gave her your time and she won't accept this for nothing. She doesn't want to be your friend. All she wanted was someone to speak Hebrew to."

How Old Are You?

*R*eiko and Yoriko had come to the first lesson of the beginners' Hebrew classes. They were shy and impossibly polite. Terribly inhibited, their eyes fixed firmly to a point on the ground before their feet, they took their seats next to each other.

There they sat, next to each other in the classroom, two hours each week, for six months, and I never once saw them exchange a word—except of course, for obligatory polite greetings.

I couldn't understand it. They looked around the same age, and they obviously belonged to the same social class. They dressed similarly, in clothes which probably had been bought in the same shops in the fashion area of Harajubu. They had similar hairstyles and their responses were identical.

Each one of them came to the lesson on her own and left that way. I never saw them walking together toward the subway.

And it went on that way, until the day I taught the class the rudiments of Hebrew conversation. We practiced a few sentences together, and I asked the two of them to interview each other in Hebrew. The girls blushed and paled and avoided looking at each other.

"Now, you are meeting for the first time," I told them. "What question would you ask each other?"

I pointed at Reiko to go first.

She looked directly at Yoriko and asked bravely: "What is your name?"

Yoriko replied, and immediately asked a question of her own: "What is your name?"

Reiko answered but her next question made my hair stand on end: "How old are you?", she asked Yoriko.

Yoriko replied and asked the same question in return. I was speechless. Asking someone's age in Japan is considered crude, tasteless, rude, invasive, impertinent, and proof of a bad upbringing. I was particularly surprised to hear such questions coming from the lips of my two dainty, well-mannered students. It's almost as bad as asking an American how much he earns!

I couldn't believe my ears, when the next question came.

"Have you got a husband?" asked Reiko, who received a negative reply. She gave the same negative reply to Yoriko's identical question.

"Have you got a boyfriend?" asked Reiko, an angelic expression on her face, as if it was the weather they were discussing.

And so the two girls continued to delve into the most intimate details of each other's lives, asking and answering in Hebrew, the kind of questions which in Japanese sound just like police interrogation.

Peals of laughter rose from their throats, when they discovered that they lived practically next door to each other, and both used the same underground station.

Tears streamed down their faces when they answered the question: "Where did you get your dress and how much did it cost?" They bought their clothes in the same branch of the same store, as I had suspected.

The other students in the class followed this mutual interrogation and did not seem at all surprised or disturbed by these disclosures.

It seemed as if a gap had suddenly been closed, and they were asking each other questions neither one had dared ask for the six months they had been sitting next to each other in class.

That evening, I went home feeling puzzled and confused. I understood the meaning of what had happened much later, after months of living in Japan.

By my oversight, the girls had not been introduced to each other at the beginning of the course. For this very reason, and because of

their conservative upbringing, they were not required to ac-
knowledge each other's existence until the moment they were
asked to make each other's acquaintance in Hebrew.

The Hebrew language helped. As languages go, it is direct, forthright, simple, and uncompromising. In Hebrew you can say what
you cannot say in Japanese, which is a complicated language, cir-
cuitious, evasive, meandering, and diplomatic. I had made it possible for the girls to interrogate each other in a language which
served that purpose well. They had obviously wanted to ask each
other those same questions for months, but social inhibitions and
custom prevented them from doing so.

Needless to say, as soon as the bell rang at the end of the lesson,
the two packed up their books and, chattering gaily, went off in the
direction of their subway station.

The following week they arrived together, looking just as if they
had known each other since first grade.

Anna

"**S**hipi Sensei?" The voice at the other end of the phone was that of my student, Anna.

Anna was a young, aristocratic-looking Japanese girl. She was very attractive and rather aloof. Unlike the rest of the students in my class, she always seemed to keep her distance. Until that moment, she had never written me a letter, or called me on the phone. She always turned up for Hebrew lessons with David, a tall, blond American, the only non-Japanese in my Hebrew class.

"Yes, Anna, how are you?" I asked, surprised at the unexpected telephone call.

Anna went straight to the point. "I need to meet you. I can't tell you why over the phone, but it is urgent."

We agreed to meet at a small café some distance from the Jewish center. She refused to come to the center itself and even made me promise that I wouldn't speak about our meeting with my colleagues. "Especially not the Israelis," she stressed.

I was early as usual, and sat there looking out of the window. She arrived on time. She nervously looked over the other customers at the café and took her place opposite me. She seemed to be sitting on pins.

"You haven't told anyone that you were meeting me," she said firmly.

298 • Shifra Horn

I promised that I hadn't.

At her request, we moved to a solitary table at the back of the room. She threw another anxious glance around the room and sat down opposite me, pushing her long, shiny hair back off her beautiful face. Unlike other Japanese girls, who usually sit with their legs pressed primly together, Anna crossed her legs (the Japanese think this way of sitting is extremely impolite) and lit a cigarette. I ordered green tea for both of us and waited for her to speak.

Without any preamble, she said in English, "I lived for several years in the United States, where I met an Israeli man. I won't tell you his name, and I don't want you to know who he is. I didn't know that he belonged to the Israeli underworld." The gesture of dismissal that she made with her hand was that used by Japanese to refer to those lower down the social scale. "We fell in love and got married. I even converted to Judaism. Natalie was born in the United States." She pulled out a photograph of a beautiful little girl, about two years old, dressed in a pink kimono.

"See, she has green eyes," she said proudly. "It's very rare in mixed marriages, because Japanese genes are usually stronger. When I realized that I was married to a crook, I asked for a divorce and we got one in the States. We agreed that the child would stay with me. A few months later, I received a letter. My ex-husband, who was by then back in Israel, begged that I come to visit with the baby. His parents had never seen her. I didn't hesitate, mostly out of respect for his parents and because he had sent me an airline ticket. A month later, I came back to Japan, without Natalie. His sister had come to pick her up for the evening and never returned her. I didn't know what to do. I had no one to turn to in Israel and couldn't do anything. His family will have nothing to do with me. They don't answer my letters, and I am told over the phone that they have moved away. I don't know if my daughter is being looked after properly and or getting all her inoculations or who's making sure she's being properly educated. And I miss her terribly. I lie awake at night worrying."

"How long has it been?"

"Almost two years. She's three and half already. She probably doesn't remember me, and doesn't know she has a mother so far away."

I understood at last why Anna wanted to learn Hebrew. Her daughter would speak only Hebrew, and if she did ever manage to meet her, she needed to have a common language to speak in. I also remembered how her eyes had misted when, during one of our first lessons, she read aloud a sentence she had written. "Mother comes to her daughter." I had thought at the time that, like many of my Japanese students, she was excited at actually reading Hebrew, after only three weeks with those strange letters. "David is my partner now, and we're going to get married," she volunteered. "I met him in Japan. He's also Jewish, as it happens," she added somewhat apologetically. "He's never learned Hebrew, so now's his chance to learn it with me. This way, he'll also be able to speak with Natalie. David is my strength. I don't think I could go on without him."

"What are you thinking of doing now?" I asked.

"Please help me to find her," she said. "You understand why I can't meet you at the Jewish center. My ex-husband is connected with organized crime in Israel, and he travels a lot in the Far East. He's been to Japan a few times as well. I'm sure people in the center know him. You'll be in danger if he finds out that you've met me. I've got to protect you."

I didn't have to tell Anna whether or not I would help her. It was a given. I was her teacher and, as such, I had a responsibility toward her. I promised to speak to an Israeli lawyer I knew who had lived in Tokyo and might be able to help her.

We met again a few days later, at another café this time. I gave Anna several addresses and telephone numbers, including that of the legal advisor to Na'amat (the women's organization connected with the National Labor Federation in Israel), and the numbers of some close friends of mine, if she should find herself in trouble. The Israeli lawyer advised her to go to Israel as soon as possible, where she must begin a legal battle for custody of her child. "Every day that goes by makes the matter more difficult." I quoted the words of the lawyer I had spoken to. Anna thanked me, an intense expression on her face, giving away no hint of emotion or weakness, with typical Japanese restraint.

That week, Anna and David did not attend their Hebrew lesson. Nor the week after. From this alone, I knew they were out of the country.

About two weeks after our last meeting, I was leafing through the Israeli paper *Ma'ariv*, which reached Tokyo four days after being published in Israel. On the back page, boxed in as a special-interest item, was the story of a Japanese mother, whose Israeli ex-husband had kidnapped their daughter. It also told how the mother—the reporter didn't know her name—had hired a private investigator to find her child. The child was snatched from a kindergarten and mother and daughter subsequently disappeared. The border police have no record of their leaving Israel.

Only two days after reading the story in the paper, I had another phone call from Anna. There was no satellite echo, and I assumed she was back in Tokyo.

"We did it. Natalie is with me. We are very happy. Thank you very much."

"How did you get out of Israel?" I asked her.

"We hired a private plane to take us to Cyprus, and from there we flew straight to Tokyo. Everything is fine." She sounded reluctant to divulge any more details.

"When can I see you and Natalie?" I asked.

"I'm sorry," she said in her aloof voice. "You'll never be able to see us. Even one meeting could be very dangerous for you. My ex-husband is a violent man and would stop at nothing. If he ever finds out that you helped me, you'll be in great danger. It's better that we part over the phone. And thank you again," she added in Hebrew and hung up.

That was the last time I ever heard from Anna. She never returned to my Hebrew class.

Konishiki

"I'm dying to marry an Israeli," declared Konishiki—complimenting me and all the rest of the women of Israel—as he contemplated dozens of plates of food being served to him. "But before I meet her, you must teach me Hebrew," he said, and patted my knee genially.

It's not every day, nor every woman, that gets to be patted genially, gently, and surprisingly, by a mountain of a man. Well over six feet tall, weighing around 560 pounds, Konishiki was one of Japan's most popular sumo wrestlers.

My acquaintance with Konishiki began when the Israeli Tourism Office in Tokyo came up with a brilliant idea to turn Israel into a mecca for thousands of Japanese tourists. The average Japanese knows almost nothing about Israel. Nonetheless, a great many people in Japan have heard of the Dead Sea. They get very excited at the prospect of floating on the sea's salty surface, the valuable minerals in the water, its healing properties, and the salt lumps which pierce the water like polished crystal swords.

Arriving in Israel, the Japanese, like many other tourists from all over the world, make a beeline for the Dead Sea, to have their photographs taken floating on the water reading a newspaper.

Our Tourist Office decided to base its promotion on this image. They decided on a publicity campaign, which would send Konishiki to the Dead Sea, where he would be photographed from every possible angle, floating on the buoyant waters of the biggest salt lake in the lowest point on the face of the earth. This would surely encourage thousands of Japanese to flock to Israel in his wake.

Negotiations with Konishiki, his agent, and manager took place in a Japanese restaurant in the expensive entertainment area of Akasaka. I went along as official photographer of the historic event and as a great admirer of the sport of sumo and of Konishiki himself.

I am not the only *gaijin* woman to admire these colossal men. The sumo wrestlers are very popular with the ladies of Japan, and also with foreign women living in Japan. I discussed the subject in Tokyo, with a foreign psychologist, who tried to explain to me that the sumo wrestler symbolizes the ideal man for Western women. On the one hand, he is very strong, masculine, competitive, and wealthy; on the other, he is chivalrous, gentle, and polite. A perfect combination. Not that the wrestlers' physical appearance is anything to get excited about. Most are huge and pinkish-skinned, heavy-jowled and covered in enormous rolls of fat, more reminiscent of the Michelin man than a real flesh-and-blood man. But who cares? A sumo wrestler embodies a rare mixture of incredible strength and the finesse of a Bolshoi ballerina.

Armed with a sophisticated camera, I waited for my idol at the entrance to the restaurant. Konishiki arrived in a convoy of limousines, sprawled in the backseat of an elegant black, high-roofed car, the kind that takes Japanese brides to the wedding chapel. The high roofs of these cars did not interfere with the brides' elaborately constructed hairstyles, and allowed them to climb out with dignity, their backs straight and their hair and white, boatlike hats intact.

This was how Konishiki appeared, dressed in a *yukata*, with a wide belt tied negligently under his huge paunch. His feet, slim compared to the rest of his body and which had more than once failed him onstage, wore huge wooden, boatlike, clogs, and seemed barely able to bear his enormous weight.

Konishiki walked in next to me, swaying like a sailor who had just disembarked from a long sea voyage. Despite his huge proportions, the handshake he gave me was gentle.

Feeling completely overwhelmed, I sat on the restaurant's silk cushion, beside the great man, carefully observing every crumb that went into his mouth and listening to every word that came out of it.

Sulvae Puoli Atisanoe, who is known in Japan by his nickname Konishiki, is not Japanese, but he has earned the esteem of the Japanese people.

Konishiko was born in American Samoa, but he is considered by the Japanese to be a foreigner from Hawaii. His Polynesian ancestry is plain in his huge size, his dark skin and wide nose. And his unruly curls refuse to be held in the traditional sumo straight, oiled, topknot.

We talked about his family in Samoa, all built like Konishiki, his Christian faith, his desire to learn the Bible in its original Hebrew and his search for a wife, "preferably Israeli, but she must be slim and gentle-natured."

Despite his genuine desire to visit Israel, he never did get to float on the mineral-rich waters of the Dead Sea. One of the biggest problems was the lengthy flight. How, for example, could a sumo wrestler fit into an aircraft toilet booth? Konishiki would have to abstain from all food and drink for at least twenty-four hours before the flight and during it, in the hope that this would keep his intestines in a state of calm.

Furthermore, a flying sumo wrestler would require at least three seats in the first-class compartment. And if he slept, his massive body might create an insurmountable obstacle for flight attendants and passengers alike.

Another reason Konishiki never made it to Israel was his increasing popularity. He won first prize at the next tournament he took part in. With each bout, he made more money. A trip to Israel would have broken his disciplined training schedule, which was leading him slowly but surely to the championship.

Thus, the Dead Sea did not overflow its banks, I lost a student of Hebrew, sumo fans got themselves a foreign-born champion, and some poor Israeli girl will remain forever single.

We heard recently that Konishiki has found his peace. He has married Sumika Shioda, a slim, twenty-six-year-old Japanese model, who weighs only 108 pounds.

Shioda is indeed fortunate. Only the Crown Prince himself is a more eligible bridegroom than a champion sumo wrestler.

Meeting of Souls

I looked in confusion at the Hondas, who stood beside their car at the entrance to my building. As far as I knew, our-end-of semester party was tomorrow, at six. I looked at my watch: it showed exactly 6:00 P.M.

I had forgotten. I invited them up, warning them of the mess and upheaval in my apartment. I hadn't even begun cooking for the party and I racked my brains trying to think of something to serve them and the rest of the students who would soon be arriving.

But they were adamant about not coming up. Satoko stuttered: "Shipi Sensei, the party is tomorrow. We know that. We only came because we wanted to know where you live."

What a relief. The Hondas, considerate and thoughtful, had never been to my home before. Since there are no street names in Tokyo, or house numbers, even the most intrepid navigators in the world could be lost in that urban labyrinth. To make matters worse, the party started at 6:00 P.M., the height of the rush hour.

The Hondas, therefore, had decided to reconnoiter a day before the party, find my place, and gauge the time it would take to arrive punctually.

At exactly 6:00 o'clock the following evening, all my students arrived together, as if they had been brought by a tour bus. It seems, or so my son told me later, that some of them had actually arrived at 5:30, but these had waited downstairs in spite of having been urged to go on up. No Japanese person would ever arrive anywhere too early, and embarrass his hosts, who surely are not ready yet. This is considered even worse than turning up late for a party.

With infinite embarrassment and thousands of apologies, they took off their shoes at the door and remained in their socks. I took an interested look at the socks and came to the conclusion that they were all clean and almost new and in spite of the heat and humidity outside, not a whiff of foot odor reached my nose. Nor was any one wearing a sock with a hole in it. I had noticed this throughout the five years I lived in Japan.

Apologizing profusely for the poor quality of their gift, they handed me a huge parcel. This contained dozens of tiny plates, each with a different-colored fruit jelly, a typical gift for the summer, when the Japanese give and receive presents. I thanked them with countless bows and led them into the living room.

By Israeli standards, my home in Tokyo would be considered modest, even small. Since I was still fairly new in Japan, and had not yet been invited to visit Japanese homes, I did not understand why my students were so excited by the sight of my living room, saying words like *"sogoi"*—huge; *"oki"*—large all over the place, accompanied by typical Japanese sighs. Later, once I had experienced more of the Japanese way of life, I realized that my living room alone could have housed three Japanese families, with an average of two children each.

After the mandatory polite words, speeches, and embarrassed murmuring, the first bottle of whiskey was brought out and opened, and the ice was soon broken. The students put their arms around each other's shoulders and began singing in Hebrew, "How good and how pleasant, to sit here together with my brothers."

The students were then invited to the table to savor Israeli delicacies I had prepared from Japanese raw material. For example, I had mixed the tahini from Japanese sesame seed paste, called *goma*, whose taste is very similar to our own unprocessed tahini. I found pita bread in a small bakery called "Arab Bread," and my hummus was made from Japanese beans called *Ejipto-Mame*—Egyptian beans.

My guests liked the unfamiliar food. The table was soon empty and cleared away for dessert. Suddenly, as if commanded, Yoko Orata walked into the middle of the room and took out a gold flute. Within seconds the whole apartment filled with the magical sounds of the flute.

Yoko had always seemed to be a nice, pleasant girl, simple and very shy. She never opened her mouth in class, and anytime I asked her anything she would blush, lower her eyes, and say nothing. It was hard to take in the enormous change in her as she stood up to play. Yoko looked very different: older, stronger, and full of self-confidence.

"Yoko is a virtuoso," the school's principal had explained to me in a whisper. "She is well-known all over the world, and she is a soloist in concerts, especially in the United States and Europe." I could now understand why she had to miss so many of her Hebrew lessons. She had a very busy schedule, and had even appeared in Israel, playing under the baton of Zubin Mehta. This was why she had decided to join my Hebrew class. Yoko wanted to speak to her Israeli colleagues in their native tongue.

When Yoko had finished her performance, she was replaced in the center of the room by Mari, a serious student who was about to leave us to take up her studies at the University of Tsukuba, the city of technology. Mari wanted to study Hebrew so as to teach Israeli students the Japanese language in the holy city of Jerusalem. A knowledge of Hebrew would make her a better teacher.

Mari brought out a guitar, and began a medley of Naomi Shemer songs in a pure, high voice.

The old gentleman, Heishero Honda was next with a harmonica performance. The tunes he played were Israeli and Japanese. His wife, Satoko, was moved to tears. "Do you know," she said to me, "Heishoro hasn't touched the harmonica for thirty years. He thought tonight was a good time to play again."

After the musical interlude, Michiko, a psychology professor at one of Tokyo's universities, retired to the back of the room and untied the furoshiki around the bulky parcel she had brought. As if by magic, she produced a painted porcelain bowl, a bamboo brush, a bronze teapot, and several jars. Michiko arranged these in front of her, and in utter silence prepared the traditional Japanese tea ceremony, as if she were alone in the room. She also taught me how to sip the bitter, green tea from the bowl, how many sips were proper, and which side the bowl should be turned to after drinking. At the end of the lengthy ceremony, she made me a gift of the dishes.

Old Tseneo got up and sang Italian arias. Akiko sang American blues, and Ono played the "Stars and Stripes Forever" on a trumpet, and a medley of American country western songs.

At exactly 10:30, as if under orders, they all stood up at once, and murmured apologies for taking so much of my precious time and causing me the trouble of cooking for them. They put on their shoes and left the house.

As they had arrived together, they left together, and the house was silent. It was as if the music, singing, and animated conversation had never happened.

Sayonara, Japan

Farewell Japan

*M*y parting from Tokyo was stormy, or more accurately, shaky.

We spent our last night in Tokyo at the house of my student, Satoko Honda. She would not hear of our returning to our empty apartment. All our belongings had been packed and sent ahead to Israel. She insisted that we sleep in her old house, which was close to her new apartment.

We had packed for twenty-four hours, stuffing cardboard boxes full of the last five years of our lives in Japan. (When we unpacked in Israel, it turned out that everything had been packed, including the wet sponges, the salt and pepper, the garbage in the cans, half-empty tins of food, empty containers of cleaning materials, and the dirty rags we used to wipe the furniture. Our Japanese packers had been more than thorough.)

It was late at night when we arrived, exhausted, at the small, typically Japanese apartment, where we found futons spread lovingly over the tatami, with starched, scented sheets, which Satoko had considerately prepared for us.

Well aware of the problem I had as a vegetarian in Japan, Satoko had filled the fridge with tofu, bottles of juice, rich cakes, various kinds of expensive, imported cheeses, and fresh fruit and vegetables. Despite these gastronomic temptations, I was far too tired to eat and made do with a few sips of cool water.

I sprawled out exhausted on the futon, dreading the day ahead, when I would leave Japan. I couldn't sleep. I dreaded flying, as always, and leaving the city I had spent five years of my life in upset me also. The terrible heat wave that had smothered the city in a summer blanket of hot steam didn't help.

"It'll happen tonight," I said gloomily to my husband, who was dozing gently on the futon beside me.

"What'll happen tonight?" he asked, half-asleep.

"The big earthquake. The one they've been predicting for five years. It will happen tonight."

"Ever the pessimist." My husband dismissed my fears and, turning over on his side, began snoring.

I felt all alone. Tomorrow I would have to suffer through a long, frightening flight, there might be a terrible earthquake and, any minute, on top of all that, it was so hot in the room that an air conditioner running full blast did nothing. I glared at my husband. "It's all right for you to sleep," I said to the body next to me. "You don't have to fly tomorrow."

It happened the next morning, at exactly 5:30. It was stronger than anything I could have imagined, vibrating my bones and churning my insides.

Books fell off the shelves, and utensils rattled noisily in the kitchen.

"What did I tell you?" I woke up my husband, who could have slept through 6.5 on the Richter scale.

He looked confused.

"It's an earthquake! Get up!" I screamed. "We've got to get out of here!"

The earthquake got stronger. As more and more things began falling in the apartment, I scooted under the heavy Japanese dining table in the corner of the room. I looked around for my husband. I saw him, in his underwear, staring at the open closet.

"Get under the table immediately!" I called to him.

"I've got to get dressed first," he said coolly.

His coolness was catching. It's better to die under a fallen object fully dressed than be caught alive and half-naked under a heavy dining table. My husband deliberated for what seemed an eternity. He decided against a suit, and chose, after many hesitations, a pair of jeans. I put on a light summer dress. Dressed and shod, we walked toward the door, ready to be rescued. As we stood in the stairwell, we noticed that it was motionless under our feet. The earthquake had been over for a while. A heavy silence had fallen over the hot, steamy city, which had awakened suddenly at this early hour of the morning.

Satoko's neighbors, who had also stepped out into the stairwell, stared at us, foreigners, and then crawled back into their futons, sweat-soaked from the heat wave which had taken over the city.

It took us three hours to reach Narita, Tokyo's busy international airport. From the state of the roads, you would think that all twelve million inhabitants of the city were trying to escape the worst summer heat wave in the city for a hundred years. The road surface was melting away under the wheels of our car and the entire city was enveloped in a stinking humidity. Narita Airport, on the other hand, welcomed me with a burst of much-needed cool air.

I went through my special passport control counter, where I was greeted amicably by the same clerk who had detained me on my first day in Tokyo. His gloved hands gave my passport a thorough going-over, paying special attention to the many times I had taken short holidays away from the island.

This time he stared at it for a long time. He felt each page separately, held it up to the light, to make sure no two pages had stuck to each other and returned it to me, stern-faced.

"There's no return visa," he said tragically.

"No need," I replied lightly.

The clerk looked at me in disbelief. "You need a visa to get back in," he insisted.

"No need," I repeated, when I noticed his serious expression, and added: "*Sayonara*, Japan."

"Ah," he said. He deliberated on this new fact and processed it in his mind, and repeated after me: "Ahaaa. *Sayonara*, Japan."

"*Hai*," I replied, smiling in confirmation.

Suddenly a tiny, hesitant smile began to crack his serious face. The smile gradually spread across his expressionless face, his small eyes disappeared completely behind the origami folds of his face and his many gold teeth sparkled.

"*Sayonara*, Japan," he called to his colleagues at the counter, holding up my passport, and then he stamped his Japanese stamp for the last time.